FAI

To: Alex
May the Wind
always be at
your Back!

FAITH ON FORTY YARDS

Anthony E. Prior

ISBN 1-59109-614-6

To my mother and father for always believing in me and to my brother, Stanley, who first inspired me and has continued to be my greatest inspiration. Stanley passed the torch to me so I could fly. That was his calling: to show me and teach me that our successes and failures are not always our own.

The later chapters in this book are dedicated to Nezzer

Contents

My life, just as yours, begins with a single breath. God has given us a journey all our own, and each breath we take brings us closer to understanding the meaning of our lives.

— Anthony E. Prior

Preface

This book is not the story of a pro football player who has had years and years of play and season after season of success. No, it is the story of a player at the peak of his game who faces setback after setback yet always manages to muster enough courage to press on. My story is about a young boy with a dream, who grew to be a man through experiences of rejection, "being cut," and waived. I have fallen victim to the numbers game and salary caps and all kinds of obstacles. But no matter what wall I run up against, I always see the possibility of a comeback. No matter what, whenever it comes time for me to make (or hope) for a comeback, all my faith is on forty yards.

My faith in forty yards started at home, when I was a kid. I used to train for hours just so I could run forty yards in four seconds. With my older brother Stanley, we'd train on the dirt track that ran along the side of our house in Riverside, California. Stanley and I always trained together and I didn't ever want to change that. Stanley was not only my brother, he was my motivator, personal trainer, and my friend. That all changed one hot summer day in August 1989.

It was late morning. The sun was beating down with such fire you could feel the heat even in the shade. Stanley suggested we jog together and then sprint on the dirt trail at the side of the house. I always hated jogging with him because he'd tell me to shut up whenever I wanted to talk, and I love to talk while jogging. Stanley said he was always too tired to talk, but I thought he was just full of it.

As we stretched in my parents' garage before our jog, Stanley began to talk about how I was going to make it in pro football. He had always dreamed of a pro football career, too, but today, for some reason, he didn't say a word about himself. It looked like his gas tank of enthusiasm had run out, leaking away like the air of life. His dream had faded. Like a child whispering in the ear of a parent, he said, "I can't do this, but I want to see you continue and make this dream a reality."

As we started to jog, Stanley set off at a fast pace, like at the beginning of the dream we always talked about. I was saying to myself, "I'm going to keep up this pace no matter what." The sun was beaming on us. Not a cloud was in the sky, and I realized the heat was going nowhere. Stanley started to slow up, but I kept going at the pace he had set. Looking back at him, I didn't say a word. He raised his right hand and waved as if to tell me to keep going. At that moment the umbilical cord was cut. I was going on the journey to the NFL by myself, with an unlimited tank of enthusiasm, full to the brim with my brother's encouragement. To this day, it's still full.

Introduction

I attended Washington State University from 1988 until I was drafted into the NFL in May 1992. I never graduated from college, considering that my sole purpose and motivation there was to have as much fun as possible before making it into the NFL. It wasn't until I got into the NFL that my real college education began. My first year with a pro team was like my freshman year. My early years as a pro football player educated me far beyond what I had learned at college, to the point that I believe college is a playground for young adults who don't yet know how to think for themselves.

My first semester in the college of the NFL took place in New Jersey, where I was drafted by the New York Giants in April 1992. The Giants cut me in 1993 and I went on to play for the New York Jets. In March 1996, the New York Jets cut me and that's how I earned my bachelor's degree in pro football.

The Cincinnati Bengals picked me up in April 1996, and I attended their mini camps during the spring. Although I was cut in July, a big shocker, I had gotten some good studying in. The San Francisco 49ers picked me up in July 1996 and I had a great pre-season but came up short and was cut in August 1996. The Minnesota Vikings picked me up and I played with them in 1996 and 1997. By then I had my master's degree.

In 1998 I was a free agent looking for a team so I could work on my doctorate. The Kansas City Chiefs chose me, but I was injured in August 1998 and cut soon after. I kept working on my doctorate and in November 1998 the Oakland Raiders picked me up. A few players dropped out and there were some empty desks so I kept studying for my doctorate. In 1999, I was ready to write my doctoral thesis but was not picked up. So in 2000, I went north to Canada and played for the Calgary Stampeders and went to the Grey Cup with them. In 2002 I was a free agent looking to write more and finish my thesis in the NFL, but the wind kept me in Canada. It was in Canada that I completed my Ph.D. This book, *Faith on Forty Yards*, is my life's thesis. These words are the reality my eyes have seen and my ears have heard.

Prologue
Beyond Forty Yards

I wake scared in the middle of the night and move my foot, looking for Ebony next to me. We always touch feet to let each other know we're there. But I stretch my leg as far as I can, find nothing, and realize I'm lying here alone. It dawns on me: Ebony and me, we're not together any more.

Getting up to use the toilet, I flip the switch and one of the bulbs blows. That's strange, I changed it yesterday. I wash my face and grab a towel. As I'm patting my face dry, I stop to stare at myself in the mirror. Alone in Canada, away from my family, friends, and kids, I wonder what I'm doing here. Am I here for selfish reasons? Yeah, I guess I needed time to do some soul searching and to figure out whether or not Ebony and I were going to take our relationship to the next level.

I look at the clock and realize it's only 4:27 a.m. What the hell am I doing up so early? I never have problems sleeping. Maybe I'm hungry and should scramble some eggs. Looking for spices in the cupboard, I smile, thinking about how Ebony turned me on to spicing up my food. Now that we're apart, I discover how much I love that woman. I'm lost in the thought of her.

I think back to September 2000, before leaving on an away trip. We'd staying up late the night before, talking about her mother as we looked through old photographs. We came across a picture of a little girl in a white dress holding a black baby doll. At first I laughed and said, "Who's the white girl holding the black baby?"

She said, "That's my mother. She always wanted a black baby."

I didn't believe her at first and continued laughing. "Are you serious?" I asked.

She looked at me and said, "Why do you think my name is Ebony?"

"You know, I could write something about that," I said.

❧

I had a lot of firsts with Ebony. She was the first woman I said "I love you" to and meant it. She was the first woman I ever prayed with. She was the first woman I ever wanted to marry. Now look at me, scrambling eggs by myself in the middle of the night.

I miss that woman and realize that when you have love around you, you're a happy person. When you find yourself in a place where there is no longer love, it's a very lonely place.

I put on some Sam Cooke, the smoothest voice ever recorded. I would have paid a thousand dollars to watch him sing live in concert. There will never be a singer who can live up to Sam Cooke. He had a style all his own.

My thoughts are all over the place as I stand at the stove, scrambling eggs. They burn as I gaze out the window at the snow coming down. There have been times when I thought I was getting over using women for my own selfish pleasure. I realize now that they were using me in the same way. When they look at me now, I'm their example of the kind of man they wouldn't want to be with. I can't change some of the things I've done, but I do find myself saying I regret this and that. I used to train for hours so I could run forty yards in four seconds and it would take time away from family and friends. I acknowledge my failures and embrace the good things I have done because the good far outweighs the bad.

When you reach a low point in your life, you see the decisions you've made that have hurt the people you love. One day you wake up, find yourself alone and feeling insecure. That hurts.

❧

Damn, I'm getting carried away. These eggs are going to be a little dark. Ebony wouldn't have eaten them. She always wanted her eggs bright yellow and fluffy and would tell me whether or not I had made them well. As I sit down to eat, I grab the seasonings and spice them up good, the way she would have liked them.

The silence around me is frustrating. Growing up, I was never alone. I always had my family, mostly my brother Stanley. I miss him. His presence in my life has been a constant breath of fresh air because he knows me like no one else. He knows when I'm up and when I'm down. Right now, I'm down because I don't know where the wind is going to take me.

I sure miss the early morning conversations with my father. He'd get me up for my track training sessions and we had a routine of making breakfast together, which lasted all through my high school years until I left for college. We'd talk about everything, from girls to sports to my life's destiny. My father has been the only man to influence me and I pride myself because of that. I can't hear my father's voice right now, but I can feel his presence. That's all I need for comfort.

Now I'm sitting, not eating, listening to Sam Cooke. I should have been married at this point in my life. I regret not working in the same city as my kids. I wonder, will the day come when my boys resent me for not being with their mother? Will they have the heart to forgive me and understand that any time a person starts off something wrong in life, it can't end right? You can spend a lifetime patching it up, trying to make it right. That's why grandparents try and raise their grandkids, trying to make their wrong right. They're trying to justify their incompetence, trying to correct a new birth in a wrong way, trying to take away some past sin that has been hovering for decades, sort of like guilt that won't go away. We see the sins of the parents in their children. That's what I believe and there's power in what you believe.

The eggs don't taste good so I throw them in the trash and decide to make over-sized pancakes instead.

I remember once I made Ebony breakfast in bed. It was a simple gesture, but she thought it was the sweetest thing. I never paid much attention to the saying, "You never miss somebody until they're gone." Damn, that is so true. I have been too proud to acknowledge my true feelings until now. I wish I would have done some things differently and, if I could, I would take some things back. But, I can't. I must live with my decisions, whether they were good or bad, because in the end, no matter what I do, I'll have to answer for them. The good decisions we make sustain us and take us to higher understanding, putting us on a path to greatness. But, the bad decisions hinder us from becoming effective in life. They shatter our character and make us less human.

Damn, we should be so far along in our relationship by now. I feel sad making this pancake for me alone. Right now, this big pancake will fill my stomach, but my heart still feels empty without her. I told her that we would be married one day. We both said that we would have a daughter and name her Chante. I even gave her a nickname, Tae Tae. We would act out scenes, as if Chante was sitting right next to us. We even talked about her having a sister, and she said we would name her Jay Jay. Now, I find myself smiling. I believe people reminisce to make themselves feel good.

I think about my mother, and the look on her face the day I told her I was going to play in the NFL. I had just come home from football practice and I was making a peanut butter and honey sandwich that hot summer afternoon. I was in the start of my senior year of high school.

Now at the age of thirty-two I find myself at a crossroad. No football contract, little interest in the NFL. Salary caps? Age? What is it that keeps me out of the NFL? It can't be my age because I just ran forty yards in 4.2 seconds a month ago. Who knows what it is?

The CFL has been good to me and I have been an impact player in this league. What drives me at this point in my life? I have finally developed a style I can call my own. I owe a lot to all the people who have helped me throughout my career. Our successes are never our own. To all those who have helped me get to this point in my life, I say thank you and at the same time, I'm sorry for not living up to my potential. Yet, that's why I find myself waiting again for another chance in the NFL.

The NFL is where the greatest athletes in the world take to the field of play and demonstrate some of the most memorable moments in history. I'm waiting, and keeping my faith on forty yards and when I get that call I'll be ready to live up to all the things my father and I talked about those mornings over breakfast. The great things to come are just around the corner for us. All we need to do is believe in that and work at a steady pace to take us there.

❧

I'm stuffed. That pancake was too big, but it sure was good. The kitchen is a mess, but outside I can still see the snow falling silently to the ground. The weather in Canada is funny. One minute, it's nice; the next, there's a blizzard.

My career is as changeable as the weather, and so is my personal life. It hasn't killed me or destroyed the goodness in me. I have taken my career and personal life and dissected them to find out where I went wrong. I put all my faith on forty yards and I thought that could sustain me, but I learned the hard way that success sustains us only for a while. If we put too much store in success, eventually we destroy ourselves and those around us.

I have gone beyond forty yards to realize that I'm not the one in control. I'm just passing through this world the same as all of us. We're on borrowed time. Now I've learned to lean on God for all my worries and concerns. I have peace now, whether I'm on a field playing football or on a track running forty yards. It's the mystery of life's journey that sustains me now.

Chapter 1
The Seeds of Me

My father, John Frank Prior, was born of a mid-wife, September 5, 1939, in an old shack on a farm in east Texas. They didn't have much, but one thing they did have was family, and the most important thing was being together on that farm.

My father loved living on the farm. "I'd go into the woods with my friends, and we would create our own little world. We would build things and let nature play with our minds. We climbed trees, hid from one another, ran, fought, and even just sat throwing rocks, wondering where our thoughts would to take us next," he said. No one showed him how to entertain himself, where to play, and what to play with, the way television does today.

My father lived on his grandparent's farm after his parents separated in 1944. His grandmother, Ms. Pearl Anthony, was a great cook who made everything from scratch. She and my father's grandfather, Eugene Anthony, were the most consistent people in my father's life, as was his mother, Ms. Ophelia.

Ms. Ophelia loved to cook as much as her mother did. Later, when I knew her as my grandmother, she would always say to me, "Come here, baby, give me some sugar," meaning a kiss. I'd run to hug my tiny grandmother with her beautiful long hair.

My father helped buy the house where my grandmother lived in Galveston, Texas. We'd go to visit her in the summer, my dad loading us all into our green wood-panel station wagon. During our summer trips to Galveston, he would never run the air conditioner, never stop at McDonalds, and always make us wait to use the bathroom until he needed to fill the gas tank.

One hot muggy summer when I was about eight years old, we were visiting my grandmother in Texas. She had made me lunch with raw bean sprouts. I told her I hated them, but she wouldn't hear of me not eating them. She said there was no way in hell I was going to get out of that kitchen until I ate all of them. I started to plug my nose to eat them but she just said, "Stop that!"

Thirty minutes passed and I still had eaten only two bean sprouts. In the back of my mind all the time I was thinking, "Where is my mom when I need her?" The next thing I hear, my mother is coming up the stairs and out of nowhere I start to cry. My mom tells me, "You don't have to eat those bean sprouts." My tears saved me! But my grandmother looked at me and raised an eyebrow in disapproval. That's all she needed to do to tell me everything that was on her mind.

My father taught us to think for ourselves and sort out our own problems. He learned that lesson himself quite early and quite painfully when he was only eight years old, in about 1947. My father used to tell us a story about his father, Mr. Bill.

John Prior Sir, or Mr. Bill, they called him, my grandfather, was a farmer who worked and traveled around Texas, farming here and there. He was some sort of journeyman on his own agenda, trying to make ends meet. They said he loved to party and his three demons were wine, women, and music. They called him a "red nigga," meaning his skin was light. He had a fair complexion, a red tone with freckles.

People might say Mr. Bill was a bad man. People might even say he was a selfish man. But if you look at my life and his, you see similarities. I have traveled the road playing football on different teams. I don't live with my kids and see them every day. Some people have said that I'm a selfish man on my own agenda, just like Mr. Bill. And I have lived a lifestyle in which wine, women, and music were my high and my motivation. I'm thankful now that I have had enough sense to realize I was becoming a slave to my own desires. Not so Mr. Bill.

One hot summer day in 1947, my grandfather, Mr. Bill, was

spending time with his three kids: my father, the eldest, and my Aunt Gene and Uncle Klide. Mr. Bill was going to take the three of them home to live with him, and my dad was all packed and ready to go. Mr. Bill took them out for ice cream. While they were out together, somehow Mr. Bill changed his mind and ended up taking all three kids back to their grandparents on the farm. My dad kept waiting on his father, but he never showed again on that hot summer day in 1947. My dad didn't see his father again until about four years later.

My father never let that disappointment affect his life. When he had his own kids, whenever he would tell my brothers and sisters, "I'll be back," he always came back. He never let us down the way his father had let him down. Yet I never heard my father say one negative thing about his dad. I think he understood his father and that gave him peace. He didn't hold a grudge for his absence and inconsistency. That's just the hand my father was dealt. He says, "In this life you take the bitter with the sweet and, when your life is over, make sure the good moments outweigh the ugly ones."

Around 1952, when my father was thirteen years old, he moved to Galveston, Texas, with his mother, Ms. Ophelia. From that time on, my dad pretty much raised himself. His mother, my grandmother, worked long, hard hours, which made it difficult for her to watch my dad's every move. He sometimes ran numbers for underground gambling to make a bit of money to help out. But during the summer, my father would get on a bus and go to east Texas and help his grandparents on the farm. That Texas heat made a man out of him, he would say. Farming gave him a chance to think about some of the things he would like to accomplish in life.

When my father got to high school and started playing sports, those summer bus rides soon stopped. My dad took up sports, which he sure loved. He said it kept him out of the streets. He played football, basketball, and even ran track. When asked what he remembers most about the sports he played, he said, "The only thing I wish was that my parents would have seen me play. My mother worked all hours and my father would pop in and out of my life. All the other students' parents would always watch their kids. I wished mine could, too."

At sixteen, my father may have been only a kid, but he was also a student, a worker, and an athlete. That's a lot for a young man. On his own, figuring out what life was all about, my father said that by the time he was sixteen he was having the time of his life. My dad worked as a bus boy at the Turf Grill, which was along the ocean in Galveston, Texas. He would clean bathrooms, wash dishes, and help wherever it was needed. Everybody knew John Prior (a.k.a. The Rock). He would also dance the night away while his mom worked. She knew her John Frank could take care of himself. My grandmother could see that John Frank was a rare breed of kid, more mature and responsible than other kids his age.

Eventually my father got fired from the Turf Grill and he started working for the coolest restaurant in town, the Balanece Room. He worked in the men's lounge and washed pots. They took care of him, even feeding him from time to time. But he got fired from that restaurant, too, this time for eating apples on the back pier. "They were gonna fire me anyways," he said. "Business was getting slow."

When high school came to an end, my father left Galveston and enrolled in college, attending Southern University, Baton Rouge, Louisiana. It was a four-year college and the largest university in the South for blacks.

My dad had the time of his life at college until one night when he got to drinking some Mad Dog wine. The rule was that you couldn't have alcohol on campus, so to hide his bottle he also bought a loaf of bread when he was at the liquor store. As he was carrying the bag home you could see the loaf of bread hanging over the side of the bag. By the time he got on campus, he was weaving from side to side, walking and smiling like a wino. A woman yelled at him, "John Frank, where in the hell you been?" He looked up at her and slurred the words, "Shut up!" Then he picked up a brick and threw it right through the window. My dad's days at Southern University were over from the moment that brick landed.

My dad left Southern and went to live with his aunt in

Tyler, Texas, where he attended Tyler College. His aunt lived next door to the grandparents of a young woman named Mae Lois, who is now my mother. If my father had never thrown that brick, I wouldn't be here writing this story. That's why I believe every action in life triggers a reaction, some good, some bad.

❧

My mother, Mae Lois Wady, was born during the war, on July 24, 1941, at a time when a loaf of bread cost five cents and the Internet wasn't even thought of yet. My mother grew up poor, in a family with seven kids. Her parents scraped to make it through. Her mother, Eva Mae Wady, was a strong Christian woman who prayed all the time. She worked as a maid for the Brightman family in Texas. My mother's father, Tommy Wady, was a minister at the local church.

As a young girl, my mother grew up not knowing sometimes where the next meal would come from. Her mother would sit on the porch, rocking back and forth in the chair, praying and singing to God, "Bread of Heaven, Bread of Heaven, feed me till I want no more." My mother says a family that prays together stays together.

My mother lived in an old wooden house, where the roof leaked. The nights were cold and she used to sleep with all her brothers and sisters to keep warm. As a little girl Mae Lois used to say to herself, "When I get grown I'll never live like this."

Childhood Christmases were not a time for opening presents. Fruit in their stockings was a celebration. An orange or an apple was a highlight. My mother delighted in that moment and, when she looks back on it now, realizes that you can't put a value on fruit nor can you place a value on a toy, for those two things can be replaced. "Now my value is in the love I have for my brothers and sisters, my mother and father," she says. "They can't be replaced and the years growing up can't be replaced either. We have to embrace those moments in which memories are made."

As a child, my mom would walk to school, with her brothers and sisters entertaining each other along the way. Kicking and throwing rocks, they'd pass down an old dirt country road where the fields were green and the air was clean.

As a young girl my mother tells the story of falling from a tree she had climbed, hitting her head on a branch, and losing the sight in her left eye. Her family didn't have any health insurance and couldn't send her to hospital. Instead they felt that prayer could change anything. They'd gather the family together in time of trouble as a support. My mom accepted what had happened to her, wore a patch over her eye, and kept on with life.

My mother also often tells the story of her near-death experience when she was about seventeen or eighteen years old. I probably heard that story once a year as I was growing up. She had gotten really sick and the doctors said they could do nothing to help her. While lying in bed sick, her father Robert knelt over her and began to read Psalm 121 from the Bible. My mother can still hear his voice as she rested her eyes and went to sleep:

1 I lift up my eyes to the hills —
From where will my help come?
2 My help comes from the Lord,
who made heaven and earth.
3 He will not let your foot be moved;
he who keeps you will not slumber.
4 He who keeps Israel
will neither slumber nor sleep.
5 The Lord is your keeper;
the Lord is your shade at your right hand.
6 The sun shall not strike you by day,
nor the moon by night.
7 The Lord will keep you from all evil;
he will keep your life.
8 The Lord will keep
your going out and your coming in
from this time on and forevermore.

That night her family huddled around my mother and prayed to God, "Jesus send your angels around her and comfort her." The whole family believed she was going to heaven that night. I'm thankful God had other plans for her. The next morning my mother awoke to the silence of the house and, for a moment, she thought she was in heaven. Then she realized she was in Tyler, Texas, lying in bed, healthy as a newborn baby.

After this teenage illness, my mother began acting like a drama queen. Now whenever she has a headache, it's a brain tumor. When she feels out of breath, she thinks she's having a heart attack. Every time she writes a check for a purchase, if the cashier asks to see some ID, they're a racist. My mother may be a drama queen, but I love every bit of it. I'm a drama case sometimes myself. We all are at times, depending on the circumstances.

As my mother gained her strength back, she says like all girls her age, she just kept on. Sundays growing up were always a full day and my mother and her family would stay in church all day long. Nowadays, two hours of church is too long, but when we need a favor from God, we change like the wind.

My mother used to stay up late Saturday nights helping my grandfather write his Sunday sermons. Her father, Tommy Elle Wady, could really preach, roaring like a lion in his youth. Inside the little white church, during the hot, humid days of summer, the congregation would be fanning themselves as the heat of day warmed the church until it felt like a sauna. Nobody complained back then, because they were on God's time and were there to praise His name, no matter how hot it was. My mother's younger sister, Nellie Mae Wade, had a voice from God, and her praises went straight to God.

Growing up in east Texas, my mother and her family had plenty to celebrate on Sundays. Not only did they celebrate the goodness of God, but they celebrated their freedom in the church. During their time in church, they didn't worry about yesterday or tomorrow. Their moment with God put them on higher ground.

That higher ground all began with my great grandfather on my mother's side, Thomas Elle Wady. He was said to be a man's man, in that he related to people from every walk of life. At a time when black folks were scared to talk to white folks,

Thomas would talk to them all the time. He wasn't fearful of any man walking God's earth. In east Texas at a time when a black man couldn't even walk the street without fear of being lynched by the Klu Klux Klan, Thomas Wady had no fear of the white man. He walked with courage. He walked with God not only on Sunday, but all through the week.

Thomas was a farmer, a laboring man, who worked long hours, but he was also the first black man to own a car in his community. Thomas was a good Christian man, who followed the motto, "If you want to succeed, love the Lord." He felt sorry for the people of the world, he said, because so many people don't understand the simple things in life.

During his later years, Thomas went completely blind with glaucoma and soon came to ill health. Father Time caught up with him and life in his aged human body became a struggle. While having dinner with the family, eating at the head of the table, one of death's demons came knocking with a stroke. After about two weeks of care, Thomas soon caught talk that some kin folks were about to come back from California and help by his bedside, but Tommy, my grandfather, told them their service was done. "There's nothing you can do," he said. "Getting on a train and spending money you don't have is useless." At that time, Tommy Elle was doing the service every man will have to face, taking care of the man who has taken care of him. Soon after that God sent his angels around Thomas and took him home, where suffering is no more.

Thomas Wady was married to Nellie, a real dark woman whose hair was as black as midnight and curled like an endless stream. She was a woman of endless riches, not in terms of silver and gold but of love and dedication to family, at a time when hell was a daily reality. Thomas's mother, Mary, my great great grandmother, was a full blood Choctaw Indian from a reserve in Oklahoma. She was so fair skinned that she would dye her face darker so she looked more native and more of color. What made the Choctaw Indians distinct was that, because they lacked horses, often they would have to run wherever they had to go. Whenever I run, whether in competition or just for pleasure, I wave my hands to the sky and touch my head, my shoulders, my chest. I'm asking God to send the spirit of my ancestors, to let them run with me. I find great strength in that gesture.

ॐ

My mother met my father as she made her way to college. At the time, he is said to have been a hell raiser, to the point that my maternal grandmother thought he was the devil incarnate. He had a reputation for partying and fighting all night long. My grandmother feared for her daughter's safety in his hands. You didn't know what was going to happen. From time to time, my parents like to tell a story about those days. My mom's version is like this.

One hot breezy night in good old Texas my mother and father were getting ready to go to a party. In those days, my parents said, they would get all decked out, with dresses for the ladies and Stacey Adam shoes for the men. At the party my father got to drinking some good old Mad Dog wine, 20/20, they called it. He was scratching the floor with his shoes, dancing like nobody's business. As the night wore on and more glasses of liquor were poured, the music got louder and the crowd got bigger.

My father was drunk, the crowd knew it, and everybody was like, "Watch out for The Rock," they said, using my dad's nickname. Well, my mother saw my father having a good old time, dancing, smiling, and laughing. Out of nowhere, she decided to leave. I think she saw my father having too much fun so she tried to yank him off the dance floor. As he was about to fall, he reached for my mother to catch his balance and tore her dress.

My mother's cousin saw what happened. They say this man was crazy and had already killed a few people. Back then black-on-black crime was just paperwork, not an investigation. My mom's cousin went to his car and grabbed his gun and was on his way to shoot my dad. But my mom stopped him and said, "He's just drunk. Leave him alone." She begged her cousin to put the gun away. My dad says he really doesn't remember too much, but he tells us, "That nigga wasn't going to hurt nobody. I would have beat his ass anyways." I like my dad's version of the story.

❧

As time passed, my parents' bond grew stronger and stronger. In 1960 they got married at the justice of the peace in Texas and, for two whole years, nobody knew they were married. During those two years of marriage, my dad continued to live with his grandmother and my mother stayed with her parents. One day my mother decided to go out for night on the town and my father couldn't find her anywhere. When he heard that his woman had gone out for the night, he decided to sing like a bird and tell everybody they had been married for two years with nobody knowing. After my father's announcement, my parents moved to a small apartment in Garland, Texas, where my father worked as a janitor and my mother was teaching school.

One night a white man showed up at my parents' front door and asked to speak to my father about the application he had put in at General Electro Dynamics. The government was about to cut back on all government-issued contracts if they didn't start hiring blacks, and they wanted to offer my dad a job. That was a good day for my father. The company trained him and paid him at the same time. You never know when fortune will come your way.

Soon after, in 1963, my parent's first child — Stacey, my oldest sister — came along. (They were going to name their first child Stacey whether it was a boy or a girl.) My mother never wanted to leave Stacey so she taught part time. While she was away teaching she would call the babysitter so often that the babysitter up and quit.

Eventually my parents said goodbye to the apartment and moved into a house in Dallas, Texas. Soon after came Joseph, my oldest brother. Texas would be home until my father's company transferred him to Lowell, Massachusetts. In Lowell, my parents recall being one of the only black families; there wasn't a black person in sight. My Dad said, "It too damn cold up there." Nevertheless, while living in Massachusetts, soon came my older brother Stanley and my sister Simone. In the family pictures taken at this time, I'm not even a thought, except for the last family picture in which my mother is pregnant with me.

❧

These are the seeds of me. On my mother's side, my grandmother Big Mamma's grandpa was the last slave liberated in Texas. The story is told in a newspaper clipping that is held in the archives of the courthouse in Tyler, Texas. It reads as follows:

The Last Old Slave Dies

The last of the one-time slaves of the late Sam Goodman died at the age of 93 at his home on the white farm where he had been born and had spent his entire life since his liberation in 1865.

Peyton Tolbert died of pneumonia at his home on his own farm last week following a week's illness. His farm was part of the Old Wade Farm, adjoining the plantation of his old master and close friend, Sam A. Goodman, reported Mrs. A. N. Callaway, 633 North Broadway, daughter of the late Sam A. Goodman.

The name of Goodman, both junior and senior, will go down in the annals of east Texas history as applying to two of the kindest and most humanitarian slave owners who ever lived in the United States. So well liked was he and his son by his slaves at the time of their liberation in 1865 after the war between the states that it was with reluctance that many of his slaves accepted their freedom and its attendant economic responsibilities.

Before the war, Sam A. Goodman gave Tolbert to his son, and they became close friends. Sam A. and Peyton used to go quail hunting together and used to enjoy many rides together on the same horse as youngsters.

So attached was Peyton to his masters, the Goodmans, father and son, that when Sam A. went to the war, little Peyton wanted to go along with "Mass" to help take care of him and share his fate with him. That was impossible for Peyton at that time was only a little boy.

When Sam Goodman moved here in 1857 from South Carolina he brought his slaves, including the parents of Peyton with him.

Peyton's funeral will be at one o'clock, Sunday, February 3, 1952, in the Mount Zion C.M.E. Church, 18 miles east of Tyler on the Kilgore Highway, with the Rev. F. C. Jones, old friend of Peyton, officiating. Burial will take place in the Goodman cemetery located on the old Goodman plantation, which had been set aside in the pre-Civil War days especially for slaves and which is still used by one-time slaves. Jones Funeral Home in Kilgore is in charge of arrangements.

Tolbert's survivors include eight living children: Waymon and Lorenzo, both of Los Angeles; Emmet, D. B. and Lawrence of Kilgore; Phillip of Gladewater; Leotha Clemmons and Mattie Lee Tolbert of Kilgore; and a sister, Eliza Ann Stokes of Route 1, Tyler. The first grandchild of Peyton Tolbert and Lillie Tolbert was Thelma Mitchell [my grandmother].

That's some history. I can wait on my reparation now.

My great grandfather Sam Goodman on my mother's side is buried on the plantation that owned him. My grandmother Eva Mae Wady is buried on the Goodman plantation as well, as are other relatives. Her family tree lays to rest there. Even my mother has a place to rest next to my grandmother Eva Mae. For one day, when life on this earth has been a celebration, my mother will be on her way to another one. And once again she'll be with those who came before her. As for my father, the Priors have their gravesite deep in the woods of Texas.

❧

I have heard these stories about my family throughout my life and I find them significant. For to really understand yourself, you first need to understand your family tree. You need to learn about the generations who lived before you because we pick up the traits of those who came before us, some good and some bad. They all fall on us.

But we can all learn from past generations about how they dealt with the issues that burdened them, or even killed them. The beautiful thing about those who have come before us in our family tree is the great sacrifices these people have endured and the strength they attained, when the world would not allow them to be human. When racism was a daily struggle, day in and day out, despite that humiliation, they rose above their circumstances and managed to find humanity in chaos. We can embrace the great things they accomplished and overcame. For history always repeats itself, and the things our ancestors have overcome, we can also overcome — our blood and our DNA are the same. The only difference between those who have come before us and ourselves is that we're living in the 21st century. The scenery may be different, but the situation is still the same.

Our family tree reflects the past and present events that have shaped your family's name. It can make that name meaningful or it can make it ugly. The problem is that we try to avoid the negative characteristics of past generations. Sometimes we lie to avoid telling the truth about where we come from.

The seeds of me, just as the seeds of yourself, can tell you a lot. When you remove the day-to-day distractions from your life and look really close, you can see that our lives are like a puzzle and the pieces you choose to believe about yourself will determine your failure and success in life.

There is power in everything you believe. I believe there are no accidents in life but that every action causes a reaction. I believe that the sins of our ancestors and past generations always fall upon us. That's why there are some things you can't avoid, let alone control.

My father is my hero. He knows his kids, our strengths and our weaknesses. He knows the character traits that we have in us. When my father sees my life and how I have traveled and how far I have gone, I believe he sees a part of his own father in me.

Chapter 2

Growing Up

I was born on March 27, 1970, at about half past four in the morning. My mother tells me I was her biggest baby, weighing in at nine and a half pounds and outweighing all my brothers and sisters. I'm the youngest of five. I have two brothers and two sisters. Stacey is the oldest, and she's been a very independent woman her whole life. Then there's Joseph; he thinks he's a millionaire. I can't blame his attitude on my parents. I guess he loves to wish. My brother Stanley is the one who has always believed in me and who has been a constant in my life. Then there's Simone. Even though she's older than me, I think of Simone as my baby sister because she always calls for advice, or needs someone to listen. She has always been my strongest fan and supporter. Every time I was cut from an NFL team, she was always upset about it but never lost faith in me.

My story starts back in Vallejo, California, that's in northern California. From what I remember, we lived in a green house on a hill with a red fence alongside it. I can still picture all the greenery. My earliest memories are of Stanley walking me home from school. Just about every day I would pee my pants during our naptime after lunch and there were times I would have to walk home with a big wet spot on my pants. It was really uncomfortable, but walking with my brother always made me feel safe.

I have an early memory of my dad riding his ten-speed bike backwards down the hill, with his little Afro blowing and his striped shirt flapping in the wind. I have an early memory of eating Hostess cakes in the garage. My dad often would bring them home and we would sit in the garage eating them like nobody's business. I remember my older brother Joseph bullying Stanley and me and once locking us in the shed for about four hours. My parents whooped all our asses that night!

I remember my father jumping over the red fence, chasing after Stanley because he was going after Joseph with a baseball bat. My dad took off like a cheetah! Dad always protected us and watched out for our best interests. I remember Mom in the kitchen screaming over a dead mouse! I was sleeping on the red couch right next to the kitchen and woke up spooked! These are a few of my earliest memories, described as I remember them as a young boy still to this day. I'll never recall them any differently and frankly, I wouldn't want to.

We spent a year in that green house and then we moved across the street down to the bottom of the hill into a black and white house. I remember being amazed to see all these black folks moving furniture down the street without a riot erupting. We had fun that day. In the back of the house was a big gutter, with trees and trash everywhere. You couldn't keep us and the neighbors' kids out of it. If we went missing, we were usually found behind the house.

One of my most vivid early memories was being at home with my dad when I was about four years old and he had been laid off from his job. I was sick. Oh, damn, can you imagine? A black man with five kids being laid off at home with a crying, sick kid. Was I in trouble? Well, no, my dad is really a great man. It was a sunny day and out of nowhere we heard a big crash and, when we ran outside, we saw two cars had smashed right into each other in a head-on collision.

I don't remember much after that until we moved to Santa Ana in southern California. Things were starting to make more sense to me, well, a little more sense anyway.

While living in Santa Ana, my brother tried to toughen me up a little by making me fight our neighbor across the street. Sometimes I won; sometimes I lost. If you asked me, though, I would have told you that I won all the time. The only thing I wanted to do was play with my toys outside and tease my sister, hitting her and letting her chase me all around the house.

I used to love the weekends when my dad would take us somewhere. The best times were spent at the beach when he would have a day off work. We would have a day of fun in the sun, with games and toys and a barbecue. I mostly remember laughing in the sun and I can't speak for the others, but again, this is what I remember and how I saw it.

In our house in Santa Ana, my dad taught me how to tie my shoes and ride a bike. I can recall the day as if it was yesterday. It was sunny, with clouds scattered in the sky late into the evening. I was learning to ride on a big old bike with a banana seat that had handlebars as long as my legs! I was nervous, but when my dad said, "Come on, I've got you," I knew I could do it. I rode all the way down the street. The bad thing was I didn't know how to turn around and I didn't want to because the thought of having to turn the front wheel of that bike with those big handlebars made me afraid.

Not long after that, we moved about ten minutes away, but still remained in Santa Ana.

I can remember my mom's cousin Leora, who always filled our lives with drama. I can still picture her throwing that brick through the front windshield of her husband's car. No need to explain, you do the math.

My parents would throw parties for their friends, and boy they used to have a funky good time. They would make us stay in our rooms. Yeah, right! We would crack the door ajar, just enough for us to peek through, and laugh at all of them. Then we would come up with an excuse so we could leave our room to see what was going on. One time my dad made me act like Flip Wilson for them. Well, I thought I was the man! Too bad I never got to stay up because right after my performance I was sent back to my room. The sounds of Motown and the blues of B. B. King filled the house. People were drinking, dancing, smoking, and laughing. To this day, I still remember hearing the sounds of people having a good time.

One day my mom took us all school shopping at Sears; we

were excited, but a bit apprehensive, too, because Mom used to go ballistic in the stores. What could you expect with five kids running around like they're in a playground, wanting this and that! I guess we thought the most important thing was to get our clothes first and then we could have peace. That wasn't the case; school shopping lasted for a week, looking for sales and bargains. Man, I'm glad my dad didn't go with us, he's the cheapest man on earth! In his opinion we didn't need clothes, the clothes we had were fine. As we saw it, there was no way we could wear the same clothes we wore the year before—we'd be the laughing stock at school. My mom would go into debt buying us stuff for school, and I believe to this day, she's still paying for it. Thanks, Mom. You're the best!

One night, my brothers and I snuck out of the house wearing only our boxer shorts. We'd never had boxer shorts before and we wanted everybody to see. We were tired of wearing those tighty whities. When our dad saw all three of us running around outside in our underwear, Man! He took all of us into the house and boy! He tore our asses up. It worked because we never went outside in our underwear again; we just wore them around inside the house.

My little eyes and mind soaked up all the wonders of life and I never knew how all these funny moments would one day make me want to write about them.

If I were to leave out this story, I would never forgive myself. It was in the late 1970s or early 1980s, Sunday morning, getting ready to go to church. My mom would deliberately turn on the vacuum cleaner around half past six in the morning to make sure everyone in the house was awake. I also believe it was a tactic to piss us off. I hated that awful noise so early in the morning.

My mother would insist that we hurry up and get ready for church. The funny thing about it, though, she was always the last one ready those Sunday mornings. She would play Super Mom, making sure we all looked presentable. My father made a point of getting us to change into something else if we didn't dress a certain way. Problem was, he only went to church with us on holidays and special occasions. I always felt like saying to him, "What do you care? You're not even going this morning." But, I never dared say something like that because he would have knocked me into next week. I have always respected my parents. I have only one set that's original.

There were times when my mother would drive to or from church as quiet as a mouse while my brothers and sisters would argue and complain: "I'm hungry," "I'm tired," "I don't feel like going to church." Out of nowhere my mom would say, "You all shut the hell up. I hate all you sons of bitches. You make me sick. I wish I never even had none of you. Hell, y'all ain't shit. I'm telling you this 'cause one day y'all gonna wake up and I'm just gonna be gone. I'm not even going to say goodbye. Yeah, I talked with my daddy last night, he said his door is always open to me and I told him I'm ready to leave these damn kids and go back to Texas!"

We never for a minute believed one word of what she said. All we did was look at each other and smile. Each of us believed that our mother was talking someone else, the one we were looking at, smiling. All my brothers and sisters would protest that she wasn't talking about them; she was always talking about the other one. She never left, nor did she go to Texas to live with her dad. My mom's actions have spoken so loud that her words of frustration—and they were only words of frustration—have no power.

As a little child, I was seeing so much as I grew up and began remembering a lot of the moments and incidents. I remember how they made me feel, sometimes angry, sometimes sad. But the good thing was that all these people and events started molding me and shaping my life.

In 1976 my parents bought their first brand new house in Riverside, California, and to this day, they live there. My fondest memories are from this house, even though moving to Riverside sucked because we had to travel all the back way to Santa Ana to go to school. Our parents didn't want us to change schools because the year was almost over.

Let me take you back to about 1978, when I was eight years old. That's when I started playing football. I wasn't that good a player and had no confidence in myself. I was skinny and scared to hit and really I was playing only because my brothers were football players and I wanted to be like them. I couldn't even hold my jock strap right! Heck, I couldn't even fall asleep in the dark by myself so how in the hell was I going to play football?

It was my destiny to ride the bench. God knows I had no talent, but I was faster than anyone else. Apparently, though, speed was not a factor. The only ones playing were those who were fearless and not afraid to hit those big guys! My dad would look at me as if I was a wimp, which, as a Prior, wouldn't stand around our house. So, I would find the courage to play a little and survived the season with no bumps or bruises.

I remember our coach was a very intense man, the kind of coach who would make you run through a brick wall. Although he was a master motivator, I was terrified to show any courage. All you could see was my big dark brown eyes through my helmet saying, "Okay," or "Yes" to everything and anything while at the same time I was thinking, "This coach is crazy." To this day, I can't recall his name but he was very overweight and used a wheelchair to get around. He didn't yell or get excited, he just talked a bunch. I never knew what he was saying; I was too worried and afraid most of the time. I played a few games but nothing to brag about.

That first year, our team won the championship for Little League in our district. I really can't take too much credit. I was a cheerleader on the sideline, watching everybody else and getting excited for them. Although I was a bench warmer, the coach would let me play when we had a big lead or there was no way we could win. I didn't mind. As long as I got dirty I would make my father smile and he would take his big hand, place it on the top of my head, and give my big head a shake. That's all I really needed.

When that first season came to an end I was so relieved and we looked forward to doing what kids do best—getting into trouble, having a few fights with the neighborhood kids, just stuff.

❦

The following year was a real rollercoaster ride. My best friend and neighbor at the time, John Thomas, was on the same team as me and my dad was the coach, so you know what that meant. I was horrified when he told me I was going to be the starting quarterback. I don't think I slept for a month. For a nine-year-old kid I was under a lot of stress. I remember very clearly we didn't win a game.

One Saturday morning ball game, it was a picture-perfect day without a cloud in the sky. I remember the sounds as our cleats hit the pavement and I can still see the freshly chalked lines drawn on the damp grass. My dad, as the offensive coach, would stay about ten yards behind me during each play. There was one play in particular when my dad would say, "32 Blast!" meaning I would hand the ball off to my right, the running back. Well, you guessed it. I went the wrong way and tried handing the ball to my left. Oops, there was nobody there. While the play continued, I nonchalantly turned and starting walking towards my father with the ball. I wanted to tell him that the running back had gone the wrong way. But my dad was jumping in the air, yelling and pointing towards the outside, shouting, "Run, damn it! Run, son!" I kept walking towards him as if the play was over and, next thing you know, Wham! I fumbled the ball. "Oh, shit!" was all I heard my father say.

After the game, which we lost, my dad said to me, "Son, what in the hell were you thinking out there?" I couldn't speak; I decided it was best to remain quiet. I sat shaking my head. "Well, get it right, Booboo," he said. Those words stuck me like a thorn and at that time I told myself I would get it right one day, not just today. While I was growing up I would always wish for tomorrow to come so that maybe then I would get it right.

When he was coaching, my father would get home from a long hard day, change into his uniform, grab his whistle, and we would all jump into the back of that old green Toyota truck.

He would be smiling the entire time. I would look at him out of the corner of my eye, realizing that this is what he loved to do: coach his boys, watching them grow into something special made him happy.

Soon as we pulled up to the practice field my dad's whole demeanor would change. He was a tough coach. The other coaches were scared of him because when he put on the coach's hat he would turn into another person. I still looked at him the same way because he was my father, I knew him, his mode, everything. Looking back I can still see my father after practices, running wind sprints and out-running everyone. To a kid that means an awful lot: seeing your father, so strong and well-built, really enjoying himself.

My father was a tough coach and once I remember him taking a switch to one of the other boys because "we," meaning the team, messed up.

I'll never forget my dad's playbook. He kept it on top of the refrigerator like it was top secret. He had some of the best plays a coach could draw up. With an old ruler and a set of markers, he would spend hours sitting on the patio in our backyard scribbling away. Maybe one play a game would work and the rest, well, need I say more? My dad would get irritated, yellin' and screamin' at us like we were at some kind of military camp. I sometimes thought to myself that maybe it was the plays that didn't work and not the players. Though I wouldn't dare say that, I sure was thinkin' it. Heck, we couldn't even buy a game to win.

We started losing so bad that one Sunday night, my dad collected all the dolls my sister didn't want and bought some ribbons at the store. The following Monday at practice my dad was in full gear. He made everyone on the team wear a bow on their helmet and carry one of my sister's dolls if they made a mistake. Three other football teams were practicing on the same field and when our team would take a jog for warm-ups they'd mock and point at us, laughing like nobody's business. Some kids laughed and some cried.

I thought for sure my dad was going to make me do the

same thing. Yeah, right, he would never do that, no matter how terrible I played. He'd always protect me, after all, he was my dad. He wouldn't humiliate me like that. All I could do was smile and laugh at the other players, even though I knew I had made mistakes during Saturday's game, too. But even though I didn't play great football all the time, my dad never made me carry a doll around or put a ribbon on my helmet.

Dad eventually got carried away and started whooping kids' asses with a ruler and parents started to complain. Since "majority rules," my dad was fired as a coach. Funny thing was, on the day he was fired, he went and sat in his green Toyota truck, the first brand new truck he ever bought and the one he put some serious miles on. I was wondering what he was doing in there, so after practice I ran over to go home. He was looking all pissed off and said, "The hell with them, they don't want to win, those sorry bastards." He still encouraged me to keep on playing, but deep down I knew the reason he wasn't coaching anymore. The parents thought he was running a suicide camp, but I carried on knowing my dad wanted us to work hard.

During one practice my dad made my friend John Thomas run a play about ten times until he was no longer afraid of it. All practice, my dad blew the whistle again and again until John started crying, and as he cried he ran the play over and over again.

The sun was going down and it was starting to get dark when we were ready to go home that day. John followed behind us as we walked to the truck together. We stopped for something to eat on the way home, talking about football and school the whole time. If I had known my dad was going to be fired as coach the next day I would have done things differently that night. The other kids' parents had decided that my dad was too much of a drill sergeant and that was the last time he would coach us. Perhaps I would do something courageous like John did. He was a different person after that day, more confident, walking taller around the neighborhood. That was the kind of coach my dad was.

I didn't realize that this would be the last time my father

would be my coach. That would be the last time my dad took his big hand and placed it on my head and gave my peanut head a shake.

The next day when my dad came home from work he never changed into his coaching uniform. He didn't even grab his playbook off the top of the refrigerator. I knew something awful was wrong and he just shook his head. A few days later the other coaches got back at my dad by making me and a few of the other boys wear ribbons during the practice. I cried while I was jogging around the field. I could hardly wait to tell my dad what had happened. The following day, my dad came to the practice like a raging bull and told everyone off. After that, I was treated like a star and the remainder of the season, no matter how badly I played, I never was made to carry a doll or wear a ribbon on my helmet. It was all because my dad got fired. My dad's tactics were so funny at the time. Occasionally when we are sitting back reminiscing about the past we still laugh about that.

The following year I turned ten. Wow! Double digits. I'm a man now, or so I thought. That year my coach was Ernest Burns. He was the most intense coach in Riverside, California. He had a passion that most people only dream about and you could see it in his eyes every time he talked about football. He would become so intense that at times he would have to wipe the tears from his eyes. He was a major influence during my career. We would meet up again when I was in high school and that became a turning point in my life.

I decided to play running back. I was a little jittery at times, and sometimes scared, but I did it and played as hard as I could. I didn't want to let my dad down or embarrass him. He came to every game, always wearing the same thing—jeans, a red windbreaker jacket, and a gray old man's hat. I was always able to pick him out in crowd. That year I played okay despite a few bad games. I could always hear Mr. Burns screaming when the defense was on the field. He would always yell, "I want my ball back!" He would sweat and drop onto his knees yelling those infamous words. There were several times when I was tempted to grab any ball and go and give it to him.

That year my dad coached my older brothers. He would watch my games, and do some coaching with me at home. I had more courage and knew what I was doing. I wasn't playing a major position, but was a backup running back and didn't play that much. Still, I loved it. I was playing football! I was with my friends and was considered cool. I was ten years old and had it going on. I even had a girlfriend down the street; her name was Janeen.

I'll never forget my last football game. Would you believe our team was undefeated and getting a chance to play in the championship? That was a big change in my life. It was a Little League playoff game and after the game had gotten under way, Dechon, our only running back, got hurt and guess who had to play? Me! I was terrified! I couldn't believe I was going to have to play the whole rest of the game. Every time I got the ball I fumbled like it was a loaf of hot bread just out of the oven. I had no idea what was wrong. The crowd and the parents were yelling, "Get him out of there!"

My dad was in the stands waving his arms and I'm sure he must have been saying, "Oh, shit, son, what the hell are you doing?" I was getting angry and frustrated with myself. I ran to the sidelines, tore off my helmet and threw it to the ground. Next went the shoulder pads. I was crying and telling myself I sucked. My dad came screaming down those bleachers yelling, "Anthony! Anthony! Get your damn helmet and put those shoulder pads on before I whoop your ass! And take your ass back out there!" Hearing that voice, the tears were gone fast.

Mr. Burns put me back in the game. The next play, I fumbled the ball again. I was devastated. My ego was crushed. The coach took me out of the game and I spent the rest of the game sitting on the bench. I wasn't worried about the game; it was my dad I was concerned about.

All the way home I remained quiet. We stopped for a burger and my Dad gave me the usual "man-to-man" talk, telling me that when you fail you always have to get back up and try again. After those encouraging words he added, "And, when we get home I'm gonna whoop your ass." He kept on eating his burger. I thought for sure by the time we got home he would have forgotten what he had promised me. I began to think I wasn't in trouble. He wouldn't take me out to eat then whoop my ass later, would he? Well, that's what happened. As soon as we walked in the door, he sent me to my room for behaving the way I did out there, embarrassing him. I got whooped and that would be the last time I played football until high school. Looking back on that hot summer day in 1980, I understand why I needed to be disciplined and would refer to that day for years to come.

❦

Bike racing was the next sport I got involved in. BMX racing was the coolest thing in the early 1980s. We started riding around the neighborhood, racing each other and the other kids in the neighborhood. Our street Big Dipper Drive was the hangout for kids from all the neighboring streets. Racing bikes would become my new thrill for the next six and a half years.

I started racing bikes because of my older brother Stanley. He was the one person I looked up to and when he started BMX, I was sure to follow. After a few months of pedaling around parks and old vacant fields, I decided it was time to give racing a try for real, and go racing at the local YMCA.

I would try to be cool but my heart would be pumping. I could only tell myself not to crash and embarrass myself, especially with Stanley and all the neighborhood kids around. All the boys from the Theriot family across the street and all their boys raced bikes and they were pretty good but they argued and complained a lot. My brother and I stayed cool. Stanley helped me practice at the track and at the age of ten I was racing as a beginner. After paying the registration fee I looked around to see who I was racing against. I was so embarrassed to see that I'd be racing against only another boy and a girl—just the three of us. I was more worried than anything about a girl beating me. The good thing was that I would at least get a trophy because there were always trophies for first, second, and third place. No way could I lose because there were only three of us. We had to race three times and I won every race. For a moment I was a hero.

That night, my brother crashed the same way he always did. He never crashed by himself but usually took about five other racers with him. He was always in first place whenever the crash would happen. It was as if he was scared to win, afraid of success like a lot of people in the world. My brother always blamed the crash on his bike. Since I was his cheerleader, I would agree with him because he was my hero. That's what big brothers are to little brothers.

Before too long I became a novice racer and the competition got tougher. We ventured out to new tracks to find more intense competition, spend more money, and waste more time fixing our bikes and healing our scrapes from falling. Our crashes were all for the glory of getting one more trophy. We were chasing plastic trophies to display in our rooms and to crown the glory we enjoyed at the track. This went on for years and years till I had darn near 500 trophies. I started storing them in my dad's barn, which he built in the backyard, and to this day there are still trophies sitting on the shelves. As the years went by and my brothers and sisters started having kids, we'd give trophies to the kids just for riding up and down the street. My dad still tells me to get rid of those damn trophies and little by little he gives them away to his grandkids.

∽✿∾

I was still bike racing when my mom came home one night eager to tell me that she was going to get me a talent agent along with a chance to do television commercials, model clothes, and all kinds of stuff. At first, it was like, "Wow, I'm going to be a star, I'm going to make movies and be rich!" Well, it didn't happen and the experience was bittersweet. But that's my mom, a headstrong pre-school teacher, always helping the down-and-out. She has always been a generous person, a woman who has helped many people even though they couldn't help her in return. She gives in the true spirit of giving.

That first year, in 1981 when I was eleven years old, my

mom would take me on casting calls after school. We'd have to sit in traffic because we lived in Riverside and Los Angeles is at least an hour's drive away. Towards the end of that year I was tired of trying to become famous; it was wearing me down. Mom and I would argue all the way there and sometimes I'd start to cry, saying, "I want to race my bike."

She'd yell, "Oh, the hell with that bike! All you're doing is wasting your time!" That made me cry even more and every time before going onto the set to act, she would tell me to smile and do well. "I'll take you to Sizzler's to have the all-you-can-eat salad bar when we're finished."

I'd go into that room, shining like a star, smiling like Sammy Davis Jr., thinking, "Boy! I can hardly wait until it's time to eat!"

This was my time to be somebody else, a moment to see if it was my turn to be lucky and get the part. My mom always told me to go and do the best I could; that's all I could do anyway. I've realized that's a good way to live. I guess that's why I never worry about what other people say about my life, about whether I'll be happy or not. I was happy before I got the auditions, I was happy eating at The Sizzler later, and I always believed that my fate was in my hands, not someone else's. I learned at an early age to enjoy the moment, because life is about lots of moments that continuously shape our character. Despite all the traffic and the crying I will never forget The Sizzler and their all-you-can-eat shrimp at the salad bar.

Our ship came in about a year and a half later, in 1982, when I landed a Kellogg's commercial with Kirk Cameron. That's when he was a nobody, and well, so was I. My mom talked with his mom and she was so happy that day. She was talking and laughing with the producers, watching the caterers serving the food, and feeling like a star herself. Mom didn't realize how closely I watched her, but seeing her reaction to my success made me realize I had really accomplished something. My experiences to this point in my life taught me that if you practice persistence with whatever challenges you face, sooner or later, heaven and earth will cooperate and seemingly, out of nowhere, all the things you wish for will come together.

A problem for many of us is that we want things right now. Being the last of five children, I have learned to be patient and wait my turn. We all look at our successes with open eyes but we close our eyes to our failures but we've got it all mixed up. Failures force us to keep going. They drive us to change bitter experiences into sweet ones. The problem is that we tend to focus too much on our successes, losing sight of how we reached success. Our failures are the stepping-stones to success. It's important to keep our eyes open to our failures and remember the path we took to become a success. This is something we all need to be conscious of.

Soon after the Kellogg's commercial I got another one with McDonald's in 1984. My mom had to work that day so our neighbor, Bob, took me to the shoot. He was an older man who worked in the meat department at a supermarket for many, many years. I think my mom felt that people didn't believe that I was really doing commercials, but everybody knew Bob and he sure didn't lie. I may be exaggerating, but that was my first experience being the envy of friends and neighbors.

The second commercial wasn't much fun. They production crew appeared to be somewhat disorganized and my mom wasn't with me, though she and dad did come later. My mom got mad at my dad because he messed up the paperwork so I didn't get all my money, but she worked that out. The crew got things rolling and it turned out to be a productive day. Eventually, I made some good money and about a year later, once I had saved up some money, I bought a new BMW. I was only fifteen and had only a learner's permit so the car stayed parked in the garage, but it was the nicest car in the house. My mom drove an old Buick Regal, and my dad drove a raggedy old Plymouth K-car. Boy, was it ugly! I sure felt like I was the man of the house with a little money and a nicer car than my parents. Yeah, I thought I was it!

☙

Racing bikes started to take its toll. I kept telling my dad I was going to make a living racing bikes. His reaction was, "Nigga, please play some football and you'll make a real living." I thought, "Football, no way. I'd kill myself or get killed!"

Around 1985, I told myself that if I didn't get a real sponsor soon to start paying for my BMX races I'd end up spending all the money I'd earned from the commercials. I wished college offered bike racing scholarships. My dad said, "Wake up, son." So I decided I was going to let it all roll in the American Bicycle Association Grand Nationals in Oklahoma City. Because I was going to pay all my expenses, flight, and hotel, I asked my mom if she knew anyone who needed work done so I could earn more money for the trip. I didn't want to spend all my life savings at the age of fifteen.

The stage was set in Oklahoma City, with racers from all over the world. I wasn't scared, just anxious to display my skills and make a good impression. I'd been racing for six years and hadn't won a national event. The closest I got was second place and I'd consider myself a failure if I didn't win at least one national race.

The scene was amazing, energy was everywhere, and I was ready to wear my crown. I felt that I deserved to win at last. The first day of qualifying, I just plain dominated. I was on a real high and felt this was my moment to shine. I'd been down long enough and it was my world that weekend The race officials could award me the trophy and the sponsors could start coming out of the woodwork. I'd wear jeans and a sweatshirt for the race because I wanted potential sponsors to notice me. Everybody else was sponsored by major corporations and had picture-perfect uniforms. I thought to myself that I'd be wearing one of those very soon.

That night, I couldn't sleep. I was sharing a hotel room with the Rockwells, a family from our neighborhood. They had two boys racing, but I don't remember how they did I was too concerned about how I was going to finish. I was thinking too much about the next morning: I'd eat, practice, and get ready for the main event.

This was the Super Bowl of BMX. The place was full to capacity and buzzed with excitement. Out of 114 racers, I was one of eight finalists and was assigned the third lane. We had about three more races to go. Having watched so many other races before mine I saw all the emotions that life presents: pain, sadness, joy, tears. My heart began to beat harder and faster; I had the look of a warrior. I was in the zone. Everything I'd put into the sport of bike racing had come down to this one moment. I really couldn't have been more prepared for anything in my life. I had no other concerns.

The gate went up and the eight of us were ready to take off like rockets. Ready and watching the lights—red, yellow, green—I got off to a good start. A feeling of quiet came over me; I reached the first jump and became aware that I was in the lead. I felt in complete control of the race, but I wasn't surprised because I expected this. All the way around the track I was in the lead and, as I came around the last corner, I heard the crowd. I felt joy come over me and I pedaled harder around the last turn. The crowd was getting louder still; I could see the finish line. Out of nowhere, I slipped a pedal and almost crashed. Two racers flew past me and I ended up in third place! Tears poured from my eyes. I didn't know what to do, or who to talk to.

Instead of the trophy I wanted so badly I was given a big wooden plaque. When I went back to the hotel room the neighbors I was sharing with congratulated me on a job well done. They didn't realize I had laid everything on the line for that one race. There would be no next week for me, just today, and the past hour had changed everything. I threw my bike down on the ground and words that my parents didn't think I knew poured out of my mouth.

The next day I didn't even qualify to race for a different title. My confidence was shot and there was no sponsor looking in my direction. The only thing I could think was, "Damn, what am I going to do now? I'm fifteen years old with no interest in school except English and writing." My oldest brother Joseph had a football scholarship to the University of Arizona. Stanley, my other brother was planning on attending Fullerton Junior College to play football. They had plans and direction in their lives, all I had was a big wooden plaque from Oklahoma City.

Throughout my life, I put so much emphasis on winning, doing everything possible to win, leaving no room for excuses. I thought I was in total control, but failed to recognize the forces I couldn't control, such as sickness, bad weather, and other people's actions. I now understand that life does throw you disappointment. Looking back, the lesson I learned that day was that no matter how much we prepare for an event, the outcome is completely unknown.

༺༻

My parents always made sure we had chores, such as lawn work, washing dishes for a week, and folding your laundry as well as everybody else's, and even putting the clean clothes in their room. That seemed brutal at the time, but it showed us you have to take care of your own first. When it came to clothes, one lesson stood out and lasted until the day I left for college. After folding the clothes, the towels, and the blankets and putting them in their proper place, the socks were a totally different story. In the front closet was a dirty old laundry bag and we would put all the socks in that bag, no matter what the color, whether they were new or old.

During my school years, when I lived at home, the mornings would be about racing to the bathroom or squabbling with my brothers and sisters. After all the chaos of trying to get ready, the last thing we would do before leaving for school was go to the closet, pull out the sock bag, and try to find a pair of matching socks. If we were rushed, hell, we would grab any two socks, even if they weren't a pair. If we had time on our hands, it became a country club around the sock bag, laughing at each other, throwing socks at one another, find each other's match. When you found your own match, you could up and leave the mess, but the last one to find a match would have to put all the socks back in the bag and put the bag back into the closet. On a typical morning when I was growing up, we'd pull out the sock bag, put it away, and leave out the front door.

My sister Simone sometimes woke up at half past five and ate up all the cereal. Then she'd smile at all of us because she knew that when we grabbed the cereal box it would be empty. A little fight would break out, a few words would be exchanged, and someone would get a slap in the back of the head. I would take off before all that started, because I knew Simone would not have left any cereal. Simone continued to set her alarm clock so she could eat up all the cereal.

Sometimes there would be plenty of cereal left, and Simone would watch you pour cereal into your bowl, open the refrigerator door, and find no milk. You'd have to scrape together something like some toast or a banana to eat. Meanwhile Simone would laugh like nobody's business and make sure you saw her pour a bowlful of milk into the sink. She'd say, "That sure was good and sugary." Then she'd run to her room to get ready for school.

さ

Every now and then I wonder why people reminisce. For me, whenever I hear a song from my youth I never feel sad. When the words from a familiar song start to whisper in my ear, then I begin to smile about yesteryear and memories begin to start forming in my mind.

Monday night football was a spectacle for my father. I think Mondays during the football season made him feel like a player himself. When we would hear our father pull up at half past four in the afternoon and the door of his car slam shut, we would all be there to greet him as he opened the door and we'd ask if he could carry us. He would carry Simone and me, Simone on his left and me on his right. We thought our father was a big strong giant and, as little as I was I believe that, and to this day I'm taller than he is but he is still my giant from yesteryear.

One particular Monday night my father was cooking dinner because my mother and Stacey had gone shopping. As the evening progressed, we found ourselves at the counter eating some spaghetti my father made. From what I remember, it was good. My mother's Buick Regal had a diesel engine, so whenever she pulled up we definitely knew it was her. As she pulled up in the driveway we all said, "Mae Lois is home!" and my father would say, "There's your momma." We patiently waited for her to come through the front door to see what she had bought us at Sears, but for some reason we could hear yelling and screaming outside, so we knew something had happened.

The screaming got louder and louder as my mother got closer to the door and we could hear our sister Stacey crying. The door flew open and my mother said, "Y'all ain't gonna believe this shit." We were all stunned with excitement, anticipating my mother's next words. "Stacey was caught shoplifting in Sears and my friends were there. Oh, hell, I'm so embarrassed." Her next words, "Stacey get your ass in your room. Take off your pants and Stanley go get me a belt. Y'all come back here and watch me tear her ass up." That's just like my mother, getting her kids to be her audience. It was like this for all of us. Whenever we stepped out of line or got in trouble, she would spank us in front of everybody and tell one of my brothers or sisters to go get a belt. We all loved that duty. An audience of brothers and sisters would laugh at whoever was getting a whompin' at the time. I think we were laughing at the fear my mother would put in the eyes of the one getting a whompin'. If we would try to run, she wouldn't ever have to run after us. One of the other kids would catch you and then we would really start to laugh.

Sometimes my mother would even have the belt in her hands. The audience watching in anticipation, my mother would pause and walk real slow and say, "You know, I brought you into this world and I will surely take you out." If you were the one in trouble you were probably saying, "Please just get this over with already." That was one of my mother's tactics, pause to get you relaxed and then out of nowhere, smack! Usually the first touch of that belt would make you scream a different scream and the audience would laugh a little louder.

Remember the names, those nicknames that your family still call you whenever you call home or go home for the holidays? Yeah, we all had nicknames. Stacey, hers was "Bub." I never knew what it stood for. Joseph, his nickname was "Sunny" and I never really understood his either. But when you have a big family, you have social groups. Simone was only two years older than me and Stanley three years, so I competed with them. Simone's nickname was "Buck" and Stanley was "Bucky Beaver." Both of them sucked their thumb until they were about fifteen and their teeth showed it. Their thumbs were raw from all the thumb sucking. My dad used to put hot sauce on their thumbs and I used to love to tease them about it. My mom even made them wear gloves and I would sit in front of them and put my thumb in my mouth and use my other hand to twirl my shirt the way they would, as if to mimic them. I couldn't do it for long, because I would be laughing so hard.

My nickname was "Pissy Papa" because I would wet the bed all the time and all my humiliation would come in the morning. I can hear my mother vacuum cleaning the house, walking towards my room and her first question was, "Hey, Pissy, you piss in the bed?" I would nod my head, "Yes," and she would sing some song she had made up: "Funky Pissy Pappa you better beware, funky Pissy Pappa you pee in my hair." The first person to come into my room to tease me was my sister Simone, with her thumb in her mouth, shaking her head, with burn marks on her forehead from the hot comb. My mother had been trying to straighten her hair for church that morning.

It got so bad I was peeing in the bed every night and I would often get up, change the sheets, and turn on the washing machine in the middle of the night. Still my oldest sister Stacey would hear me and say, "Pissy," real loud as I would be putting new sheets on the bed. There were times I would wet the bed, change the sheets, and wet the bed again all in one night. I tell you, growing up I wet the bed everywhere. I was too nervous to sleep over at friends' houses. I would try and stay up all night long to avoid having an accident. We laugh now at those days. My family calculated that I have wet the bed in hotels, motels, all our relatives' houses, on my brothers' and sisters' beds, and even on them, in my parents' bed and on them, too. There were times I would cry I was so frustrated. I wasn't scared of the dark but for some reason I would fall asleep and pee on myself and on whoever was next to me. To this day, "Pissy Pappa" is a legend in my family.

My bedwetting was a condition of weak abdominal muscles, a doctor told me during my career in the NFL. That's why I've had numerous problems with pulled groin and lower abdominal muscles. The weakness in those muscles had to be strengthened.

❦

My father has always been a straight up man. One evening in 1979, when I was about eight years old, it became very clear that he wanted us to know the history of black people. My father called us from our rooms and said, "You come in here and watch this show on television." It was a school night and we had just got done eating dinner. The first time he called we didn't really pay attention because our father didn't care about the TV unless football was on. Before you knew it my dad was standing in the hallway with his chest out, yelling, "Get y'all asses in the front room right now." We all jumped up and ran into the front room to watch television, even though we didn't know what we were about to see.

It was a television documentary of Martin Luther King Jr. and the Civil Rights Movement of the 1960s. When Martin Luther King Jr. appeared on the TV screen, my dad said, "I bet they're not teaching you about this man in school," and he was right. We couldn't use the bathroom or even get a snack that night. My dad made us watch the entire show.

I was stunned by some of the things I saw. What captivated me most was the original footage of firefighters turning up the pressure on their water hoses, knocking people to the ground and tearing the clothes off their bodies. I saw white police officers beating black women, men, and even children. I saw a white police officer beat a heavy-set black woman, who reminded me of my own mother. I thought about what I would do if a cop was beating her for no reason. Without a doubt, I'd kill him. Then I saw a white police officer strike a little black man in the back of the head, for no reason except that he was walking down the street. I saw that black man retaliate with force, hitting the police officer and I thought about my father. I said to myself, "Nobody could beat up my dad. He would fight all those police officers by himself."

Only eight years old, I saw some disturbing things on TV that night. I really didn't understand until I got older. One thing was solid—my father made us all feel safe growing up. Anytime we heard a noise in the night and it frightened us, as long as we knew our father was in the next room, it really didn't bother us.

The next morning, walking to the bus stop, I was looking strange at white people. My best friend, a white boy, asked, "What's wrong?" But all I could say was, "Nothing," because I didn't know how to express what I was feeling.

That same day I looked at my white teacher and wondered, "Was that her dad or cousin in the footage I saw last night?" I looked at white people much different from that day on. I looked at them with knowledge well beyond that of an eight year old. I was suspicious and didn't trust them and that was the weekend I asked my dad to build a doghouse for King, our family dog.

❦

My brothers and sisters loved our dog King. He would run away every day, but when he got hungry he'd make his way back home. My father would have to tie King up all the time.

What made King so unusual was that he hated white people. Every time a white person would pass by our house, let alone try and come up to the front door, King would bark out of control. In the back of our minds, we would be laughing. King was a racist dog. We couldn't be that way, but I guess we sort of applauded King whenever he'd bark at white people.

We all loved King. My dad built that doghouse and it even

had carpet on the floor. Soon after the doghouse was finished, King took off one cold night. We all yelled, "King, get back here, you stupid dog." We could see his eyes light up as we chased him and the streetlight from up reflected in his eyes. I guess King thought we were playing with him as we chased and yelled at him. King looked back, with his tongue hanging out his mouth, but whenever he looked ahead he ran faster and faster until he was so far ahead of us, we lost sight of him in the night. We never saw King again.

The holidays were spectacular events. During the seventies, my father was a master at wearing sideburns and his Afro was as natural as his turquoise rings and bracelet. Carving the turkey was a big distraction for him, considering Thanksgiving was Cowboy day and the Cowboys were often playing on TV. Before eating and while saying grace you could always hear the TV. A crowd would always join us for Thanksgiving dinner and whenever there was a touchdown, half of the table would get up to watch the replay. That's one thing my dad loved about watching games on TV: the replay. The turkey was always dry, but dessert seemed to satisfy everybody. If the Cowboys lost on Thanksgiving Day, my father would leave the house and go to the barn in the backyard. I'd watch him walk and talk to himself and wave his hands in the air as if he were cursing the referees himself. On the other hand, if they won, he'd just sit there and fall asleep.

Nothing really changed in the eighties. My father lost the turquoise jewelry and the Afro turned into a Gerry curl. The Cowboys were still the Thanksgiving Day show and his routine stayed the same.

Thanksgiving may have been my father's holiday, but Christmas was for my mother, the drama queen. She either made it wonderful or miserable, especially if one of us talked about gifts we didn't get. Look out!

When we were really young, my brothers and sisters would wake up at about half past one or two in the morning. We all would sleep in the same room, anticipating Santa's arrival. I remember talking through the night, saying, "I hope I get this or that." Sleep was impossible. Only after we had seen our presents could we fall asleep.

My oldest sister Stacey would always walk into our parent's room to wake them up while the rest of us stood at the door, waiting to run to the front room to open our presents. As soon as our parents were awake, we would all storm into the front room and tear away at the presents until we were all satisfied.

A Christmas drama would erupt if there were no batteries for an electric car or if somebody got a gift that cost more than yours. That was the way Christmas went in the seventies, when it all was fun. By the eighties we were all a little older. Gifts got more expensive.

My mother was gaining weight and one particular Christmas, my dad bought her a stationary bike. That sure was the wrong gift to buy. My mother believed that if anybody could use something that was given to them then it wasn't really a gift, it was a tool everybody could use. My mom sure yelled that morning. "That gift was for you, damn it," she shouted. I guess my mom was right because that evening my father was riding the bike out in the barn. My mom insisted there was no way in hell she was going to ride a bike in the barn where mice ran free and dust sat in the air and junk surrounded you like a bad habit.

The following Christmas was the most memorable. We were all old enough to wait until morning to open up our gifts. The excitement of getting up in the middle of the night had worn off. By the eighties I had figured out that Santa Claus lived in the room beside me.

That morning, my oldest brother Joseph jumped up out of the bed and ran outside. He ran to the backyard, looked into the garage and said, "Where's my car?" My parents looked at him like he was crazy. Somehow he believed he was getting a brand new Camaro for Christmas. Even I thought that was odd, since my mother drove a Buick Regal and my dad by that time had moved on to a Volkswagen Rabbit. Joseph looked at my mother and said, "Damn, did we go bankrupt this year?" That set my mother off. "You ungrateful son-of-a-bitch, get your ass out of here," she shouted. The rest of us were laughing. My dad seemed to be a little puzzled and confused.

My mother was already in a ballistic state of mind, so there was no way that any of us were going to complain about our gifts. For some reason, my father left the room when my mother was about to open her gift from him. You would think he'd have learned his lesson from the previous year. All we heard from my mother as she began to open her present from him was, "This son-of-a-bitch bought me pots and pans. I don't want this shit. Take this back and give me the money. I'll buy my own gift. I can't believe this shit." My father shook his head and smiled a little. We all looked at him, while eating breakfast, thinking to ourselves, "What was he thinking?" But we never would question our parents' motives. As a black man my father was not too respected in society, but then what black man is? When he walked into our house and into our presence, we all respected him. My mother and all her outbursts always made sure of that.

I sometimes look back and think of those Christmas nights when my sisters and brothers would stay up through the night, whispering and trying to keep our laughter low. It was a time when we didn't care whose house was bigger than the other and whose kids were smarter. We didn't care who made more money, who finished college and who didn't, whose wife, girlfriend, husband, or boyfriend we didn't like. It was a time when youth and innocence were as carefree as strolling through the park. Now with families of our own, it takes a week to get a call back, birthdays are forgotten, holidays are a reason to show up. The business of life and mainstream living take us far from who we are, when all in all it was about being together and laughing in the sun.

❧

When we're young, we never look back. We're too busy anticipating the next big event, a new toy, a trip to the park, or playing with friends from the neighborhood. The innocence of youth happens for us only once. During that time, all responsibility falls on our parents or guardians. We find excuses for breaking a window or fighting, and we even find a good reason to lie, because we are protected in our youth. When youth is gone and we become young adults, responsibility takes on a major role.

I often find myself daydreaming of my youth, often while I'm driving. Now I know why my car's windshield is so big and wide—it looks into the future. On the other hand, the rearview mirror is small and oftentimes forgotten, but you always know it's there. Every once in a while when I'm driving, listening to some good old music, and my life seems a little out of balance, I find myself smiling, looking in the rearview mirror at my childhood and remembering the innocence I once had, with my brothers and sisters.

Chapter 3
High School Sports

During my freshman year in high school, all I wanted to do was go home, watch TV, clown around, ride my bike, and then get up the next day and do the same stuff all over again. I had no clue what was going on. My brother Stanley was a senior when I was a freshman but I recall never seeing him at school. Not once can I remember passing him in the halls. I guessed he was probably in the library most of the time. Yeah, right! He'd tell me to keep his report card hidden from my parents. I always wondered why until I opened it one time and saw his grades. Well, Stanley had a girlfriend named Jamie—they're married now—but at that time, she used to follow him around like a hawk. I used to think she was a lunatic. One night when we were out in his truck and she was in her car she chased us all over for about an hour. Stanley and Jamie are married now with three beautiful girls. I always knew he would marry her; she was the only one who'd put up with his bullshit.

At the end of my freshman year, after a year of being a regular student, with no after-school activities, no job, no nothing—just living one day at a time, Stanley asked me, "Why don't you run track?"

My reaction was, "Yeah, right!" and I got embarrassed. Joining in the conversation, my dad said, "Why don't you play some football?" I responded, "I hate football. I'll run track next year."

So the first thing I started to do was lift weights. My parents had bought some cheap plastic weights awhile back and

Stanley became my trainer. After dinner, we would go out to the barn in the back and Stanley would help me work out, starting with ten sets of ten for every body part. He damn near killed me the first time, but with regular workouts, both my confidence and strength increased.

After about a month, I thought I was buff. Every time I'd lift by myself, I'd run into the house, take my shirt off, stand in front of the mirror and flex the body part I was lifting on. That used to set me off and I'd run back and forth until I was too tired to continue.

The habits I started in high school shaped my life and eventually brought me money but also a lot of pain. Little did I know that tunnel vision, and focusing only on myself, would haunt me for many years to come. I learned that honest hard work pays off. Hard work at a steady pace is a habit we have to develop. Miracles happen on a moment's notice, and we are usually proud of our determination and commitment to hard work and goals. My father showed me through his actions that patience and work with a steady hand will help you attain your goals.. Memories of my father working to attain something out of reach are embedded in my heart.

The summer months passed, the new school year got going, and I began to settle into ways I never thought possible for me. On the first day of track practice, the coaches were quite excited to see me trying out. I guess they thought that because my brothers were on the track team I was supposed to be some speed demon. The events I entered were the 100-, 200-, and 400-meter relay.

When I started practice and got familiar with these events, wow! I didn't realize how slow I was. I naturally thought I would be as fast as my brothers because, you know, the apple doesn't fall far from the tree. Well, I started to think that I must have not only fallen from the tree but rolled down the hill in slow motion! I always believed I could run fast, but for some odd reason my body wouldn't let me. I didn't know what was wrong and after a few practices the coaches put me on the junior varsity team. Now that was a low blow to my ego! I didn't know why I couldn't run fast enough for varsity. I thought that because my brothers were at the varsity level, I should be there too. From that moment, I realized from here on I would have to work for everything in my life, one way or another, and maybe even outwork everybody else.

When my dad asked if I was running varsity, I had to say no, I was running junior varsity. He sort of lifted an eyebrow and said, "That's okay, you will eventually get a chance to run varsity."

Coming from my dad, that was so inspiring. He could have made a negative comment to make me feel bad, but instead, his positive reaction put me on higher ground and helped me create a goal, a vision, a road to follow in order to grow. And that I did. I put all I had into track from that moment on.

On the day of my first track meet, that morning, my dad woke me up early and made me breakfast, as he was getting ready for work. This routine of making breakfast together eventually become a daily ritual for the both of us, lasting all through my high school years until I would leave for college. Our breakfast time was fifteen minutes before six in the morning and we'd talk about everything from school, girls, sports, and yeah, yard work, and what chores he wanted done on the weekends. Those twenty minutes each morning were a valuable contribution in helping me grow up and put focus into my life. During breakfast, the talks with my father gave me direction as we talked about life and things to come. That particular morning, I didn't even think about the track meet until I got to school. All I could think about was that I didn't want to be in last place.

It was a cloudy day, a Thursday to be exact, and as I warmed up I started feeling tired and wondered how would I run in front of all those people? I was nervous and started making excuses saying I didn't feel well and wanted to go home. Eventually, my event came up and I placed fourth in the 100-metre dash and fifth in the 200-metres. Considering my history racing BMX bikes, I should have been crushed, but I knew I'd done the best I could. Still, I wasn't proud of myself. I knew I could run a whole lot faster; I didn't know how yet.

Throughout the season, I continued to place third and fourth. All year long I often became dissatisfied with my performance because I knew I could do better. It was all a matter of time. I kept arguing with myself that this was only my first year and I've got to be patient and give myself a break, but I didn't have time for a break. I wanted to win. Then I settled down and reminded myself that I didn't have to be a high school star, the stud on campus, that I was an ordinary boy trying to find direction. I didn't need the approval of other people. As long as I focused on my own course, I'd eventually get where I wanted to go. At the time, I didn't know where I was headed, I knew I was going somewhere and all I had to do was keep on running.

As my second year in high school was drawing to a close, track was beginning to get exciting. Not only was my speed increasing, so was my confidence and I could feel myself growing up. As the end of the season approached, we were preparing for the city track meet, where all the schools in our district competed and gave us a chance to show our stuff in front of everybody. I told my family about the meet, but I didn't expect them to attend. In fact, I didn't really want them to be there because I was only running junior varsity. Well, they not only decided to attend, they decided to take me there and all I could do was think about how I was going to embarrass them.

When we drove up I could see the stands filled with people and the athletes warming up. It was a beautiful Saturday in May, not a cloud in the sky, not even the slightest breeze to use as an excuse for losing.

I could feel the excitement in the air and the knots in my stomach as the meet got under way. I kept telling myself that I could do this: that there would be other moments in my life that would be bigger than this; that all I had to do was run like I know how and move on to the next big event. I didn't even know what that next big event would be. I was trying to pump myself up.

In the first heat, I qualified for the junior varsity 100-metre semi-finals and made it to the finals. I was so happy! There were nine of us competing in the finals and as I started warming up for the race I could see my dad in the stands. He always wore his gray "old man" hat and red windbreaker jacket, so he was easy to spot in a crowd. The lights were on all around the stadium and the crowd was energized, not for us junior varsity runners, but for the varsity finals. I knew they weren't excited about seeing us run but I was set to run the race of my life. As we set up at our blocks I asked myself how the hell I had got this far. Why was I running? I should quit now because I didn't want to embarrass myself. Then I started to smile because I realized that someday I'd be really fast and people would respect me for that. I had to run this race first; then I'd be a little closer to that place in my dreams.

The gunman yelled, "Get into your lanes and to your blocks!"

My arms began to shake as I took my starting position, my body was all tensed up, and my heart was beating so fast. Before I knew it, the gun went off and I couldn't hear a thing, all I could do was look at the finish line that seemed so far away. I was running hard and out of control. I wanted to win for my dad so he would be proud. I could see people jumping and screaming but still couldn't hear anything. I could see the finish line getting closer and the other racers ahead of me. What position was I in? Were people laughing at me? Finally, I started to hear the crowd and how loud they were as I reached the finish line. I crossed it, wondering what place I took but wouldn't look into the stands. It was only right to look into the stands when you know you've finished first; never look into the stands if you don't know where you've placed. I walked over and asked the official and he said I took fifth place. I looked at him as if he was wrong. That was my way of saying I wasn't satisfied and as I looked around and waved to my dad, glancing at the guys I beat. Three of the guys I beat used to beat me earlier in the season. At that moment, I knew I was heading in the right direction. I realized that a little hard work does pay off and from that point on, I started to believe that I had potential and there would come a time when I'd realize the reality of it.

With the track season over, with such a positive ending, I said to myself that maybe I could try out for football.

It was the summer going into my senior year and there was a new coach named Wayne Cochran. He was fair and most important, believed in hard work and that's what I needed. I felt my journey was beginning to take shape and before long I'd see some change. Our coach decided we needed to learn form running and that day. I listened and concentrated so intently with fierce determination because I wanted to maximize my potential, achieve something and be somebody, leaving no opportunity for excuses. I learned an awful lot and it seemed I could feel my body move forward like a deer, finally experiencing the speed I always knew I had, like it was in my dreams.

It took an ordinary man, Coach Tim Titus, sharing an article about speed and showing us how to run in such a way that would continue to greatly benefit us. However, I believed that day he showed only me how to develop speed, even though there were about sixty other guys there. I hardly remember them being there. I couldn't believe what I was learning. If only Id known this earlier, I could've been running varsity in the past year, but there are events we encounter in life that are only presented to us when we're ready. We either believe in their purpose or fail to recognize the importance of their role in helping us get to the level we want to reach. I'm so thankful that I recognized the opportunity the coach was demonstrating that day and that I took that lesson and ran with it.

As the summer practices continued, I began to lose interest and hinted to my mom that I was going to quit. Her reaction was, "Do whatever you want."

Let me take you back to one hot summer day. It couldn't have been any hotter. The grass was so dry it felt like straw, the water was warm, and I was tired. I started wondering to myself why I was trying to play this stupid game of football. "I'm not even good," I thought. "I don't even have a starting position and I'm not good at catching the ball either." But I finally knew how to run and I believed I was the fastest on the team. Speed was the only thing I had going for me. "I should just quit right now and prepare for track season," I told myself.

That day we were doing up-downs: running in place, falling to the ground and getting up to do it all over again. On each whistle, I became more determined that this would be my last practice. When I got home I told my mom that I quit, and all she said was, "Fine."

When my dad got home I was in my sister's room, joking around and making her laugh like I always did. My dad came in and asked, "What are you doing home?"

"I quit," I replied. "I can't stand football. It's too hot and too hard. I don't like the coach and they don't like me." I was saying everything I could think of to make him feel I needed sympathy. But that wasn't his reaction. My father told me firmly, "Son, you take your ass back out there. Quit? Quit for what? You're going to play!"

I asked myself if he was insane or something. I just told him that I didn't want to play, but like a champ I went back out there and straightened things out with the coach. I couldn't believe I was back out there in the hot sun like a slave down south. I asked myself why my dad would push me back out there. He must've known something I didn't. Maybe he saw the potential in me, but all I knew was that I hadn't played football since I was ten years old and what was I doing out here?

You guessed it, I was riding the bench. That's what I did throughout my junior year. The coach and players always encouraged me because they saw my speed and potential. But potential is useless and gets you nowhere. It's an excuse to keep players around for a while to see if the potential actually develops and produces results. Counting on potential can sometimes result in an individual feeling, "I almost did it." They said I've always had potential. Having potential is like having something only until someone else takes it away. All I could do that year was work on my potential. I grew to hate that word with a passion and yet would hear it for years to come. We had a reasonable season that year considering it was our coach's first year. I was impressed and felt that he had potential too, and was glad he would stay on.

When football season ended, I started training for track.

Stanley and I would run together up and down the long dirt path that ran along the side of our house. Occasionally we'd stop to watch each other. I'd watch his form in awe and he'd do the same. At that time in our lives, we figured we were the fastest guys on earth! Nobody knew we told ourselves that, constantly pumping each other up. We'd just lift and run, not having any specific direction or goal, just enjoying it. We considered this fun, not work. We used to make up stuff to try. To this day, I still don't share my secret about sprinting. In those early years, we had no idea how far either of us would go in our sports endeavors. Heck, we were just two kids trying to stay out of trouble, because my dad didn't allow us to lie around the house all day. In fact, we weren't allowed to lie around and he'd find chores for us to do so we decided it was smart to train our butts off instead.

With all our training my brother and I thought we were kings with no crown. Someday, we'd get noticed, maybe him, maybe me. Or maybe we'd both go unnoticed. At the time, our older brother Joe was at the University of Arizona tearing it up. He was a fullback, six-foot-one, 240 pounds, with good speed, great strong hands, and a big head. I never saw him train because every time he came home on college break he'd chill out, gain weight, and talk about how much money he was going to make. My mom was all excited because he'd be able to buy her a Mercedes and we'd all be asking for things. Joe was like a modern day Moses around the family and he'd even have his girlfriend over to our house and she'd be saying, "Yeah, Joe's going to get me this and that."

We all really believed and counted on Joe. I even asked for a few things and he said, "Yeah, I'll kick you down being a senior in college."

He sure had a lot going for him and a whole lot of people were putting their faith in him. So like most younger brothers I asked my older brother Joe for advice. I wish I never had, but at the time he was one of my heroes and our family would always talk about Joe and pro football. One cloudy afternoon my Stanley, and I were lifting weights on the patio, doing arm-curls when Joseph came into the backyard. He was walking like a king and I almost felt I should be bowing to him. He looked at Stanley and me and started to laugh, asking, "What are you guys doing? You might as well stop all that nonsense. I'm going to be the one to make it, so stop wasting your time!"

Stanley and I kept on lifting. Joe went into the front yard to wait for a friend to pick him up. I was all pumped from working out and, fishing for a compliment from him, I decided to go ask him a question. "Joe, do you think I could get a scholarship like you?"

He looked at me and laughed. I didn't see what was so funny; I thought I had asked a serious question. I was looking for some encouragement to make the journey worth the effort. I was hoping for some direction from an older brother to a younger brother, but he laughed and said I'd amount to nothing. I'd never be anything. He shouted, "Scholarship, hell, no. I'm the one who's going to do it!"

All I heard was that I'd amount to nothing. I was shocked! Stanley heard what Joseph said and was furious! "Why would you say such a thing, you fat bastard!" He was hot and getting in Stanley's face.

I started yelling and broke them up because brothers don't need to fight with each other. I remember Stanley grabbed a pipe, and was going to beat his ass. I was crying and yelling at them to stop. Eventually, they started to cool down and Joseph took off. It was then that Stanley won my heart. He stood up for me and made me believe that I could do whatever I put my mind to.

I didn't hate my brother Joe for what he said. It made me work harder and I realized I didn't have to prove anything to anybody. I only had to prove to myself that I could attain the desires I'd dream about. If Joseph had reacted positively, I might have become complacent and lost my ambition for hard work. I could've started thinking achievements should just be given to me. However, it didn't happen that way. I don't harbor events of the past and allow the less good ones to influence me. but in this circumstance, I used something negative and degrading as a motivating force in my life. Some people accept similar negative comments from loved ones and, throughout their lives, actually believe the false view of themselves and end up being stuck in life situations they dislike. In my case, I knew I was headed somewhere in life no matter how much anyone might try to discourage me. I realized such individuals probably didn't want me to succeed. I also realized people and situations can change like the weather and the world doesn't stop turning because of it, so I kept on running, getting closer to my goal.

჉

I was starting my second year of running track and I was so excited to see how far I had advanced. I knew that my speed had improved a whole lot. My form was nearly flawless, at least that's what Stanley told me. I ran varsity in our first track meet and won the 100-metre and 200-metre races. Not only was I winning, I would ask my team members how far behind me they were. I not only wanted to win, I wanted to make it look easy. Of course, I wasn't the fastest man in the world, but I was in my own world and loving the results of my hard work. I was finally seeing my potential come alive and it was such a relief for me because I knew I had the speed in me. I just needed some help developing it. I continued to practice at home after school, sprinting on the path beside my house. My attitude was that if I did extra practice, I'd keep a step ahead of everybody else.

I won a lot of races in my junior year, including a win at the city meet making one of the fastest in the country. I wasn't really surprised because I didn't believe in luck. I had learned that we get what we deserve and what we work hard for. No matter what, if you are fair and treat people right, they will treat you the same way. On the other hand, if you are hateful towards people and treat them unfairly, that's how they will treat you. I've always tried to live that way, recalling the saying, "What goes around comes around." I have seen and experienced the glory and headaches that can result from that theory.

I was really on a high that spring of 1987. Our track team won the district title and the city meet. Recalling my fifth place in junior varsity the previous year, I was thrilled at my second place finish this time. Too many times, we emphasize whether we win or lose. It's not until we find a way to measure our improvement that we find satisfaction, realizing that we have to lose sometimes in order to win. For me, losing was a time to get myself together and get ready to improve, face a new challenge, making new strategies, and plan for the next event.

During track practice that year, I was introduced to the forty-yard dash. I was excited to show that I was the fastest on the team. That morning, the grass was a little damp with the morning dew and everybody was stretching and warming up. I ran my fastest time in the forty-yard dash that morning; my time was 4.4 or 4.3 seconds, I don't recall exactly. I knew I had run the fastest that day. Everyone patted me on the back and I certainly felt proud. At seventeen years old, I had no idea that the forty-yard dash would be central to my career or that my major achievements would evolve around forty yards and my success with this particular event.

The summer after that track season, I would be a senior in high school, with no colleges noticing me or knocking on my door. All I had was an awesome time for the forty yards but no game film, just a word-of-mouth reputation. That was the year Coach Burns came into my life, constantly telling me I was great, that this would be my year, my time, and my chance to make it all happen. Coach Burns was very influential in getting me on the field of play when others thought I could only run. He made me believe in myself. I would never have guessed this man would help me surpass my own expectations.

During my freshman year at high school I started lifting weights frequently because my older brother Stanley was buffed. He used to flex in the mirror all the time. By the time I was in my sophomore year, my body began to change. I was excited about finally developing muscles. I ran track that year and got dusted, but finished strong. I kept on lifting weights during the summer months and, during my junior year, decided to give football one more shot. I was a little nervous because I thought about what had happened between my dad and my brother Stanley during my freshman year.

Stanley kept complaining that he did not get enough playing time, so one evening my dad and I decided to go watch him practice. My dad was walking fast, like he was going do something important. They were practicing behind the bleachers so we climbed to the top and watched. We watched his every move, from his stretching to warm ups, and during the whole practice my brother Stanley held a big yellow bag while his teammates lay into him. I took a peek at my dad's face. He said, "Look at this shit. My son is a human dummy out there. That's embarrassing." We turned and walked away. To this day, those words and the look of disgust on my dad's face are embedded in my mind. When my brother Stanley got home, my dad never said a word. I decided at that time, I would never hold a bag during a practice if my dad was in the stands watching.

❧

My junior year was a real learning experience. I discovered how fast I really was. One of our coaches decided to show us form running and after that, when it came to running, my confidence skyrocketed. I knew I wasn't that good of a football player, but I had something then that no one else possessed: speed to burn. I was more excited about learning how to run than I was about football.

The following morning, practice was so hard and several of the guys threw up. I was on the verge of quitting. It was getting too tough, especially after learning the techniques of running. I felt my job on the football field was done. That afternoon when I got home, I told my mom I was going to quit football and get a track scholarship and run in the Olympics. She said that was fine and I didn't have to play football. Later that afternoon I was in my sister's room making her laugh when my dad came home. He asked me why I was home so early and I began to tell him that I had quit football. I told him the coaches were crazy and they didn't like me. He knew the part about the coaches not liking me was a lie. "You take your ass back out there. Quit? Quit for what? I'm not raising no quitters so you're gonna take your ass right back out there." I begged my mom and she remained silent.

Well, I went right back out there the next day. That was sixteen years ago and I'm still playing. About a week after my dad told me "to get back out there" I was in the kitchen making myself a peanut butter and honey sandwich. I said to my mom, "I'm going to play in the NFL. Watch me." She gave me a look that I will never forget. I didn't have to say those words; she already knew I would play in the NFL.

In my junior year I was a receiver. I didn't get the ball much, but on film you would see me fly across the screen like a deer and that got me excited. The play could be going the other way and all of a sudden you would see a flash of lightning that would be me. Day by day I was getting better, faster. But it still wasn't fast enough to have college scouts look my way. At times I would think back to what my dad had said, "Sooner or later you'll get it right." I held onto those words and kept running, knowing that something would happen.

That summer I watched some of the guys get letters from colleges all over the country. I didn't get anything, but I still had something they didn't have. And then one day there was a letter from UCLA. I was stunned and thought it only takes a single drop of water to start a waterfall. And I knew that this one drop was about to start that waterfall. That year Mr. Burns told me I'd be kick-off returner, running back flanker, and cornerback. Frankly, I thought he was nuts, but he told me to demonstrate my speed every chance I could, "Run like a deer, fear nothing. This is your last high school year. It's over for many of the guys after this year but I believe you can go on to the next level."

I gained so much confidence from Mr. Burns' influence because he was the first coach who really believed in me. That year, I ran like a scared rabbit every time I caught a kick-off. Whenever the ball was in my hands I ran as fast as I could. I had no great moves, no style, just raw speed, running and running to get to that place.

That year, I also met Dechon Burns and Ryan Phelps. These guys were my teenage homies. We all met in high school and, with John Howard, we would be called the "four homies." To this day, these guys are in all my teenage memories.

I received my first college letter that year from UCLA, letting me know that they'd be watching my senior year. That I was all I needed! I took that letter and ran all the way to the NFL! Most guys would get lots of letters from colleges, but because I didn't get a lot of recognition, that one letter changed everything. It motivated me. I didn't need to see the whole picture to believe in the possibility. It gave me a glimmer of hope. Whatever the outcome, I would accept it. If you don't believe in the little things that happen first, the big events will overwhelm and swallow you up.

My senior year proved to be a good one, perhaps because I was running scared as I only had that year to attract interest from some colleges. I ran with as much speed as I had. I even developed some good football skills on the field. I have never believed that something would work in my favor, no matter what; individuals have to take an interest in themselves, realize their potential first and then begin to grow. Without water, a plant won't grow. So, I watered my speed, and it grew.

Lots of people can run fast, they just can't run like me. We are all distinct in our own way and I found that out in my senior year during football season. I recognized that when things are on the line I'd come through. Often, we don't know this until we're up against a wall. The choice is yours to give up or spend a lifetime saying I could have or I should have. Forget finding excuses, never get discouraged, and just do it. I refuse to give into excuses and I don't leave room for negative thoughts. I'll jump without a net and, if I fall, I'll fall hard.

Letters started arriving from all over the country that year. Each time I read one I would work a bit harder at practice and run a little further. Those letters not only inspired me, they suggested I was finally heading somewhere. I didn't know where, but I wanted to be prepared. I didn't brag or boast about the tons of letters I received. By the end of the football season two colleges still showed interest in me. I was quite satisfied with that, considering I had only played one year of football.

My first recruiting trip was to Reno, Nevada. It was cold there and I didn't like it much. Out of nowhere, Coach Karm from Washington State University showed interest and invited me for a visit. Well, I fell in love with the place and was so excited I couldn't wait to get home to tell everybody about it. I knew I'd end up there; it was the place I saw in my dreams. I can't describe the feeling, but I can tell you it was a moment when everything in my life seemed to make sense. Reality started to brighten up but I knew there'd be lots of hard work ahead. The emotions and excitement of achieving a goal can make you crazy, but at the same time, bring you comfort.

Back at school on Monday morning, I told everybody I had decided to attend Washington State University and I signed my letter of intent on February 15. Hah! I got the scholarship that I had asked Joe about and I didn't stick it in his face. I had bigger plans.

When track season started, I hesitated about continuing. After all, I had nothing to prove. At the same time, I knew that running track had started my football career. I love running and without running track, I probably wouldn't have gotten my scholarship. That track season, others looked at me and wondered why I was running when I already had a full scholarship. But, that didn't matter. When you have a love for something, you don't need a motive. Most people are motivated because of what they'll get in return, fame or maybe fortune, but I proved to myself that it's okay to do something out of pure love without looking for reward. My reward was that God gave me my speed and I wanted to share that. My attitude has always been that if you love what you do, it shouldn't matter where you do it, whether you get paid a lot, or not at all because love has no limits, only people do. That's why we have to be aware of what motivates us and the real reason we do what we do. That's the question we have to ask ourselves.

My running statistics were solid that year; we won the city meet and the conference title. I not only ran for the love of it,

I ran to say thank you to my coaches and teammates. I knew I was off to greater horizons. Not only did I surprise myself that year, I also inspired a younger teammate. I don't remember his name, but do recall that we used to talk about life, the forces of nature, our dreams and aspirations. Once the track season ended, I proceeded to prepare myself for going to Washington State.

❧

During that time, I was really struggling to get a high enough score on my SAT tests to qualify for eligibility to play. Unfortunately, I never took the tests seriously and didn't attain the necessary marks. So I was admitted to WSU as a freshman under the restrictions of Proposition 48, which the National Collegiate Athletic Association had put in place in 1983 to create eligibility standards for incoming freshmen. In order to get into college and play college sports, all I had to do was maintain a "C" high school average in eleven core curriculum courses, and score above 700 on the combined verbal and math sections of the Scholastic Aptitude Test or above fifteen on the American College Test. Under Proposition 48, an athlete could not play in the first year.

I lost a year of eligibility in my freshman year and had to watch from the stands. I couldn't be involved with the team. All I would be allowed to do was to attend school and live like a regular student, even though I still had my scholarship. That was emotionally draining, being on such a high and then dropping to a low. As in years past, I found myself on the comeback although I recognized this comeback would be tougher than the others. Considering the talent at the college level and with my lack of experience I felt disadvantaged; however, I soon found the strength to stumble my way through the competition, where many athletes want promotions just given to them.

Chapter 4
College Years

The summer of 1988, my parents drove with me to Washington State University in Pullman, in eastern Washington state. Was that fun! We argued and fought the whole way. Looking back on it now, I had the time of my life. As we got nearer the university, I began to feel a bit sad. All we saw for about four hours was wheat fields and my mom laughed, "Where in the hell is this place?"

My dad was enjoying the long drive. He always looked forward to long drives, saying they were time to reflect on things, get things off his mind, and sometimes even figure out solutions to certain problems. I would never have guessed that in the years to come the road would become my friend too, chasing that place I wanted to find.

During our drive to WSU, I contemplated the various events that had led me to WSU. I kept thinking about all the things I could do if I believed in myself and left the outcome to God. When we share our dreams with certain people they try to destroy them, so I believe we should keep our dreams to ourselves, letting people watch us live them; then they will realize how blessed we truly are.

We finally arrived on campus. It sure was big in comparison to high school. I think my parents were more excited than me about my going to college, probably because they didn't have to pay for it! They just had to drop me off. I checked into the dorm and my parents helped me move in. Once I was settled, we walked over to the football field and watched a practice. It was summer training camp. I was amazed at the size of some of those guys out there; they were huge! They looked so much like a professional team and all I could think was that I had a year to prepare myself to be out there. Again, I felt a little sad because my parents would be leaving shortly. We had some lunch and said our goodbyes in front of the football office. My mom's eyes filled with tears and my dad, trying to be a man and not let his emotions show patted me on the back and simply said, "Give 'em hell, son, and make us proud." Those words stuck with me.

❧

My first semester at college was a big party. I had been considered a square in high school. I had never been drunk before, I wasn't allowed to go out on weeknights, and my curfew was half past midnight on weekends. Well, that first semester, I gave 'em hell all right. I missed a lot of classes and spent lots of time talking to my roommate, Mickey. To this day Mickey and I are still close friends. I'd tell him over and over how fast I could run, that I could run the forty yards all day and as for the football forty record, I'd blow that away. He'd hear that every night. On weekends Mickey and I would have about twenty people in our room, drinking and dancing all night long and, out of nowhere, I'd go crazy and sprint down the hall while everyone would watch with their heads out the door. I would tell them, "You haven't seen anything yet." I guess I just wanted to be accepted and, since I wasn't able to be part of the football team, I decided to get noticed by talking a lot.

One night when we were partying, I remember telling everybody that I could outrun a car. They all said, "Yeah, right!" Mickey would always laugh because he knew I would try and do it.

That night, they all walked out of the dorm with me wearing my tighty whities, barefoot, with no shirt. There I was, a brother at an all-white college, out in the middle of the night running up and down the street racing cars in my underwear. I knew I was fast and they all agreed. I would find myself running at night for no reason at all. I couldn't play football. I had nothing to prove; I just enjoyed sprinting forty yards. I'd even drag Mickey out to watch and he always came no matter what; I think he felt he needed to support me. Having been admitted to college under Proposition 48, I would tell other students I hurt my knee and that's why I wasn't playing this year. I felt stupid to tell them that my SAT scores were too low to make me eligible to play. I really didn't like school that much. However, my English teacher and Anthropology teacher always found ways to make those classes fun. I could see they were passionate about their work just like I was passionate about football and even more passionate about sprinting the forty yards.

There were a lot of alcohol on campus and I drank like a fish. But I still managed to get my running and workouts in and, on weekends that first semester, I would get drunk and loud, sprint up and down the hall and occasionally, I would go outside in my underwear and race cars.

One evening, I was wearing some new clothes my mom had bought for me. One of the girls that came over started drinking and, before long, she was really drunk. I was a little tipsy myself, but not terribly drunk and certainly aware of what was happening when she leaned over and threw up all over me. All over my brand new clothes! I jumped up, she staggered into the bathroom, and everybody began to laugh and scream. I was so mad when I saw her leaning over the toilet, throwing up in it, and everybody looking at me and asking what I was going to do, I said, "Come into the bathroom and watch this."

I proceeded to throw up on her back, on her face, and on her neck and put everyone into hysterics; they were shocked, laughing, screaming, and running all over and all I could do was scream too. Can you believe I got high-fives from the guys? The girls were less crazy and soon no one on the floor said a word. I believe they were too scared to say anything because they thought I was real crazy. At times I guess I did get out of hand during college, but I had Mickey to tell me to chill out when I'd lose control and that's what I'd do.

When Christmas break was coming up, I really looked forward to going home and seeing everybody again—too bad the college sent my grades home to my parents. I told them my parents had just moved and to send my grades to my dorm address. Guess what? They sent it to my parents anyway and my dad opened it. I had been home for a few days when my dad came in from the back room, walking fast; he must have heard my voice. He asked, "Anthony, what the hell are you doing up there?"

I said, "I'm not doing anything!" To which he replied rather loudly, "Hell, I can see that!" He waved my first semester report in my face, advising that I was on academic probation and, if I didn't improve my grades immediately, I would lose my scholarship. That pretty much ruined my Christmas break. Later that night, I sat with my brother in his car at the side of the house. We had a few beers and talked about a lot of things. It was a really nice, clear night and I commented that I could sit here and talk for the rest of my life, enjoying the soft music and being at home. I was consumed with enjoying the moment. As I've learned through the years, that's what life's all about. I think that people reminisce because it takes them back to moments in their life when time and events seemed to make sense and life was somewhat peaceful. At times, I love to reminisce. That particular night, I didn't care about college, my girlfriend, or anything else. I was buzzed from the beer and felt at peace.

I returned to school after Christmas break with a whole new game plan. I worked at improving my grades and cut down on our weekend rendezvous. Since I was on academic probation, I had to attend the Student Advising and Learning Center and felt like a zero going there. I wasn't irritated with them; I was more frustrated and angry with myself. I had set myself up for this situation. In my second semester, though, I made a complete turnaround and got things back in order. I realized my back was against the wall and I had no net to catch me if I fell.

When the semester was drawing to a close my grades were good and I was going to be eligible to play next year. Even though I had no idea what position I would be playing, I was excited knowing I could play. I told myself, I have to go out with a bang. So that night, Mickey and I went crazy in our room. He pretended to be Lawrence Taylor, running through people, and I was Carl Lewis. It didn't take long before we were both out of control. I asked Mickey to break something so he flipped up his bed. After that, I took over. Everyone on the floor came by to watch the spectacle and wondered what was wrong with me. I tore the desk out of the wall and tried to throw it through the window, breaking the glass. I tore apart the closet and smashed the chair into pieces. Mickey was breaking stuff too, and before we knew it, Mickey ran into the washroom, grabbed the ironing board, and threw it out the smashed window. Other people on the floor became excited and handed me things to toss out the window—fans, books. We headed for the girl's dormitory, drunk as hell, on a mission to destroy whatever we could get our hands on. I was taking karate at the time, so I was into kicking and started smashing mirrors and windows. I kicked a huge mirror right next to the elevator, shattering it to pieces as everyone who lived on the floor looked on.

"Whoever tells, I'll kill you!" I yelled at them.

Mickey and I proceeded to another dorm. We saw a big mirror outside the women's elevator. I yelled, "Break that bitch!"

Mickey kicked it about three times before it finally shattered. He went crazy; it was almost like relief that the term was over. For me, I was on a high and felt destructive that night. Why, I don't know.

Mickey and I stayed at our girlfriends' places that night because the police and fire department were investigating our rooms, looking at all the destruction. In my frightened excitement I found the energy to run all the way to my girlfriend's place and, as I was running, I realized how close I'd come to losing my scholarship. But like so often in the past, I somehow got through this episode. It was a clear night and I knew people were driving past, wondering why I was running like a deer in the wind, dressed in jeans and not in typical running attire. Little did they know I had just destroyed a dorm room and might be kicked out of college! At the time, I didn't care; I was just running, reminiscing, and thinking about what was to come.

The next day I was questioned by the authorities and, of course, denied it all. They said that people saw me tear the place apart and that Mickey was an innocent bystander. Yeah, right! I was kicked out of the dorm and was no longer allowed in there, but I still had my scholarship and that was the most important part. I figured out that I had acted like a wild dog that night, something I did whenever I got excited. I still feel like breaking things sometimes. It reminds me of my college days and, to this day, I'm still a legend on the fourth floor of Streit Hall, all due to raising hell a few times and pushing extremes to the limit.

My first year of playing college football was a big learning experience. I didn't play that much in 1990, but that didn't take away from my dad wanting to come up, visit, and watch a game. I told him no at first, because I felt embarrassed. I wasn't a starter and I didn't even play that much. I didn't want him to fly all the way up to watch me ride the bench and, besides, the game was going to be on national television. Well, he insisted that he come. I was excited to see my father and I promised myself that I was going to do something in that game on national television that would get my name called.

In years past I would always see my father in the stands wearing his gray old man's hat and red windbreaker, but that game I couldn't see him for the longest time because everyone was wearing red, the school color. Finally, I spotted that gray old man's hat, the only one in the stands.

Late in the second half, I deliberately hit a guy late. My name was called, they showed it on national television, and they even showed a replay. For one moment I was in the spotlight and after the game my dad and I had something big to talk about. I called friends that night and they all said, "I saw you hit that guy late." My response was, "No, that was just a bad call." I knew what I had done. My motive may not have been great, but I got the reaction I was looking for.

※

The spring semester of 1991 was the funniest time of my life. When I think back to 1991 I find myself smiling and laughing all over again.

When the pro scouts timed us in late February, I broke all the forty-yard time records for WSU. The record was 4.3 seconds and that day I ran a blistering 4.21. To this day, that record still stands and I'm very proud it is mine.

A few days after that, my roommate Randy and I were talking about going to a frat party. Randy said he was a little tired that evening and he would take a nap. We agreed that I would wake him in a few hours. Randy walked up the stairs and I went to go sit on the couch to watch television. I sat on the couch flipping channels unsure of what to watch and I began think about how fast I had ran a few days ago. My heart started to beat faster and all of a sudden a rage came over me, like a mighty wind. Before you knew it, I was destroying everything in sight. I threw the lamp, then picked up the stand next to the couch, and threw it against the wall. I took the entertainment center that held the television and stereo and pulled it to the floor, breaking everything. The grand finale was going to be big: I picked up the couch, heaved it onto my back, and tried to run it through the wall to say "Hi" to our neighbors. As I was running towards the wall with the couch on my back before I got to the wall I slipped and the couch fell on top of me. I lay there for a minute, stunned and out of breath. I heard footsteps begin to come down the stairs and then stop. Randy leaned over the stairwell and said, "What the hell is wrong with you?"

I pulled my head out from under the couch and said, "Man, I just got a little excited."

Randy shook his head and muttered, "You're crazy," and went back upstairs to bed.

I lay there under the couch and fell asleep. When I woke

up we got ready for the party and left the place just as it was. We had fun that night.

The next morning we decided to clean up because Randy had some friends coming to visit from Seattle. It sure was hot that day. That afternoon Randy's friend went to the store to get some beer and chips. We all just sat around telling each other how great we were and that we were all going to graduate with honors. Yeah, right. Randy gets complaining how hot it was and that, if it wasn't for my outburst last night, we would have had some curtains around here. I looked at him said, "Nigga, you need some shade. You son of a bitch, I'll go pull a tree out of the ground for you."

I had a lot of beer in me by this time and was capable of doing almost anything. Just outside the door was a young tree, maybe only a couple of years old. I stormed outside, started yelling and screaming, "You want shade, you little bitch," until I had a crowd watching me shake and pull that tree back and forth for forty-five minutes. I kept doing the same thing until finally, I pulled it out of the ground and put it in the apartment roots, dirt and all. I set it up against the window and said, "You happy now, you little bitch." We all sat around drinking beers and wasting time.

The following morning, the phone kept ringing and ringing but we were all hung over. The only phone we had left was the one in my bedroom because I broke the rest of them. Randy got up to use the bathroom and the phone was still ringing. He yelled so loud to answer the fucking phone. Damn it, it was his phone and, when I heard him yelling, I jumped up, ripped the phone out of the wall, and threw it out the second story window. I walked outside and told Randy to look out the window. He looked out the window and saw me pissing on the phone and I said, "I bet you this damn phone will never ring again." He just looked at me and smiled, told me I was crazy, and went back to bed.

Chapter 5

Women

The first woman I ever loved was my mother and I still love her dearly; she was the first woman to show me what love is. As I was growing up, I remember my mother always going out of her way to help others in need. My mom still hasn't slowed down one bit. She's a smart woman, who has a great mind even though I don't always agree with her opinions and advice. My mom believes in what she knows and I can't fault her for that. The way an individual is raised contributes to their view of life. All we can do is accept their point of view and not judge them, but rather respect our differences in opinions.

When I was twelve years old, my bike had been stolen. A friend of mind said he could get me a new bike and I told my mom about it. Well, she was rather confused and asked if I had any money. I said, "No, he's going to give it to me." I really believed this kid; I wanted a bike so bad since mine had been stolen and everybody else was riding except me. So one day after school, my mom picked me up to take me to the supermarket where my friend said he'd meet me. Mom and I waited for hours but he didn't show. I was crushed. As we drove home, my mom said she'd try to get me a bicycle that week even though I knew she couldn't afford it. She ended up buying me a GT, the best bike made, worth at that time about five hundred dollars! She agreed to make payments weekly so I was able to take delivery of the bike in advance. To me, that's definitely a reflection of love at its finest. Sometimes you figure out how to find a way to help those you love.

My mom would repeat similar kindnesses over and over through my years both at home and at college, always finding a way to help out her kids. As with most mothers, my mother was always giving advice. Even though I would always listen, I had the attitude, "I'm going to do what I think is right, no matter what." Now that I look back, I wish had listened to a few things she warned me about. But that's life. We learn to grow from our mistakes and celebrate our accomplishments. It's too bad the effects of our mistakes last longer than our accomplishments.

❧

Way back 1976, when I was six years old, was the first time I kissed a girl. It happened one Tuesday afternoon after school, with a girl named Janeen. My brother Stanley and my sister Simone kept spying on us. I guess they were jealous that I wasn't paying any attention to them. Janeen and I were standing at the foot of the bunk beds that Stanley and I shared when we kissed! Boy! I felt like a man, then all of a sudden, we kissed again, falling down at the same time. The weird thing was that as we fell down, our lips stayed together. That was my first kiss as a young boy and I remember it like it was yesterday even though it was twenty-six years ago. Janeen moved away a couple years later and I never saw or heard from her again. I'm still curious after so many years, and I would like to ask her why she suggested we kiss and fall down.

❧

By the time I was in grade school, my curiosity started to get the best of me. I couldn't understand why I would get a hard-on during class. When the bell rang to dismiss us, I would always be the last to leave. Once I remember a teacher asking me to go up to the blackboard to write a sentence but I sat there like an idiot; she must have thought I was stupid. Little did she know my monster was waking up at his own will.

When I was in eighth grade, in I met a girl named "Sugar Bear." Boy! She really was a sugar bear. Real pretty and all the boys around the school liked her but she didn't like any other boy except me. We would eat lunch together and talk about things. She would look at me as if I was a walking angel. I was intimidated by her and could never muster the courage to actually ask her to be my girlfriend. At that time, I was a shy momma's boy. Sugar Bear moved away and I never got a chance to kiss her. I was a little disappointed though I didn't have time to think about it much because I was getting ready to go to high school.

I was thinking that I'd better find a girlfriend soon considering every guy in high school had one. So that summer, I was on the hunt to find myself a soul mate. Stanley and I still shared a room that summer; the good thing was that my older brother Joe had a scholarship to University of Arizona and would be leaving at the end of the summer, giving me my first chance to have my own room. Having my own room now was a big deal in high school, a big thing for me, considering I had always shared a room.

That summer, I used to hear my brother Stanley and his friends talking after a night out with the girls. They would share stories about where they did it and how. I took in every word as if my life depended on it. One night, they were talking so dirty, I started laughing a little so Stanley asked me if I was awake and I said I was. He and his friend started interrogating me about women and asked if I ever had sex with a girl. I hesitated with my answer and said yes; they knew I was lying so they started asking all kinds of questions, like if I knew what it felt like to be inside a woman. I said, "It feels good." "No shit," my brother said, "but in your own words, how does it feel?" Everybody would say it felt a certain way so I said, "It feels bumpy when I'm inside a woman." Well, they laughed at me, asking who she was, where she lived and, again hesitating, I told them she moved to Texas. They started laughing again, told me to stop lying, and to go to sleep. I tried to listen a little more to what they were talking about but my little body was too tired to say awake.

Stanley kept after me that summer, saying over and over that he was going to "get me some," meaning he was going to find me a woman so I could lose my virginity. I would smile, hoping it would be soon. Every time I'd look at a girl, I'd try to imagine what it would be like; my mind played lots of tricks on me that summer. Finally, when we were reaching the start of the school year, my brother said he had a candidate. Little did he know that I'd been doing some searching myself. She was a girl I had been friends with during the summer who was as excited about high school as I was. One day, we had kissed. I never told anybody about Kemisha, but we got to be friends and started talking about sex, that she was a virgin and so was I. I told my brother about it and right away he started talking about when I would have sex with her. He suggested we do it one Saturday night in the barn in my parents' backyard. I was so scared that day. Stanley and I planned the whole thing. He gave me some rubber and demonstrated how to put it on and gave me the advice that once I had it on to give it to her real hard and she'd never forget me. This was like the Super Bowl for me. Stanley wanted to make sure that I did it with Kemisha so he was waiting downstairs listening because he didn't want to be fooled. "I want to make sure you do it right," he said.

That was one of the longest days of my life. As the sun was setting, I started to get cold feet and asked my brother to just stay in the house or something. I didn't want him downstairs. Again, he pressured me and I gave in. Plans stayed as they were. As it got later, Kemisha and I snuck into the barn. I could see my brother hiding because he told me where he would be. I couldn't believe I was finally going to be a man. As we got upstairs, I got cold feet again so I told her that I had to go to the bathroom. I ended up going downstairs and outside. My brother followed me outside the barn and I whispered to him, "Are you sure about this?" He looked at me and whispered back, "She's up there waiting for you." This was my moment of truth.

When I returned to Kemisha, she was laying there. The funny thing was we both were virgins but she thought I wasn't. So, I had to make it look like I knew what I was doing. I leaned over and kissed her, caressed her, and we must have kissed for about an hour. I knew my brother was getting impatient because

I heard a thump that sounded like hurry up. I knew that was my key. I put the condom on and the next thing you know, we were having sex. I couldn't believe it. I didn't even have hair on my nuts, let alone know anything about having sex. Kemisha was moaning, oohing, and ahhing. Next thing you know, I come to think that I pissed on myself, but this kind of pissing felt really good. After we have lay there awhile, arm in arm, we got our clothes on and then she went home. I went back to the barn to celebrate with my brother. We gave each other high fives and, from that point on, I was never the same. I felt I was a mature adult.

Now little did I know that there was a lot of growing up to do. That first year of high school was fun. All I did was look at all the students and realize the differences in all of us. I didn't play any sports that first year in high school. All I did my first year was race bikes all the time. I could remember the girls had big hair, lots of make-up, and wore tight jeans. It looked like every girl was trying to outdo the next girl. They were competing with each other for what I guessed was attention. My first year of high school, you didn't need all that extra stuff, as long as you were a girl you had my attention, no questions asked. I guess the first year was a chance to see what would be expected in years to come.

High school would be a place to prepare for the future. I realized that after my first and second year, I realized that, Wow! I only had three years to make something of myself. I was kind of afraid, but fear often puts you in a hurry to do something to change what you're fearful of. I didn't want to be a bum, or a nobody. That second year, I tried out for track and met, Celine, the girl who would be my high school sweetheart.

The first year of college I met a girl named Susan, two days before my nineteenth birthday. Meeting Susan was one of the highest points in my college career. She was the finest girl on campus, two years older than me. Susan and I were inseparable and did everything together, even working out at the gym, during the first year of our relationship. I thought I had it made, but Susan and my mother didn't get along, and my father told me that he didn't have a good feeling about us.

During the next semester at school, Susan and I lived together secretly. Eventually she went off the pill and pregnant, Susan moved home with her parents until the fall semester, when we shared family housing on campus. That fall semester, Susan gave birth to my son, Jordan Prior. It was an exciting day. Susan and I both looked at each other, not knowing what to say. We were both very happy that day bringing a new person into the world; however, I was still juggling where we were going from here. I thought Susan and I would always be together, however, you can't make promises that you can't keep. From January 1991 until January 1995, we stayed together and then broke up, continuing the same pattern, back and forth. She would even come to New York and leave on numerous occasions because of silly arguments. In January 1995, Susan and my son went to the airport and never came back to try to make it right. We battled in court for custody of Jordan and all that stupid stuff. Then she finally got married and went on with her life.

Lavonda I've known half my life. She is the mother of my two other sons, Jonathan and James. We first met in high school, I was her first, and then I went away to college. Every time I would come home for break from college we would get together. I thought she was cool considering she knew I had a girlfriend and she never said anything. This went on for about eight or nine years, until one night she told me her period was late. I was like, "Oh, no, not again, another kid without being married." I was like, "Damn! I'm a typical athlete having kids everywhere." Even though Lavonda told me she would have an abortion, one night I got a pager call from my mother, who had just had a surprise visit from Lavonda's mother and her four-month-old grandson. My mother said, "Damn, son, you really did it now! Jonathan looks just like you." I felt so betrayed by Lavonda that I felt I could never trust her again. If she could keep something like this from me, who knows what else she was capable of doing?

As Jonathan got older, I tried to do the family thing one minute and still go out on dates. Lavonda knew what I was doing. We never talked about being together. Instead we would laugh and never have a real conversation, mainly because for years our relationship was only about sex and nothing else.

Jonathan turned two in October 1998 and the following year I started to ask myself if I could see myself marrying Lavonda. I thought nobody would want a man with two kids by two different women. That's baggage at its worst, so I tried to force myself to love Lavonda. How can you love someone you never respected, considering she knew I had girlfriends all the time and she never protested? How can you trust someone who didn't tell you about your own child until he was four months old? How could I make myself love her?

Around April 1999 Lavonda went to Europe and when she got back, my mother called to tell me that Lavonda was pregnant again. I called her at work, saying, "This is my business, not my mother's. Why can't you tell me what was going on? No one likes to hear things like this from another source."

I tried to do the right thing with Lavonda, or so I called it. I didn't play football that season: I had pulled my hamstring during the summer and besides I had personal problems to deal with. I was excited about being with Lavonda for the delivery since I hadn't seen Jonathan born. Heck! I hadn't known he existed until four months after the fact. I was determined to be in the delivery room for this second baby.

I called repeatedly to find out if Lavonda was ready for the hospital but all I got was, "She's not here." One afternoon I called and her brother answered the phone and said, "Congratulations, you have a beautiful son named James!" He told me that James had been born five days before.

Again I was in shock. Why hadn't anybody called me? How could anybody in his or her right mind deny someone the chance to attend the birth of his son? I just told myself I'd just leave it at that. Finally, I went to see James and, as with Jonathan, I was won over the moment I saw him. At that moment I didn't care that I hadn't been there at his birth. I just wanted to enjoy my new son. I looked at Lavonda and said, "Wow!" and smiled, but inside I was saying to myself, "Did you know what you just did, having the baby without telling me?" Like a man I tried to love

Lavonda again. But the saddest thing in life is trying to force a relationship.

Due to my present situation, in consideration of the mothers of my children and the respect I have for them, I have given only a few details from our relationships together. Because my children will read this book some day, I have left out the rest of our story. Writing the conclusion will be up to them. As life goes on, I'll let my children form their own opinion of their mothers. I had full control of the outcome of our relationships so it's not my call to comment on or point a finger at their motives. If I say negative things about the mothers of my children, in turn I would destroy their character as well as my own. How can I say I love my kids and say I hate their mother, for their mother lives in them? If I hate the parent, in turn I hate my own child and that simply is not true. Mother and child go hand in hand, like sex and fire. If you abuse sex, it can kill you. If you respect it, it will bring things alive for you.

∼⋆∽

My pen has come to a sudden halt. I have nowhere to begin on these creatures of the night, these snakes by day, these beautiful manipulative beasts who have persuaded my mind, taken me into the night, and robbed my thoughts. Her smile took my mind and her eyes seized my body with lust and temptation, her whole being has at times awakened the beast in me. Then I look around me and see my collection of books and I realize that maybe I see a parallel between the women in my life and the books on that shelf.

I have read some books and skipped through others. Some of my books have looked better than others; some are big, some small, some thick. Sometimes I felt like reading a small book for a while and at the end of the evening, I put it back in its place. Then I had those big books that collect dust and every now and again I would pick them up and read a chapter or two, just because it was there. And then I had that thick book, the one I never read but kept around, just in case. Some books on the shelf I kept there because the cover was so mesmerizing, so beautiful I was amazed to have it in my collection, even though, when I flipped through the pages, it seemed to have no plot or story line. The conclusion sucked and I know there would be no sequel. I kept it on the shelf because it was spineless, its chapters had no history, no character, no esteem, but I kept it on the shelf to make the other books look beautiful. Its cover was so fine and, when I needed it, I could access it at will.

Some books don't have great-looking covers. They're not appealing to the eye, so many people walk right past them. But once you begin to read this kind of book, you realize that it is spiritual, it's motivating, its story is powerful, and it will make you change. But you don't change because you have access to all the other books and you can always pick this one up when you feel like getting deep and spiritual or when things aren't going so smoothly in your life. You can always pick it up and choose whatever chapter you want to read.

Sometimes we have so many books on our shelves, we sometimes can't think straight. We spread ourselves thin, trying to make sure all the books are property aligned. When we have one book in our hand, how can we read two or three books at a time? How can we make sure the books on the shelf aren't being read by somebody else? Books can be like football coaches: they mess with your mind and your money. You have people buying books to stimulate their minds, buying bookmarks so you can pick up where you left off. Some of us need to lose some books. Our shelves are too full, but having more than one always seemed to make me more of a man.

Some people pick up books that have ten chapters but read only the chapters that interest them. Why read chapters three and seven, then jump to the conclusion and think this book will always be on the shelf? If you would have read chapter five, you might have noticed this book has esteem problems. This book has mental illness and unresolved issues. This book shows abuse in the family. This book shows divorce, insanity, and even selfishness, but you didn't see or read it because chapter three and seven were so appealing that you missed the other chapters. Reading them would have saved you money, energy, and a big headache.

I believe a real man has one book on his shelf and he knows that book in and out. He takes his time with that particular book. He starts from the beginning. He doesn't skip chapters as I have done. He reads all the way through, right up to the conclusion. Sometimes it takes years to read through the book. After he's done, he places it on the shelf and with honor it stays up there until the day he dies. He never loses respect for the book's content. Although he sees books that look better than his, he's content with the book he has chosen.

If he keeps replacing his chosen book with new books (which by the way cost money and mind damage), the new books will always ask, "Why did you get rid of your old book?" And you have to constantly baby sit the new book until you buy another one. The cycle continues until the day you die. The smart man has one book on the shelf and he respects it, for that book is his partner for life, not something you replace.

The most damaging books on the shelf are the books with a kid's version. Sometimes you don't read through the books carefully enough and by accident a kid's version comes along. No matter what, that book will always be on the shelf, whether you pick it up or not. You have an obligation to make sure that kid's book develops into an adult book.

If you have no commitment to the book with whom you made a kid's version, the other books on the shelf look even better because you feel the first book wants a permanent space on the shelf. And you lose respect for the first book because the first book watches you read other books and place them on the shelf right next to it? And the first book lets this go on for years and years.

The first book appears comfortable with your reading style until one day she makes you throw away the other books and insists that you read only her book from now on. And then you're in conflict. When you chose that book, it saw that you had other books in your hands. That was okay with her then because that book had a plan in mind. "If I let him read me at his leisure and never complain, I'll sit on the shelf one night, opened to his favorite chapter. I'll make sure all the other books are closed and I'll open up to him and let him read me all night long. I'll let him read whatever chapter he wants and with that he will get caught up in me. A kid's version will be made and the other books will be thrown in the trash." But that doesn't happen. The first book is defeated by her own plots and schemes to get you all caught up in the moment.

As a pro football player, well, hell, you can have a small library of books if you want. During my first years in the pros, I thought of books like my own personal roster. I had a first rounder and second rounder and the most important book was my free agent, because they were down for anything.

When you try and have too many books on the shelf you'll never be productive. If you read more than one book at a time, they will be in conflict with each other. No matter how far apart you try to separate them on the shelf, they always know about the other. The more books on the shelf, the more problems, the more kid's versions, the more stress, and the less success.

Chapter 6

Faith on Forty Yards

Ask any football player in the world which question his peers ask him most often and he'll tell you it is, "What time can you run the forty in?" Most of the time football players will say they are faster than they really are. If any player says speed doesn't count, they never have possessed it. Half my life has been based on forty yards. I have been blessed on many occasions just because of my speed. I have also worked very hard to achieve that four-second time; it's funny what motivates us sometimes. I used to train for hours just for four seconds and it would take away from family and friends. Now I'm a free agent in football and once again it's all coming down to faith on forty yards.

As a teenager in high school all I heard my brothers and father talk about when it came to football was their "forty" time. I never really understood the significance until I was older. My brothers were pretty fast, often racing against each other in the street. They would yell and scream loud enough until a crowd of neighbors and friends gathered to watch. I was the one who hollered, "Go!" and it usually took several tries because one of them would always jump the gun and take off down the street too soon. I stood at the finish line waving my arms every which way while they argued about who won the race.

As I began to succeed at track and field, I trained on my forty with my brother Stanley on the 100-yard long dirt track at the side of the house. Every day after school I would run up and down until I was too tired to run anymore. I would always run more than my brother Stanley. At that time, he was faster than me. Then one summer before my first college season I started giving Stanley a head start and I would catch him like nobody's business. Towards the end of that summer, my brother Stanley stopped training and playing football. While nodding his head yes with a big smile, he told me that I was faster than he was and that he wanted me to go all the way to the pros. "If you have to rely on your speed, ride it all the way to the top, Anthony," he said. "Run so damn fast the coaches will have to make a spot for you." After that, and to this very day, I still haven't stopped running.

The first time I was clocked running forty yards was in my junior year in high school during spring football. Going into my second year, I ran a 4.3 and everyone was like, "Wow, did you see that!" They asked me to run it again and I did. I think they just loved my form and, when I run forty yards, I love to look good.

During my senior year at high school, when I got a football scholarship to Washington State University, the coaches told me I had a lot of potential. What they really meant was, "You're so damn fast we have time to see if you will develop into something." They also told me that I played pretty well in my senior year, but they just didn't know where to put me because I didn't catch well enough to play as a receiver and didn't cover well enough to be a cornerback. "But, damn you can run like a deer," they said. Without my forty yards, they told me I wouldn't have had a scholarship sitting in front of me. I thought that was okay and said, "Let's just see how far my speed with take me."

At that point in my life, everything would evolve around my speed, whether I was studying for a test, eating too much pizza, or staying out too late. Whenever it came down to forty testing, the only place you would see me was at the gym, on the track, or in bed asleep. I would meditate on those forty yards day and night because I knew if I wanted to be great at anything, then I had to have tunnel vision and no distractions.

Some memories stand out. A week before the NFL scouts were coming to Washington State University to test players on the forty and other drills, my roommate was throwing a party.

About ten o'clock that evening, a lot of the guys on the team were partying and they asked me to relax and just party with them. "Are you crazy?" I said. "The scouts will be here in a week. I need to train." "What the hell are you going to do? Run the hill outside?" they responded. So I took my roommate's truck and turned on the lights so they shone towards the hill. I ran up that hill and walked down all evening long. I could see people going into my apartment drunk and laughing about nothing. I enjoyed listening to the loud music while I ran. My brother's words filled my mind. "Let your speed take you where you want to go." The following week I ran a 4.21 in the forty and to this day it still stands as the fastest recorded forty time in the history of WSU. The men who were partying that night made their own choices, we all do. At that young age I learned to see possibilities before they became evident.

I did not become a starter on the football field until my senior year at college, when I played safety. I couldn't cover that well, but the coaches saw in me a kid who was not afraid to hit and who could run like a deer. I'm thankful for my coach Mike Zimmer, who now is a coach for the Dallas Cowboys. He recognized my ability and gave me a chance to shine. In 1992, after my senior year, I was invited to the NFL Combine in Indiana. It was a dream come true. All I had to do was run the fastest forty and I knew I would have a chance at the big show, the NFL. Well, at the Combine I didn't run the fastest, I ran very average. Most of the time I felt like a pigeon in the pack with the others, and I thought that when it came to the forty, I would be an eagle. Usually I soar alone—there is me and then there is everybody else—but for some odd reason I don't know what happened to me. I couldn't sleep all a week. The forty is all I had going for me. I wasn't one of those players who had four great seasons all through college to fall back on. As someone who entered college under Proposition 48, I had lost a year of eligibility and only started in my senior year. My only stronghold was my speed and it disappeared that afternoon.

That evening in the hotel lobby in Indiana I sat with a man named Sutherland. He bought me a Coke. At first he asked me if I wanted a beer but I said, "Yeah, right, in front of a pro scout," who would have about my priorities. He said, "You ran pretty good," Average is what he really meant. I told him that I was way faster than that. He told me that he would be at my school in a few weeks to see.

When I arrived back at school I broke up with my girlfriend and didn't bother going to school. I lived with my friends Eric and Gabe. Some of my other friends used to say to me, "Man, don't you ever go to school?" I said that I had to train because the NFL scouts would be here soon. I told them that school was going nowhere, and that I needed to find my 4.2 speed and find it fast. I could always go to school. They asked what I would do if football didn't work out and I replied by telling them that something would always come up. Greatness is always around the corner and it all depends on whether you're brave enough to go and look for it. We can always look for the negative things in life. But I have looked for great things and, with that attitude, I have done great things.

Finally the scouts made their way back to WSU and I was thrilled to have an opportunity to redeem my crown. I ran a 4.2. Even though it was a cloudy day, I knew that somewhere behind all those clouds was sunshine. That is how I live my life. I felt really good about myself after that day; the scouts and Merv seemed to be impressed. I was fortunate to have the New York Giants draft me because I ran such a great forty that day.

When I was alone the night I got drafted, I cried and my thoughts took me back to the days when it all started, running with my brother beside my parents' house. I thought of my brother Stanley, who inspired me and encouraged me every step of the way. I didn't get a big million dollar contract, I wasn't even on ESPN, and there were no major endorsements coming my way, but the reality of achieving my dream was far more rewarding than money. Along the way there were people who were full of doubt and envy because I was living my dreams.

I went home to California for about a month before leaving for New York and I trained the whole time. I trained while Stanley watched, always with a smile on his face. Running at the side of the house was such a special time because it took me back to where the dream started.

On my arrival in New York, all the other rookies talked about their college stats and accolades. The only thing I could say was that I couldn't wait to run the forty. Early one afternoon all the rookies had a big workout running forties and doing drills and all I could think about was the forty. All my faith has been on forty yards. Everywhere I have been I've been the fastest, my drills were okay, but I was the best at the forty. My fast time is what was getting me the attention and I was lucky to be interviewed by the media on several occasions because of my speed.

After a long, tough, grueling training camp I was cut. I was devastated. Damn, I was playing pretty darn good, making good plays, hitting hard, but in the end I came up short. I called my parents and then my agent to tell them what happened. I started the long drive home.

As I drove across the country I would do a little form running every time I stopped for gas because my agent told me that I could get called anytime and I needed to keep in shape. I stopped at a rest area in North Dakota to do some drills in the grass. People were looking at me like I was crazy. While I was on that journey, passion took over and I knew failure was not an option.

I finally arrived back in Washington and stayed with my son, Jordan, and his mother. I was so excited that night that I couldn't sleep so I marked off forty yards in the snow and I started running back and forth, pulling Jordan in his sled while his small laughter eased my concern. I still felt like I was losing because I couldn't run full speed in the snow. The next night Jordan's mother and I got into an argument, so I called my friend Gabe at WSU. I asked if I could stay at his place for a while because I had no money and needed a place to train. I had used the signing bonus to buy a Porsche. That might not have been a good idea. It sure looked good though.

I spent the next day running "forties" in the gym. When I got to Gabe's apartment, my agent called to tell me that the New

York Jets wanted to work me out. I knew this time something was going to happen and, once again, it was coming down to running the forty. I was confident. I did a lot of running while driving across the country and had been training while back in Washington. I was ready to fly to New York in the morning.

That morning I woke up late and the airport was all the way in Spokane, about seventy miles east, an hour-and-a-half drive. My plane was leaving at a quarter to nine in the morning and I woke up twenty minutes before eight. I jumped out of bed like a wild animal. "Oh, my God, I'm going to miss the plane!" I ran to the car with my bag. I was speeding the whole way there in my Porsche. I didn't care; I had to be on that plane. This was my opportunity to show the Jets what I could do. After all the rush, I missed the plane. I had to make myself look good so I called the Jets and said there had been a mix-up at the airport. This was fine they said and put me on the ten o'clock flight. I could only think about running the forty in four seconds and I forgot to buy a ticket when I left my Porsche in the airport parkade.

When I arrived back in New York, the gentleman who picked me up by a gentleman told me what was expected of me: eight o'clock wake-up and nine o'clock work out. That night at the hotel, I asked a taxi driver to take me to the Jets' facility. I hopped the fence about ten o'clock that night and walked along the turf where they said I would be running the forty yards. I didn't know exactly where I would be running so I walked every corner and closed my eyes and thought about that dirt trail at the side of mom and dad's house. The facility was close to the hotel so I walked back to my room. I slept well that night knowing in my heart that this time I wasn't going home.

I got up the next morning and, with the scouts and coaches watching, I ran one forty so fast that they didn't tell me my time. He said, "I'll be right back." He got a few of the coaches, did a few drills, and we signed a contract that afternoon. At that time in my life, all I was leaning on was forty yards. I thought about forty yards all the time.

Being on the Jets was great. All of WSU's running and lifting records were held by James Hasty, who now played for the New York Jets. I had never met him until now, but he would eventually help further my career and make me a better football player.

After spending some time with the Jets I was cut the same year. I first signed considering I was only on the practice squad. They said that was because of the numbers game. "Oh, well," I said and flew back to Washington.

I had some money in my pocket and Susan and I had made up, so I went back to stay with her. I spent my first night there running in the snow with my son Jordan, again pulling him in his sled. The following morning my agent called and said a team in Canada wanted to take a look at me. It was the Calgary Stampeders. The next morning I was on a plane headed for Calgary, Alberta. I wasn't too excited about going because it wasn't the NFL, just the Canadian Football League. I flew into Calgary the next morning and was supposed to work out the next day. I didn't want to be there. I had convinced myself that I didn't like the place at all. I didn't like the guys around me, the food, or the hotel. I had decided that my forty was in a class all by itself and all I wanted to do was embarrass those other players. I didn't want their times to be close to mine. That night I was so focused on running that forty that I couldn't even think about football.

The next morning I ran the fastest time ever on Calgary's hard-ass cold turf. When they asked me to sign a contract I said, "No, thanks." The general manager at that time, Roy Shivers, asked me why I wouldn't sign. I responded by saying, "It's not the NFL and I don't want you. I'll take my chances." So, the next morning I went back home to Susan and my son.

I spent the following week resting and complaining about I should be on a NFL team because nobody can run as fast as I can. I decided that I'm young, that I've always been a late bloomer, and since this year is just about over, I'll start getting ready for next year. After a few weeks of relaxing and running off at the mouth I decided to run in an all-comers' meet in Cheney, Washington. It was a 5.5-meter indoor dash and I won it. I called the Jets to let them know and several weeks later I was living in New York getting ready for mini camp.

I didn't know the mini-camp schedule until a couple of weeks before it started and realized that we would be running the forty. Next thing you know, I stopped doing football drills and started training once again for forty yards. I realized that this was my time to show everybody who the king of speed was. I needed to get the respect from the veterans on the team and I decided that I would run so fast that they would have to acknowledge it. Our trainer would occasionally ask if I wanted to do some cornerback drills. "No," I would say. I would drive to a local high school and train for the upcoming forty. All my energy was focused on the four seconds that would bring me fame, not those damn football drills. Whoever got acknowledged for his skills by doing drills? No one. On the other hand, you get much more recognition by the way you run that forty yards.

I remember that spring day I had a sore ankle. Still I ran a 4.2 in the forty and everybody knew me. I made the team that year and was an outstanding New York Jets player. Once again I placed all my faith in forty yards.

As the years went by, I began to develop into a good football player. The Jets had a few coaching changes that year, bringing in different personalities with new philosophies. In life there are some things we have no control over and so one spring morning after four years with the Jets I got a call saying I had been cut. I thought to myself, "Damn, here I go again!" The next morning at the crack of dawn I was training once again for another shot and all my attention went back to running the forty yards.

About a week later I got a call from the Cincinnati Bengals saying that they would honor my contract and I was excited. They sent me a schedule of their mini camp and the first thing that caught my attention was they wanted everyone to run the forty at least twice. At that moment, I called my brother Stanley to let him know. "Man, I'm going to show that organization who's the king when it comes to running the 'forty.' " I didn't care about football drills, all I could think of was those four seconds that had been so good to me up until now. I began to call the forty my friend as a means of getting instant attention.

Arriving in Cincinnati for the Bengals mini camp, I thought it was an ugly city. When I got to the hotel I waited until about ten in the evening before calling a taxi to take me to the training facility. As in the past, I walked along the turf reminiscing about where my journey began: the dirt trail at the side of my parent's home. I got back in the taxi and headed back to the hotel. Perhaps the taxi driver thought I was a little weird but, when you're on a mission, you do what needs to be done.

Confident, I smiled at myself in the mirror the following morning and thought that if anyone in Cincinnati didn't know who I was they were going to get to know me in about three-and-a-half hours. That afternoon I ran the fastest time in Bengal history. Hands down, I was the fastest. I made the six o'clock news that night and once again those forty yards brought me back to the place I wanted to be. I couldn't wait to get home and tell my friends and family about my success. A couple of days before training camp was about to begin I got a call first thing in the morning and was told I had been cut because of a salary cap. I was stunned because teams already had their rosters together for camp. Once again, I found myself training for forty yards.

The days passed and I got a call from the San Francisco 49ers. The following day I flew to their training camp in Sacramento, California. I was a late arrival and I knew I faced an uphill battle. They told me where and when I would be working out. I was told the workout would be held on the grass. So that evening I walked along the grass with my eyes closed and thought only of my beginnings and that dirt trail.

The following morning I warmed up and was ready to go. They told me they were going to put me through some drills and that would be all. "Don't you want me to run a forty?" I asked. "No, just drills," they responded. Even though they signed me that morning, I was disappointed because I wanted the chance to wear the crown of the fastest man on the team. I wanted to run that forty.

I played my ass off and had a great camp. I made big plays, I hit hard, but despite all of this, I came up short and was cut before the regular season began. I drove home that night. It was a seven-hour drive and I got home about nine in the morning and by noon was at the local high school training again for another shot at running the forty. I trained in silence for the next few months.

There were no calls from teams or from my agent and then one day, out of the blue, the Broncos called. I was thrilled because they were the hottest team in the NFL. When I arrived in Colorado it was a cold day, but I didn't care. The next morning I would wear the crown once again in the forty.

The following morning when I woke up I felt weird, to the point of throwing up and for what reason I didn't know. I ran that morning on wet grass and ran so fast that they had me wait for three hours in the lobby while they tried to work some things out. I came up short. I was told that they were not going to release anyone and make any changes for the time being. I was crushed; my faith on forty yards had failed me this time. I spent the next day in a state of confusion. But like a warrior, I got back home to Washington and began believing in those forty yards once again.

The following week, the Minnesota Vikings called and asked if I was in shape. Was I in shape! They flew me out there the next day. When I arrived in Minnesota I was a little tired, but still had enough gas in the tank to feel good about everything. Arriving at the Viking facility, I was told, "Head Coach Dennis Green doesn't like to wait so be ready to run as soon as he opens the door." I warmed up as fast as I could, got a good sweat going, and began to think about my life's journey. A feeling of peace came over me like never before and I thought of all the events that had brought me to this point in my life. I realized it didn't matter how fast I ran last week, or eight years ago, but what was important was how fast I could run the forty yards right now.

Dennis Green opened the door. I threw my hand up in the air and said, "Let's do this now!" I had nothing to fear. I told myself, "I'm not good at the forty yards, I'm great," and at that moment I ran great. At first they wanted me to run two forty-yard times, but after running just one all they could say was, "Wow! Let's do some drills." I did some drills and by that afternoon I had signed with the Minnesota Vikings. That year I played in my first career playoff game. It didn't matter how I started off, but how strong I finished. Once again, I had placed all of my faith in those forty yards and what they had brought me at this point in my life. I wanted to ride those forty yards for as long as I could.

After being in Minnesota for a couple of years I found myself as a free agent. Finally I had a chance to run for treasure and blaze the forty. I went to Carolina for a free-agent workout. I blazed the forty once again, but they didn't sign me. I was not disappointed because there were plenty of other teams. A week later my agent called and said, "The Chiefs want to work you out." I was excited because by that time James Hasty was playing with the Kansas City Chiefs. I called him and said I would be flying out in a few days. I arrived in Kansas City with an old Vikings teammate who was also a free agent. The personnel director and coach said they wanted me. I called my agent and, while they were working out a deal, I waited in the hotel thinking about forty yards, not the contract. I wanted more of a signing bonus and a chance to run the forty, telling them that I wanted them to know who the fastest man on the team was. I didn't sleep that night and all I could think about was forty yards. Once again I was placing all of my trust in those forty yards.

The following morning, I ran those forty yards. I ran so fast the Kansas City Chiefs gave me a signing bonus that was better than I had imagined. While riding back to the hotel, all I could think of was that I maybe could have run a little faster. Forty yards once again came up big for me and, before I knew it, I was at training camp.

I was having a great training camp until I hurt my lower

abdominal muscle and was forced to miss a week of practice. I played average in the last pre-season game and was cut the following morning. I flew home to Washington that evening and once again was at the local high school training for forty yards. After a month-and-a-half a few friends called pretending to be NFL scouts. Shortly after that, the Oakland Raiders called while I was potty-training my middle child Jonathan. I thought my friends were trying to be funny and up to playing tricks again. Only this time, it was real and later that evening I was on a plane ready to showcase some real speed. I was somewhat intimidated considering some of the fastest players in the NFL had gone through and played with the Raiders. We all knew Davis Laves' speed, but then it hit me, they haven't seen speed like mine.

I packed a lot of stuff because I knew I would be staying in Oakland. I said to myself, "I train for moments like this; it's my time to shine." The following morning when I warmed up a good crowd and a few players were watching. I kept telling myself to get scared because after I run this forty, things are about to get shaken up around here. It was a cold morning and the grass was wet, but it didn't slow me down. They timed me and were shocked. I was put in the same category as all of the other world-class forty-yard runners.

The Oakland Raiders came through and, by the following Sunday afternoon, I was playing on the field. I had to applaud those four seconds. The faith I had in forty yards would get even stronger over time. They didn't offer me a contract and I was released.

The next stop was San Diego. The funny thing about this was that the finish line was part of the building, so I would have to slow down very fast. I asked the General Manager, Bobby Beathrad, if we could back up a little because there was not enough room for me to slow down. He kind of smiled and said, "Okay." As I have done time and time again, I shot out like a cannon and ran, some say the fastest, or one of the fastest times. I didn't sign with San Diego because I wanted more of a signing bonus, and well, that was stupid. My agent got mad and during the summer I strained by hamstring and ended up sitting out the whole season. No phone calls. No thrills. Even though I didn't play football that season I trained as if I was going to get a call at a moment's notice. I had decided to always be prepared so that when the call came I would be ready. The season was over and I was in shape to run forty yards but nobody was calling.

I decided one morning to drive to the UCLA campus because they were having a pro timing event. I showed up like a thief in the night with only my running shoes in hand. At first, they weren't going to let me run. Then I found the athletic director of football operations. He must have seen the look of desperation and hunger in my eyes when I explained to him that I needed to do this. He went to speak with the scouts to make sure it would be okay for me to run. They agreed. I blew everyone away in the race, but still there were no calls and no interest. I had been out of the loop for close to a year. The following week I showed up at the campus of San Diego State again toting my running shoes. I blazed in the forty. There was some strong interest and I wanted to run in front of the general manager, but I first had to impress the scouts. I was beginning to get worried about not having an opportunity to play football, but I wasn't worried about running those forty yards. I knew I had that in the bag.

Several weeks later, that Canadian team called me again. Remember way back when? Yes, the Calgary Stampeders. They were having a big workout in Los Angeles, right in my backyard, and nobody can outdo me in my own backyard. I showed up and met with the coaches. During the warm up I looked around at the other players trying out. These guys didn't stand a chance. I thought about every individual there and how they all have dreams like I do. Before you knew it, we were all running the forty. When they called my name I wasn't ready. I wanted to run last and I did. When I ran that forty I couldn't hear a thing. After I ran, I spoke with the head coach, Wally Buono, and he was in shock because the coach who was standing at the twenty-yard line said he didn't hear my feet hit the ground. We did some drills and some one-on-ones.

A few days later they wanted to sign me to a contract but I didn't want to play in Canada. "I was after the NFL," I told my dad. He said, "If you love what you do, it shouldn't matter where you do it. A bird in the hand beats two in the bush." So, what I did was pack my bags and head up north to Canada to relight the candle.

When I arrived in Canada I was in awe with the Rocky Mountains and Banff, Alberta. I got the schedule for testing day and, would you believe it? The entire team had to test for forty yards. As in the past, it was time for me to wear the king's crown once again and become the fastest man on the team.

I decided I would isolate myself by standing in the corner of the end zone the following morning during the testing. Even though I was wearing sunglasses while I was warming up I could feel everyone's eyes on me, saying who in the hell does he think he is? I watched the other players run and only smiled because I knew when I ran everybody would be at the finish line and they were. It was a beautiful day. The sun was shining and the sky was blue. The turf was wet but, you know, it didn't slow me down one bit because I wanted everyone on this team to know who I was. When they called my name I ran that forty in 4.28, wet turf and all. Yeah, life is funny sometimes. You never know where it will take you and, in my case, you never know where forty yards will lead you.

Chapter 7

Football Stories

I n my opinion football is simply a bunch of men knocking the hell out of each other. Others will tell you that it's the ultimate team sport. I believe that each individual player has to take a certain amount of responsibility and then, collectively, we win as a team.

From my first year of football, when I was eight years old, and scared, through the years when my father coached our Little League team I knew I was a fast runner. Then I met Coach Burns in high school football, and he showed me how to make the most of my speed. My coach Mr. Burns made me his project. I remember that summer I was on a mission. I felt that I was so far behind the other players because most of them were starters from the previous year. They considered me an extra body, but all of that would change. Every day Mr. Burns would get in my face like a mad man, telling me how fast and great I was. He told me that over and over again and, before long, I believed him. I was the best player on the team and not playing the previous year soon meant nothing. Mr. Burns knew that this year was all I had and he was going to make somebody notice me. Like a soldier I started working, lifting, practicing hard, and telling myself that there was no net to catch me if I fell and this was the year I had to excel.

I can recall practicing one hot summer day. The smog was thick and everybody was tired. When practice was over we all sat around drinking Gatorade and talking about the upcoming football season, knowing we wanted to dominate it. We started talking about the NFL and all the great players we admired. I began to think about how awesome it would be to play on the same field with some of the great players like Lawrence Taylor, Ronnie Lott, Phil Sims, Art Monk, Al Toon, Everson Walls, Darly Green, and Joe Montana.

What made this so inspiring is that, of all the teammates who were before me, and even better than me, out of the bunch it would be me who would go all the way to the NFL and get a chance to play with all of these great players we talked about on that summer afternoon. The chance to even get in the huddle as teammates and play on national television in front of millions of people and have your name called, that would all come five years later. You never know where your dreams may take you; they took me all the way to the NFL. We all have something great inside, that's where we put our faith. The thing I am great at is running forty yards and I truly believed that forty yards would get me where I wanted to go.

In my senior year of football the grace of God must have been with me because, out of nowhere, I had a great season. I was even named most valuable player. I have to give a lot of the credit to Coach Burns and his habit of getting in my face like a mad man every game, telling me that this was my game and my time to shine. I believe that he saw something great in me and helped pull it out. He took my potential and presented it to every college in America and because of his actions I got a scholarship. Thanks, Coach Burns, for pushing me so hard.

The biggest constant that year was that I would look into the stands and see my dad's face. He was there in that red windbreaker and his gray old man's hat. Looking up there helped to put everything into perspective. Even at my young age I would think back to all those Little League games in the late seventies when I continuously fumbled the ball and how I wanted to quit, but my dad pushed me forward. It was almost as if history was repeating itself, only this time it was Coach Burns urging me on and not my dad. And in a way it was. That year ended on a good note when our team made the playoffs. We lost, but damn we played our hearts out. I cried all the way home on the bus and I can still feel the hands patting me on the back. I remember before that game our head coach Wayne CoChaun said to all the seniors, "This could be your last high school game and for some of you the last time you will ever put on a football uniform, so I want you to go out there tonight and play your asses off." And we did. That night we were a team and every senior on that team was a king.

I thought having to sit out my first year of college football, because of my low SAT scores and the college entry requirements under Proposition 48, was a bunch of you know what. After the first college season was over the coaching staff who had recruited me took a better coaching position in Miami, Florida. I was devastated that they left without me having a chance to show them my stuff. WSU hired a man named Mike Price out of Weber State and it was a God-send that they did. Even though I was a Proposition 48 student, Mike Price gave me a fair opportunity. I still wasn't that good and considered my high school senior year an act of God. The only thing I had going for me was that I was in good shape.

Coach Price was hired in the spring. Some of the players were upset because they had put all of their trust in the previous coaching staff, but I felt lucky. All of us had to start at zero and prove ourselves to the new coach. I couldn't participate in spring football but what I did was make up a plan. I couldn't wait for the summer and to go home to California. The summer before I got to training camp all I did was sprint forty yards beside my parent's house. The plan was to become so fast that the coach would have no choice but to put me somewhere out on the field. I refused to do one single football drill that entire summer because I was afraid it might slow me down. I had no idea what position I was going to play. My brother Stanley encouraged me and never once tried to make me do drills. He was on my side. He encouraged me to run and left the decisions up to the coaching staff.

The first day of training camp I ran so fast the coaches were confused. First they put me in as a receiver, the problem being I kept jumping offside because I couldn't stand still, not to mention that I couldn't catch all that well. During one particular practice, whenever he got the ball, every wide receiver would move back and try to make the defensive back miss him. When they gave me the ball, I took off like lightning and ran the defensive back over, putting him on his ass. Everyone was in awe. I asked myself, how did I do that? The next day the coaches moved me to defensive back, or cornerback. That is when I met Mike Zimmer, my defensive back coach. He was chewing tobacco and cursing every second. Funny thing, whenever he screamed, his voice would get so high you couldn't help but laugh. Zimmer took me, as bad as I was, and turned me into a wrecking machine. That first year I played on specialty teams. I was a maniac. Every time I stepped on the field I made a point to always be in there and make the first hit. I even had the chance to play some corner.

The game that sticks out most in my mind that first year was our last game against University of Washington for the Apple Cup. I got a sack for twelve yards. This was not another day at the office for me. It was a play that I would go over and over again in my mind to motivate myself. I began to realize that if you do a great thing once, you can do it the second time, then the third, and so on and so on. That is a personal philosophy I have used over and over again in my life.

In my junior year at college I started to see things finally coming together, with Coach Zimmer screaming at me trying to bring out the best of me. The athletic ability that Coach Burns saw in me during high school was actually elevated by the drills Coach Zimmer put me through in college. One day Zimmer said to me, "You have the speed and strength of an NFL player but, once I bring out more of the football skills, you might one day play in the big show." I took those words very seriously.

Towards the end of my junior year I once again found myself facing my last chance for another miracle. It was all coming down to my senior year, which would be my final year. That spring Coach Zimmer called me into his office and said I would be playing strong safety. I was a little discouraged about having to change positions in my senior year, but he promised me that he would make it very easy for me to do this and that I would be in the starting position in the up and coming season. I was a bit nervous at first. My stomach churned. "I'm finally a starter," I thought.

That spring in training camp I really thought that I would give Zimmer a heart attack. He screamed, he cursed, and he put so much tobacco in his mouth that I thought for sure he would choke. Eventually I got the hang of things and I found my new position made more sense. By the time spring training camp was over, Zimmer seemed pleased with my progress so I kept on training and watching films until summer camp. I thought a lot about the NFL during summer camp and knew the possibility of me playing in the NFL in less than twelve months was a reality. That camp I got a letter from the Dallas Cowboys. I thought about the letter I got from UCLA when I was in high school. A feeling came over me and I knew I would not fail. I called my old high school coach Mr. Burns to tell him my news. He was thrilled and his words inspired me in such a way that I felt like I could run right through a brick wall.

During our last game in senior year, I missed eleven tackles and must have looked like a chicken with his head cut off. I don't know what I was thinking, but nothing made any sense that game. Calls from the huddle sounded like a different language and I started questioning my abilities. Am I good enough to be a starter? Zimmer grabbed me by the helmet and asked, "What the hell is wrong with you? You've busted your ass so hard to get to play. I know you're better that that."

After the game and during our next practice I felt so low. Coach Zimmer made me tackle a bag every day until I was dog-tired. All the other players laughed. Here was a senior who was supposed to be a leader tackling a bag like a freshman. Little did they know I never had any practice tackling because I've always practiced on sprinting forty yards. But in tacking, my speed didn't matter. The football drills I had been running from started to catch up with me. I tackled that bag all week and, boy, it was hot in Pullman. The following game I had ten tackles, unassisted, and the rest is history.

Zimmer saw that I wasn't going to quit. Until we find a way to measure the heart of a man we will never know one's true character. That year Zimmer encouraged me and I played as hard as I possibly could. I did become a good football player during my years at WSU thanks to Zimmer and the entire coaching staff for not giving up on me.

During my senior year I got some awards here and there, but that's not important. The important thing is that I believed in myself. The next thing on my mind was what everybody calls the "show," meaning the NFL. After the season I trained and trained some more. The only thing that was on my mind was forty yards and that the NFL scouts were on their way to our camps to time and test the senior players.

March 13, I will never forget that day: I ran a 4.26. (On March 13, 2002, ten years later to the day, I ran the same time: 4.26. I tied my old record in hopes of getting another shot, this time as a free agent. Forty yards once again put me in a place I wanted to be.) That spring, the New York Giants drafted me. On draft day, my friends were playing games with me, pretending to NFL teams calling me. They were trying to get me all excited, and yes, they did fool me several times. By the next day I was feeling somewhat discouraged. A friend by the name of Curtis Geathers was over talking with me when the phone rang. I said, "Well, that's probably somebody trying to play games with me." I told Curtis to answer the phone. He picked up the phone and said, "Hello." His eyes kept getting bigger and he passed me the phone saying, "A.P., it's the Giants." I was shaking. When I hung up the phone I began jumping up and down and screaming. All I could say was, "4.2 is going to the Giants!" I meant that my forty was going, not me.

That night we celebrated, the party lasting until almost dawn. And the next morning I was on the run. I called everyone I knew, even people I hadn't seen in years, to tell them I was going to the NFL. I could hardly believe it myself. When you take time for yourself, begin to meditate on a dream, and start to believe in it, a certain power is created.

The first day of camp in the NFL, I was more "star-struck"

than anything else. I remembered playing football as a kid and how we would all pick a player from the NFL and pretend that's who we were during the game. I always picked Everson Wells. Well, to be able to actually practice with him! I was in heaven looking around at the likes of Lawrence Taylor, Phil Simms, Carl Banks, and Otis Anderson. These guys were pioneers of football, the big names who played on a level so high, year in, and year out. I even thought about that one hot day in my senior year at high school when we were sitting under the bleachers talking about the NFL greats and here I was playing with some of them. "Wow, you never know where forty yards is going to take you," I thought to myself. It has taken me to this strange land called the NFL and here I am enjoying the scenery and being surrounded by all the greats.

During mini camp I blazed the forty and from that day on they knew who I was. As training camp pressed on my body was becoming tired and weary. Some of the players left without even saying goodbye. I was starting to feel like doing the same because it was pretty tough. But, my roommate Corey Raymond, a free agent who was making a big impact during his rookie year, encouraged me to stay and not give up without a good fight. I found myself fading, and fading fast; even the newspapers let me know my fate. I had the attitude that I was going to finish what I had started and see this through with a fight.

During training camp, the rookies had to get taped at a quarter to six in the morning. This went on for weeks on end and I was becoming more and more tired. Then, there was a practice. The thought of waking up and walking damn near a mile to get taped and eat while the veterans were taped at a quarter after eight was becoming too much.

One morning towards the end of the camp I said, "The hell with this, I'm the fastest on the team and I'm going to get taped with the veterans." That morning, Corey said, "Come on, A.P., let's go." "No, Dog, I'm sleepin'. I'll get taped later." Corey left and several hours later I walked into the training room and sat down on the table. All the trainers ignored me. I wanted somebody to tape my ankles. The head trainer at the time was a black man. I thought he was just a college student helping out, so I told him to tape my ankles. He said no because I was supposed to have been in at a quarter past six. I told him, "I'm tired of this shit. Tape my ankles before I beat your ass." He looked at me and said, "Wow! Did you guys hear that this rookie is going to beat my ass?"

After that day everyone knew I was the fastest and now I was making threats. All of the veterans had a good laugh over this. I guess you could say I was just tired and frustrated. Hell, I had been there for four weeks and I still didn't know the defense completely. Rod Russ's defense was so complex you had to be a rocket scientist to figure it out. Come on, we're football players, not scientists. Rod Russ is one of the greatest minds in football when it comes to defense. He gave me my first shot to enter the NFL. Thanks, Rod.

Towards the end of the training camp I was cut. At first I thought I had made the team. They made all the cuts and, one morning, Roy Handly said he had to cut one more person. I spoke first, and said, "Not me, I'm the fastest guy out there."

The next morning I wasn't feeling so good and something came over me, almost like a dark cloud in the distance. Next thing you know, it's hovering right over your head. That morning I was cut. I realized forty yards didn't prevail this time. I walked back to the hotel, the only thing on my mind was, "Damn, I can't believe that this happened." Then I said to myself, "If I can come this close on forty yards, imagine how far I can go if I had somebody show me some better techniques."

That technique thought fell out of my head so fast. I thought, "Who can be the next team to see this speed and do something with it?" That team would be the Jets. I would run and work out for them a week later after being cut by the Giants. I signed and spent time that first year on the practice squad. I just ran wide receiver routes and ran plays that they would be defending that week. I was what was called a "utility man," helping out and getting paid. I was also learning from the other great players.

The following year, 1993, my second NFL training camp, and my first with the New York Jets, my football skills would escalate with the help of James Hasty, Ronnie Lott, and Eric Thomas, to name only a few players. I began to rely on technique and not just raw speed. That year I worked my way onto the defense playing nickel and dime, and would become a monster on special teams with the help of Al Roberts, the toughest special teams coach in football. He was also considered the toughest at any level. He believed in me when others didn't, he fought for me to be on the team, and because of this I wanted to prove him right every chance I got. When another person puts their reputation on the line for you, you should be thankful and show it in a manner so loud that words don't have to be spoken.

One player, Marcus Turner, to this day I'll call him just to talk or if I have something on my mind. Marcus and I would always talk about life and the meaning behind it. He was the one who gave me the nickname Junky. It all started during a pre-season game against the Red Skins. All the players had nice handbags and were wearing nice clothes. All I had on was a T-shirt and jeans. You could see my toothbrush hanging out of the front pocket on my shirt. Marcus asked where my clothes were. I replied rather loudly, "I'm going to play my ass off. I don't need to look nice." He referred to me as a Junk Yard Dog, which over time was shortened to Junky. Every time my technique on the field would get bad he started calling me Junky. At first, I didn't like it but, after a while, I just took it to the limit. I began to try and dress for games. To this day I look junky in my uniform, but don't let that fool you.

James Hasty was the first face I saw on the record board at Washington State, yet I never met him until I got to New York with the Jets. He also started calling me Junky and I said, "Ah, come on, man, you're up here training and teaching me all this technique, if I'm junky it's because of you." From that moment on he started calling me J.Y. I was okay with that. Everybody looked up to James. I figured everyone was scared of him. During games when James would mess up, or get beat, he would come and sit by me and say, "J. Y., did you see that shit? No safety help." I would always agree, even if I didn't see the play. I would sit there and say, "James, he sold you out, left you to dry, now you gonna be on ESPN's highlight." He'd smile for a moment, then go out to play and dominate. James has helped me more than anybody trying to develop a style all my own.

That 1993 season was going well. I remember we were flying out to Los Angeles to play the Raiders. At last my whole family was going to watch me play. Stanley had front row seats. My sister Stacey was eight months pregnant with her son Joshua. Everybody came except my brother Joseph. His kids really wanted to come, but he didn't let my mom take them. That didn't bother me because I knew he had his reasons for not coming. I never questioned him, or asked why. People have their own reasons for not doing things. He missed a good game. My dad just smiled the whole time; I knew he was proud of me.

As my season with the New York Jets came to an end, I couldn't believe that I had played an entire NFL season. After all, I was still learning how to play football. My second season with the Jets was also good. I was getting better and better with the help of James, Ronnie, Marcus, and the coaches. I was even rotating with the starters. Everybody knew special teams were my game but, I wanted a bigger role and that year I played a lot of defense. The following year there were a lot of changes. James, Ronnie, and Eric were all gone. Marcus got hurt and then there was me. That year we had all new coaching staff and different players, new faces. All this brought new attitudes, and changes. I felt I was going to start that year. Victor Green, my partner in crime, won the starting job at safety. I always thought we would be on the field at the same time, not just playing special teams, but playing defense where respect is earned from your peers. Victor went on to have a great career and is still playing.

During training camp in 1995 a player who I used to watch during my freshman year at WSU came in late to training camp. He began to talk about his journey with football and how he had been with this team and that team. He talked about Canada and the CFL. I told my roommate that I would never take that road. I would just give it all up, with all those teams he's been on. Eventually, I would have to swallow those words and take the same road. I would even join some of the teams that player had passed through.

After training camp and as the 1995 season got under way, I felt I was having a pro-bowl season. Unfortunately, I was deactivated a few times, and my timing began to fade and, along with it, my enthusiasm. I played hard, but when you play football without any heart it shows. Little did I know I was about to walk a path I had never imagined.

It all started after the 1995 season. The following March I was cut by the Jets right out of the blue. I remember talking with the coach about the off-season program and how it would be starting soon and he looked forward in seeing me. A few days later he called to tell me I had been cut. I was upset, but it was still early in the year and that gave me the chance to get picked up. The Cincinnati Bengals picked me up. I was feeling pretty good, but deep down after visiting Cincinnati and going through mini camp I didn't feel any good vibes about the place. I felt as if I was in a foreign country, almost sleepwalking. I just wanted to wake up and be back in New York. But, that didn't happen and, just before training camp, the most important day in the NFL, I got cut from the Bengals.

I was about to leave for Cincinnati when I got the call. I had been at the local high school track that day training. I was shocked when I heard the news. I knew I had to fight to stay alive in the NFL, but the next day I didn't even run. All I could do was walk around the track, as if I was lost and trying to find my way. It was hot and the sun was bright. My mind was racing and I was full of rage. When I got home, I got a call from the Carolina Panthers telling me to be there on Thursday. An hour passed and the San Francisco 49ers called telling me to get on a plane that night. I chose to go with the 49ers because I figured the Panthers would change their mind anyway.

I arrived at the 49ers' training camp in Sacramento. The coaches told me I would be in a dogfight for the spot. I knew

ANTHONY E. PRIOR

that would be the case, considering I didn't know the playbook, names of any of the players, or the coaches. The only coach I knew was Pete Carrol, the first coach to show me how to relax and play at the same time. He taught me that in 1994 when he was head coach for the New York Jets. At times during games in New York he would pull me aside and say, "Go out there and just say fuck it, and play like you know how, and when you get a chance to hit someone, hit them hard." That was one of my best training camps. I started making an impression with the 49ers the first day. I was the new kid on the block and I had to show them something fast. That I did.

A most memorable time was when I needed somebody to drive my truck up to San Francisco. I had all my stuff in the truck ready to go to Cincinnati and then my plans changed. I called friends and family promising them fifty-yard line seats right behind the bench, but everyone was too busy and couldn't get away. The person to step up to the plate was my eldest brother Joseph and at first I thought he was joking. I practiced extra hard that week knowing that he was going to be in the stands that Sunday watching me play. I played an awesome game. I made plays that I only make in my dreams. I could see him getting excited and he even called home on his cell phone to ask if they had seen Anthony make that play. At the end of the game Pete came up to me and said, "Hell of game, A.P." I knew they had their roster already set, they told me that before I got there, but I wasn't concerned about that. All I could think of was ten years ago when I had asked my brother Joseph if I had a chance to get a scholarship and play football. He had laughed in my face and told me that I would never amount to anything. And he hadn't even come to watch me play as a rookie in LA when the Jets played the Raiders.

Having Joseph in the stands made that training camp a remarkable experience. I never did tell Joseph how deeply the words he had spoken ten years ago had hurt my feelings. That never would have achieved anything. And now, because Joseph had reached out to help me, it was time to put the past to rest and get back to what is important in life, supporting one another like only family can. I got cut from the team, but that didn't matter because if God sent me to San Francisco just to experience that moment of forgiveness, I'd do it all over again.

I was cut from the 49ers after that last pre-season game so I just packed it all up half past one that afternoon and took off for my parents' home in Riverside, California. When a state trooper pulled me over I explained to him that I had just been cut by the 49ers and I just wanted to get home. He let me off and said, "Speed on until you get to Fresno." It was a bright clear night and the stars were brighter than ever. I was fumbling with the radio and came across that old song by Ben E. King, "Stand by Me":

When the night has come
And the land is dark
And the moon is the only light you'll see

That was a long night. In the morning I stopped to talk with Marcus Turner. He said, "Junky, keep your head up. You're young and you can still run." I drove home with his words running through my mind. Once again I began to think about where forty yards would take me next.

I was tired, but not too tired to run. So like a warrior I dusted myself off and got back to the basics despite the fact that the football season was in full swing. Every Sunday after church I would take my Sony Walkman and go down to the local high school. As I ran around the football field I would be listening to the Sunday afternoon games just as if I was out there playing. I needed to stay in shape if I wanted to get back onto the battlefield. I would do this routine for weeks on end. I remember one particular Sunday after working out I called my mom and told her that I would be playing the next Sunday. Somehow I just knew and I packed my bag anticipating a call. The following morning I was staring out the window and said, "God, I need a miracle right now," and then the phone rang. It was the Minnesota Vikings. They wanted to work me out and asked if could make the two o'clock flight. I told him, "Yes, I packed last night."

I wasn't concerned about the forty yards. I somehow knew

I'd take care of that. I just wanted to be playing on Sunday night. And wouldn't you know it, that following Sunday night I was suiting up once again. I had to fight back the tears during the singing of the national anthem that night. Only the previous week, I had been wearing my Walkman and running around on the football field just as if I was playing. That vision had now become a reality that I could see, hear, feel, and touch. That year, I played in the playoffs for the first time in my career. I also realized that things can throw us off track in life, but if you look at each year of our lives as a chapter in a book, it doesn't matter how you start off, but rather how you finish.

After the 1996 football season nothing was too big for me. I never did doubt that I wouldn't play that year. There is power in whatever you believe in. I believed that I would step onto a field somewhere in the NFL, and that I did.

The 1997 football season was approaching and I found myself on a whole new level. I had no idea what to expect considering I was on my way to a new training camp with the Vikings. During mini camp I started to feel comfortable with the playbook, players, and coaches. Since I came into the 1996 season late, their off season and their way of doing thing were all knew to me. My coach with the Vikings was Richard Solomon, everybody called him Sollie. He was a short man and walked with a limp. He would often get mad with us and during his outbursts he would use words that weren't even in the dictionary. He would then begin to stutter and I would struggle to hold the laughter in. We had a great group of guys: Robert Griffin, Corey Fuller, Dewayne Washington, and Leonard Wheeler, just to name a few. That was the year Leonard and I became close friends.

For some reason, during summer training camp I seemed to have a cloud over my head. I was at a crossroad. I began to think of this football thing as a way to avoid the things that were dearer to me, like my eldest son, Jordan. I thought that I could just get a job and be with him. Then there was my son Jonathan who I just heard about five months ago. I began to ask myself whether my destiny was to struggle trying to become famous.

I began to question my motives. "Why do I play football, for the money, celebrity status, the women," I asked myself. I was unable to answer any of those questions at that time.

Practice got harder as time went by, Sollie yelled more, and the sun became hotter. During one of the practices Corey Fuller got hurt and all of a sudden I was in the starting position. I didn't know if I should get excited or just walk out the door and say, "I quit."

That night I began to reflect on something great players have told me, "Even though you're not a starter there may come a time when your number will be called." I knew it would be a temporary thing, considering Corey wasn't hurt that badly. I decided to take on more responsibility. I was only the starter for about a week-and-a-half and then Corey came back.

That experience was a little sample of what it would be like to be a starter in the NFL. I haven't got a full taste yet. That will come the day they call my name in front of thousands and say, "The starting corner, Anthony Prior," and I will jog onto the field hearing the crowd roar with excitement and my teammates forming a tunnel for me to run through. I will hold my hands out and slap hands with my teammates, letting me know they believe in me, and I believe in them. At that point I will have achieved my goal and until then, I'll just be another player who has played in the NFL. When that day will come, I don't know. But I can guarantee one thing, I will be ready.

When I was the starter in training camp for that short week-and-a-half that's all I thought about. "If the game were tomorrow, they'd call my name," I thought. That may sound foolish to some people, but it has always been the little things in life that have given me much joy. The big things in life we always have to work for and anticipate their creativity, but the little things often make us stop and realize that they touch us on a personal level. The little things are intended for us and the big things are for everyone who has helped us along the way.

I had a good season with the Minnesota Vikings that year. I played hard and made a lot of good plays, but my name was never called. On the other hand I heard some of the most inspiring stories and phrases from Vikings head coach Denny Green. He would often say things before the game that would make you want to run charging through a brick wall.

The latter part of the season I strained my groin and was sidelined for the last three games. I was forced to sit and watch players do the things that I could do. That year we went to the playoffs and won the first playoff game in Denny's career. I was happy because if he hadn't taken an interest in me that morning in 1996 I wouldn't even be here. I couldn't feel bad about being injured; it was just the nature of this game.

We lost the next playoff game. I felt that if I had been healthy I may have been able to do something to prevent that loss, but we all feel that way when we can't perform. It's a time when most athletes think, "I could do this or that better," and we try to push ourselves, but reality sets in and we realize how fragile our bodies really are. Sometimes, we wish for a miracle, but we all know miracles happen on a moment's notice.

After the 1997 season I realized that sometimes we can't control everything. There are some forces that can't be stopped no matter how hard we try to fight. Certain things have to happen in life so that we learn. We may have all the best intentions in the world, but there are forces out there that we can't avoid, and we are lead into personal growth, no matter how tough the lesson. The time must pass and one day you will get to a level of understanding. At that time you can move forward with your life. Until then you will remain in the same old place, wondering where to go from here.

1997 was a good year and early in 1998 I found myself a free agent. I was healthy and confident. The only thing that was on my mind was forty yards. I thought to myself, I haven't thrilled anyone since 1996. It's been two years since I last called the forty my friend. "Anthony, you don't have to do this. All you have to do is show up," my friend "Forty" said, but I didn't listen to him. Instead I surrounded myself again; the tunnel vision became clear, and the only thing I could see was forty yards. Now I felt braver than ever before. I had my friend "Forty," the one that has never let me down. I trained and trained until one day the Carolina Panthers called. I went down there and had a good workout, but they weren't ready to make any decisions because they were still working out other free agents. I did like I always do, shake hands, say thank-you for the opportunity, and get ready to run somewhere else.

The following week I got a call from the Kansas City Chiefs. "Great," I thought. "I'll have the chance to play with James Hasty again," the player I have always looked up to. I called to let James know and he said, "Go up there and handle your business." I showed up and took a physical; I passed it and they were ready to sign me. I was shocked and I asked, "Do you want me to run?" They implied, "No, you don't have to." I refused to ignore that and said, "No, I want to work out because I want you to know who the fastest player on the team is." That next morning I worked out. They were impressed with my times. I signed that afternoon and once again I could wear the crown of the king of forty yards.

On the flight back home I realized that I didn't have to do that. I ran because I felt I needed to. Often in life we do things, not for the sake of others, but for our own need. We must do certain things to fill a void in our lives. They could be anything, but mine was running that damn forty. It was then that I realized I had become a slave to four seconds.

During spring training I lived in Kansas for about three months. We lifted and ran often. I was in great shape. But I have always been a realist. During that spring camp I realized that the Chiefs had three pro bowl corners, Mark "Mighty Mouse" McMillan, James Hasty, and Dale Carter, and they had even drafted a couple of young guys. I laughed at myself and thought, "My entire NFL career, I've been in a fight. What makes this one different? Nothing."

I made my presence known fast. I ran and I hit. The coaches noticed. Marty, the head coach, said after a pre-season game in front of all the other players, "There are fifty-two roster spots left. Anthony Prior has one of them."

A few days later I hurt my lower abdominal muscle. I was unable to run at full speed, and without my speed I'm nothing.

Marty's training camp was hell. Practice was long and meetings were even longer, but I knew that long before I even signed. I was just happy to be playing again with Hasty and to be learning the new things I was learning. I kept trying to practice, but it just made my injury worse. I tried taking painkillers to help get me through practice, but then I just stopped trying to practice. During one practice I sat far off and watched everybody. I had to laugh at some of the guys and then I started to feel sad because I knew I wasn't going to be here much longer. "You don't make the club just sitting in the tub," I realized. I began to think back on my career and felt proud of myself. Even though I was hurt, I knew this wasn't the end of me, only a time to make another comeback. I thought about the rough times and some of the bad decisions I had made. The only thing I could say was, "I'm sorry." I couldn't make the bad decisions go away, only embrace them for they had brought me all this way, to a hot sunny field in Kansas City. A few days later, I was cut, but not cut out. I had a couple of good games and at that time I just leaned on that.

When I got home I was actually relieved. I knew I had to regroup. The day I got cut one of the personnel directors took me downstairs to the training room to have my physical before I could leave. When the elevator got to the bottom he stepped out first and then quickly jumped back in the elevator and said, "Do you want to go the other way, because the offence is in there?" I said, "Hell, no, I'm a man and those men in there will see me again, maybe not in the same uniform, but they will see me again." I turned and walked towards the offensive players in the training room. I could see in their eyes that they felt sorry for me. I shook a few hands and said, "Good luck." They didn't realize that I was about to do something I also love. When I got home I called on my friend once again, forty yards.

At that time I was trying to potty-train my son Jonathan at home. I remember one Monday night I was watching a little football and my son was on the toilet and yelled, "Dad, look." I went into the bathroom and, yes, finally he had succeeded. "Yeah, I wished I were out on the football field at play, but this shit I couldn't miss," I thought. As I healed up pretty strong and my changing diapers days were over, out of the blue I got a call from the Oakland Raiders.

The inspiring thing about this call was that the evening before I had been working out at the park and Donna and her son were also at the park. Her son Devon came up to me as I was working out and asked, "Anthony, are you going to be playing soon?"

I told the little boy, "The great thing about football is that when you're in my situation you never know what's around the corner. You can only hope it's something great." Devon started rollerblading and I asked if he would race me around the lake. I took off so fast he couldn't believe his little eyes. I slowed up to let him pass me and there we were. I was running behind Devon around the lake on a beautiful warm evening just as the sun was beginning to set in a perfectly clear sky. Devon started to get tired and when I caught up to him he was sitting on the bench with his mom. I was tired too so I joined them for a while. We started to talk about life and I remember telling Devon," If you're going to dream about anything, dream big. When you dream big, big things happen in your life. On the other hand, when you dream little things, little things will happen." Then Devon asked me why the sky was so big. "You're gonna have to ask God that one," I said and we raced back. I let him win. That night a good feeling came over me. The next day I got a call from the Raiders and the scout told me, "If you can't run 4.3 in the forty, don't bother getting on the plane." I laughed and went to pack my bags.

I flew to Alameda, California, that night and an old man met me at the airport. I don't recall his name, but he looked at me at said, "Oh, you're a confident one."

"Why did you say that?" I responded.

"Well, you packed as if you plan to be here a while," he said.

"Oh, yes I do," I answered.

"Can you run?" he asked.

"You'll see in the morning," I told him, leaning back in the car listening to Frank Sinatra as we drove away.

The next morning I got up feeling like I was brand new. When we got to the complex there were a group of people and some of the others players looking at me as if to say, "Who in the hell is that?" I was like, "You're about to see who I am when I run this forty." The grass was a little wet that morning and I was a little concerned about that, but I thought of my conversation with Devon the other day. When you're in my situation you never know what's around the corner, you can only hope it's something great and, at that moment, I realized this was "my around the corner," and it was great. All I had to do is do what I do best, call upon my friend "Forty," get that tunnel vision, and see the finish line.

It all came on time. I ran. They said my speed was very fast and, to top it off, the grass was wet. After that I did some ball drills and foot drills. I was told that I all I needed to do now was get a physical and they'd welcome me to the Oakland Raiders. On the ride to the hospital to get my physical the old man with his Frank Sinatra CD playing said, "I see now why you packed to stay a while." Even though I was called because somebody got hurt I realized the importance of always being prepared, whether in life or in football, because if you're prepared, you will have nothing to fear. Some players let training camp beat them because of a lack of preparation. My biggest fear has been letting opportunities pass me by. If I were not in shape I would have let that opportunity pass me by. The following Sunday I was playing in front of thousands once again, perhaps a million this because the game was broadcast on national television. During the warm-ups I was walking around the field and realized that only one week ago I had been watching these games on television at home. And a week ago I was working out at the park across the street from my house wishing and hoping that I would be on the field of play. And here I was again. As I started to jog I thought that some people are more fortunate than others. I struggled for a moment then I came up with this: In life you get what you deserve whether it is something great or horrible. Luck is a word that is not in my vocabulary. Luck has a lover named Bad Luck and the two go hand in hand. That's why there are some things you can't believe in, because they will always be links on the chains you can't avoid, the two always come together.

The football season flew by and I had a lot of fun with the Los Angeles Raiders. I played hard, let my presence be known, and they all saw it. When I say "let my presence be known," sometimes I am referring to my speed, because everywhere I've been on the field of play, other players have seen it. I'm not talking about anything magical; every person walking this earth has something great in them. The problem is that too many don't know what that is. My advice is to think back to your youth, the days of innocence and humility. What was it that really made you happy? The things that brought you great joy then are the things you should be doing now. Stop what you're doing and get back to what you were meant to do. We all have a duty in this life to present our gift to the world and let it be known what gift lies within. You already know what my gift is: it's a simple forty yards, getting from point A to point B faster than any one. Rekindle your gift for the sake of the person who needs to see it.

As the 1998 season came to a close I found myself a free agent once again. I worked out for the San Diego Chargers, but didn't sign a contract. Playing in San Diego would have been convenient considering I lived in Riverside, forty-five minutes from the facility.

In 1999 I had to take a step back in order to stay a step ahead. That year I didn't even play. I was nowhere near a NFL field. Instead, I took one of my best friends on a Mexican cruise for a week and we had the time of our lives. Only in the still of the night would I miss my best friend, "Forty" yards. He would never leave me; he's always with me and in my thoughts. I spent time with family and friends. Like never before we laughed, we ate, we even sat together in silence at times. Often people would say to me, "Anthony, it's weird seeing you this time of year." I would just smile. I called teams and tried to get on with somebody, but nothing was happening so I just kept on living, laughing, and loving.

Late in October 1999 I was having thoughts of hanging up my football cleats and taking on a new career. I said to myself, "I've been cut seven times. Maybe that's telling me something." But, I've always said to myself I would play until I was forty years old and when you set goals for yourself and they are long-term goals, there may be times in the middle when you're going to have a setback, or God will throw a curve ball at you every once in a while. I was reading the Bible that night and I just happened to turn to Proverbs 24:16, which says, "The righteous man may fall seven times, but each time they will rise again. But the wicked shall fall by calamity." Let me tell you, the next morning I called up my friend "Forty" yards. I said to him, we can't stop now, there is too much to look forward to. At that moment I realized that on my journey I would be a fool not to see how everything would turn out one day. A few weeks later I heard about the birth of my third son, James (I call him Guegee), on December 11, 1999. That's the same day Sam Cooke was killed in 1964 and one day after Otis Redding was killed three years later. At that time I was very confused about my personal life. However, I was not going to let it slow me down, so I acknowledged it and moved on. I have come to realize that anything you start off wrong in life, you can't end right. All you can do is the best you can.

As my training started to improve, my speed came back at where I left it. All I had to do to find it is was keep on running until I felt it kick in. I have never timed myself while training. I just know when the speed is there. It's a feeling that I only know, I can't even explain it clearly, and all I can say is that my speed is with me. When I run and I can't feel my feet touch the ground, it's almost like I'm floating on air.

The new millennium arrived. I had a new attitude about life, love, and football. I wasn't getting too much interest from NFL teams considering I hadn't played the previous year and there were salary cap issues. So one day I heard UCLA was having NFL tryouts. I just showed up and made my presence known. I got some interest here and there and a week later I showed up during the San Diego State University NFL tryout date. I did the same thing: I generated a bit of interest. But I started to get a little impatient and a week later I heard the Calgary Stampeders were having a tryout in the Los Angeles area. The CFL has turned out some great NFL players and I decided to check it out.

I showed up with my friend "Forty" yards and stole the show. A week later the Calgary Stampeders offered me a contract. I took it and people were saying to me, "Are you sure you want to go all that way to Canada? They don't even pay good money." I believe if you truly love what you do, it shouldn't matter where you do it. I stood on those words, I packed my truck, took along my friend "Forty" yards, and said, "Let's make some noise so loud they will hear it all the way down south."

When you know you're truly on a journey it doesn't matter where you go. When you're on a journey it will take you places only seen in your dreams. I never heard of anyone whose journey kept them in the same place.

The first day of training camp was testing day and, yes, part of the test was running forty yards. I was thrilled to hear that. I said to myself, "Damn, I'm international now." That afternoon all the players were warming up at the north side of the stadium; I was on the south side wearing my glasses. Guys were looking at me as if they were thinking, "Who in the hell is that? Somebody needs to tell that fool this is not a track meet." After I ran the forty, wide receiver Travis Moore said, "You don't have to tell him a damn thing running that fast." Once again I was the king of the forty, but this time in a different country.

That season, I put it all together and played my ass off. I even got my name called before the games as a starter. Canada is a beautiful place that will always have a special place in my heart. I would have never guessed that my friend "Forty" yards would take me so far north. It's all part of the journey. I led in a couple of categories as a player. I played no special teams, just corner full-time.

Of all the great players I've played with, let me name just a few: Ronnie Lott, James Hasty, Everson Walls. I could go on, but I'd run out of room. I thought that, learning lessons about football from these players, my skills should have kicked in long ago. I guess I had to come to a foreign country to realize that I had arrived. The year 2000 was the year that all their advice came together. I had learned things from all these players. I took a little from this guy and a little from that guy and developed a style I could call my own. We all learn from others and it's a cycle that has been going on since the beginning of time. That's why our successes and failures are not always our own.

In the year 2000 football became fun and so I put forty yards aside and focused on the things that made me a better football player. And I became a technician, it all clued in. During one practice Calgary Stampeders Head Coach Wally Buono said, "Don't rely entirely on your speed. It will become your enemy." At that point, it all came together. I just wish those words had been spoken to me years ago. If God sent me all the way to Canada to hear those words to change my attitude, then I'm thankful. I changed that day. I know now that my speed sits at my side and never leaves me, but my football technique has arrived. Buono's words changed everything. Technique has become a cousin to my speed. In my opinion, speed will always be first in my book. It was and still is my first love and we always cherish our first love.

I made a lot of noise in 2000 and finally played the way I knew I could. Towards the end of the season we lost the semi-finals and missed an opportunity to play in the championship game, the Grey Cup. A few days later, I packed up my truck and headed home. I was sad and happy at the same time. Sad because I was leaving my girlfriend who I had met in Canada. She was the first woman with whom I ever said "I love you" before she said it. I had a lot of firsts in Canada. Yet, I was happy to be going home to see my family.

While driving home, I realized that the scriptures I read were a powerful source in leading me to this point. Was that chance, fate, or just God trying to tell me something? At that moment the only thing I could have done was act and that I did. Too many times, when a clear sign is in front of us, we want to question it and make sure that it's in our best interests. The surest way to ruin a miracle is to question it.

As the 2000 season was ending, I was getting ready for the 2001 season. I had an option in my contract that gave me a window of opportunity to sign a NFL contract within a period of time. My girlfriend and I did everything possible to make that happen; however, it didn't. I have to give her a ton of credit, not once did she discourage me. She was my rock at that time in my life. I lived with her for a little more than a month and during that time we called and sent tapes, faxes, you name it. I even went to Head Coach Wally Buono asking him to release me so I could call upon my friend "Forty" yards and prove to myself that I could get my name called as a starter in the NFL, even if it was only for one game. After that one game I would have hung up my cleats and never set foot on a football field again. That is the moment I have been waiting my whole life for.

Wally told me I had two options. "Either come here and play, or don't play at all. I wouldn't have a team because too many players think of the CFL as a farm league to the NFL. If we were a farm league, I'd say go for it, Anthony, and good luck, but I can't." I shook his hand and said, "I'll see you in June." Like a soldier, I showed up for the 2001 season ready to continue the journey.

That year we had a lot of new faces and young legs to go with them. They called me "the old man." I realized I have become a journeyman. I laughed a lot that year. A lot of these guys were a good nine to ten years younger than me. When you get to that stage of life, you realize just how quickly time passes. It's true what they say, time goes fast when you do what you're meant to do because there is no time clock ticking when you're enjoying life. It takes only a moment to realize that the years have gone by when you look around at the young faces. When you look into a mirror and see the lines coming in on your face, you're happy to see that they're all laugh lines because this has been a wonderfully fun journey.

The 2001 season with the Calgary Stampeders was a

rollercoaster ride but we all stayed together until the end. One thing stands out. A rookie by the name of Dechon Austin was on the practice squad during the entire season. He came up to me one day and said, "A.P., damn, I sure need to get on the field." I was quick to tell him, "Where you are now doesn't mean you will stay there. You never know what's in store for you. Look around the next corner."

As the season progressed, I played hard and consistent for sixty minutes every game. The last game of the season I strained my groin badly. I was devastated. We won the game and I was out. The playoff games were just around the corner. I tried to run and heal, but Mother Nature said, "Sit back, Anthony." I thought about what Dechon had said to me earlier in the season. With my strained groin, here was his opportunity. That's why I believe our successes and failures are not always our own. Even though I was hurt and wanted to play, I was actually giving Dechon his opportunity to shine. And he shone. I watched every play and wished him success.

The next event was the championship game: the Grey Cup. I tried once again to run and get well, but my friend "Forty" yards decided to take a vacation. I had no speed, just a desire to play. I packed my bags and traveled with the team to play the Alouettes in Montreal, a city I enjoyed. I still thought and hoped I could play. My mind was saying Yes but my body was saying No. My body won.

The day of the big game was electrifying. Excitement was everywhere. I walked up to Dechon and said, "Look at you. You've been on practice squad all year and now look at you playing in the championship game, you bastard." I laughed and gave him a big hug. "Now go get me my ring."

The Grey Cup game was a classic, the kind that keeps you on your feet. All I could do was pace from side to side, wishing I was out there the whole time. As the game was coming to an end we all knew we had won. The celebration was under way. We hugged, jumped up and down, and some of us even cried. I was happy for my teammates, but sad that I wasn't out there on the battlefield.

Watching the championship game from the sidelines was frustrating, but seeing Dechon in action made me think of one of the greatest Bible stories, in the book of Joshua. Young Joshua was an unknown slave who lived in the time of Moses. In the story, the two men come to meet and Joshua looks up to Moses as the leader of Israel and a man who is performing miracles in the eyes of many. In the end, Joshua succeeds Moses as leader and leads his people to the Promised Land. Moses had seen the Promised Land only from a distance; Joshua actually led his people to the Promised Land. In the same way, Dechon led the Stampeders to the Grey Cup championship and I stood on the sidelines, watching it from a distance.

After the Grey Cup championship, once again, I found myself a free agent, with my friend "Forty" yards close by my side. Again I searched the NFL for a chance to prove to myself that I have what it takes. In the past two seasons combined in the CFL I held the record as the "Most Passes Defended" and "Tackles as Corner." However, that went down in books and remained unnoticed until I could prove my talent and abilities on a field somewhere in the NFL.

It took a long time for me to get where I am. Finally I have a style all my own. I have my speed, but more importantly, I believe in myself. Where I go from here God only knows. I promise you one thing, I will be ready.

Chapter 8

Hasty Dog

James Hasty. Some know him as Haste, Hasty Dog, number forty. I call him James. He is my mentor as a football player.

James Hasty spent seven seasons with the New York Jets and six with the New York Chiefs. He was released by the Chiefs after the 2000 season and signed with the Oakland Raiders in 2001. James Hasty, in my opinion (and many of the current players would agree), was one of the best bump-and-run corners of the 1990s. His peers voted him into the pro bowl.

James was the first person I could relate to when I got to Washington State University even though I only knew him because of a picture on the wall next to the gym, where the record-setters were on display. James' picture was plastered all over the defensive back section. He had all the strength records and the speed record for forty yards. Since I was admitted to college under the requirements of Proposition 48, I didn't play my freshman year. Instead I lifted weights and ran on my own. Before I would lift, I always passed the WSU hall of fame and I was determined to make my mark on that board and shatter James' records. That was the only thing motivating me: a picture of a man I had never met.

I soon came to break James records and in 1992 I was picked up by the New York Jets after being released by the New York Giants. I was more excited about meeting the man on the board than about being with the Jets. The day after I signed with the Jets, the whole team was in the locker room and there he was. I saw him and introduced myself. He said, "Hey, Dog," shook my hand, turned around and walked away. I was like, "This son-of-a-bitch." But after a few days, I saw that Hasty was like that with everybody, touch-and-go. After being in the NFL five years, I guess touch-and-go is the norm.

I spent a short time in the practice squad in 1992. The following year, in 1993, Hasty showed me how to be a better football player. He said my speed would only take me so far. "Technique and the weight room will keep you around this game a long time," he said. I had the weight room down. What was killing me was my weak ass technique.

After the 1993 season, Hasty was in the last year of his contract. In 1994, during training camp, Hasty not only won players' respect, but he got me thinking, "I wonder. Will I ever have to defend a team's pride and self-respect from racist comments?"

During a training camp practice, a coach told a rookie player, "Hell, all you're doing is raping women and stealing food." The coach said it loud. I was stunned but I didn't have enough money saved to say anything and we all looked around at Hasty because everybody respected him. Not all players liked him. Some thought he was a narcissistic son-of-a-bitch. Some said he didn't smile enough. Some thought he spoke his mind too much; others hated him. I loved him because on that day he said, "Hell, no, we don't need that shit out here." We all stared but, inside, all of us young black soldiers took pride in James' heroic act, to let that coach know, "I don't take no shit out here, from nobody."

You couldn't really say too much to James Hasty, the man. He was a beast or freak of nature to some players and a nightmare to wide receivers. He stood six foot, one inch, weighed 205 pounds, had arms like a linebacker, strength like a lineman, and speed like a sprinter, and he carried it all on the field. A pro bowler, he walked the walk and not only earned the respect from media and fans but earned the biggest honor of all: the respect of his peers, the players he went to war with.

In 1994, Hasty was our franchise player and his roommate

on the road was Marcus Turner. I will never forget Marcus coming to let me know what Hasty had done. Marcus said, "You're not going to believe this." I asked, "What you did?" "You would not believe it but Hasty just asked for the fifty cents in change left over from our hotel bill." Marcus was like, "That cheap rascal—fifty cents! Yeah, he was like, 'Give me my money!' " And the whole time we were getting ready for the game we weren't concerned about our opponents, ready to rip our heads off. We kept shaking our heads and smiling, saying, "Fifty cents, and he's the highest paid player on the team." We talked about that for weeks.

During that year Hasty and I would lift together. On our days off and during that time, we just talked about life and things to come. That would be our last year together, but the short time I spent with the man I learned technique and how to think on the field. At thirty-two years of age, playing in Canada, I still use those techniques from ten years ago. They must hold true because I'm still playing.

Hasty and I met up again in 1998, when I signed with the Kansas City Chiefs, the team he joined after leaving the Jets. My time with the Chiefs would be a short-lived plantation experience, but the lessons learned will last a lifetime. Not too many players get a chance to suit up with their mentors. Football is short lived, it doesn't last forever, so I try to embrace the good moments and stay close to the people who inspire me.

Chapter 9
Being a Black Athlete

As I lie on my back I feel the grass against my neck, I hear my coaches and the other players talking and laughing. I watch the quieter players, knowing that they're wondering what the coaches really think of them. I'm supposed to be stretching, but I'm having a moment of recognition and heightened consciousness. I ask myself, "Why am I out here? What am I trying to prove to these coaches and players?" The sweat runs down my face, over my ear, and down my neck. I sure would like to be in an air-conditioned building behind a desk, telling people where to go, what to do, and when to do it. Instead, I'm here on the football field. It's the seventh day of training camp.

During training camp, before the football season starts, the weather is always hot and the mosquitoes bite like hell. The pressure to perform can sometimes burn like fire if you let it. At training camp, coaches and personnel evaluate new talent to see if the new players have got what it takes to be a soldier on the battlefield of play. Training camp is like playing war games: the soldier who can stand the pressure and always have enough enthusiasm and tenacity to withstand day in and day out and perform under any circumstances, wins the crown and finds himself on the team. He gets a numbered jersey that bears his name but really, that's all he has in the end, a name on a jersey.

The coaches and scouts double the roster for training camp. Going into camp, you sell your soul and some of us even burn bridges for this opportunity. You leave your family behind and some of us even leave our unwed girlfriends with our kids, thinking we have made it to the Promised Land. But when camp is over, half of the players are jobless. I've been on that side of the fence and I've seen players let that one bad experience alter their whole life. For when training camp is over, football is over for some players forever.

The sad thing about training camp is the relationships that are broken. At training camp you share a room with a stranger. You develop a bond with that person. You stay up all night long, talking about life, love, women, and football. And then it dawns on you that your roommate is the man you're competing with. He stands between you and your childhood dream of becoming a pro football player. On the field he becomes your enemy even though off the field he's your friend. You watch his every move on the field as you practice and, when he slips up or makes a mistake, in your mind you celebrate his misfortunes. You chalk up one for yourself, because the player who makes the fewest mistakes wins the crown and wears his name on the back of his jersey. When it comes down to making the team and the coaches having to choose, we only hope for ourselves that we make the cut. It's sad, but it's so true.

During one training camp, on a hot afternoon in August, the coach seemed to lose track of time and, after practice was over, he said to us, "Tomorrow I'm giving you guys the day off, but remember this, men, your bodies belong to me." After hearing that I felt a little uneasy and perplexed as I walked towards the locker room. I heard the wind in the trees speak to me. I could hear the cry of my ancestors. I could feel the sway of the slave ships. I may have been a little dehydrated at the time, but a spirit had come upon me. I looked at my brothers around me, sweating like slaves, fighting each other like animals on the fields, disrespecting each other, all in the name of fame. Listen and let me take you into my thoughts, and hear the spirit of slavery that today is modern-day football.

People have written and said that black athletes are the finest-tuned machines in the world. Many say we were created by God to do things many of us can't do. I believe that black athletes are just entertainers who get dirty outside. I know we pose no threat to anybody. I feel like a king with no crown. I'm just a product on the shelf. For every Anthony Prior on the field, there are another 200 more around the corner. The positions we hold as football players are short lived. Our bodies are not our own when it comes to big contracts and fame. That's why being a black athlete today I can't help but think back to slavery. In my opinion slavery is one of the worst crimes done to humanity and America still hasn't given us blacks an apology. That's sad. I have no problem writing about what my eyes have seen and my ears have heard. For one, I'm black, and I've been involved in pro football for ten years. I've seen a lot and heard a lot. Most important, I have the knowledge and experience to back it all up.

To really get a good understanding of football and slavery, let's go back to the slave ships, a time and place in history when a mindset was created. The mindset of fearing your master was set by beatings and torture, with hangings for slaves who didn't obey and who refused to cooperate. Now they don't beat us on the field; instead they just cut us and say, "He was uncoachable," or "He had a bad attitude." History tells us these stories. I'm just putting them in today's context. Four hundred years ago the slave ships told us that our bodies were not our own, our lives would be forever changed, our families would be separated, and see what lay before us. This attitude has been a mindset towards blacks all over the world and has also been a mindset in football at all levels—high school, college, and the pros. It's most relevant in locker rooms, where the mentality of some black athletes have made me laugh but has also driven me into a silent rage.

Many southern black athletes refer to their coaches as "Boss" and forget about the fight in which many young and strong black men died at the hands of their boss. They wanted to be respected as a man first, not as an animal. So they stood and faced life and death. I believe those men would rather crawl in freedom than walk as a possession. And if their boss couldn't give them that respect, death was fine with them. That's courage at its highest level, damn it.

When we slaves first stepped foot on white America, the field slave was a runner. We had left behind a land of our own, and we took off in the night, following the stars during desperate hours of darkness, hoping that when the sun came up we would be with our people, our land, our home. Unfortunately that story doesn't have a sweet ending. The only ending it has was Harriet Tubman and the Underground Railroad, by which some of us made it to Canada. We even caught hell there, too.

The house slave just stayed at his master's plantation and said, "Don't run. We got it good here." He feared his master and took an ass beating, and made his roots there and came under the authority of his master, who set all boundaries and standards for him, his family, and for generations to come. I see the mindset and fear of the house slave most prevalent in black athletes from the southern states.

We are all God's children and we are one under his authority and no one else's. Through my experience and continued observation I find the majority of all black athletes who have lived their lives in the southern states carry most strongly the old mentality of the house slave. Some southern black athletes always seem to be fearful around coaches. They're always saying "Yes, sir" and "No, sir." They sit up front of meeting rooms, trying to show their master they really want to be there. They are always asking questions they already know the answer to. It's a way of showing their master, "I'm listening to you. I fear you. I respect you. All my hope is in you, Boss." This is not a way of respect. It's fear that drives these men. Their minds have been transformed to fear their master (the coach).

These athletes embarrass the black athlete as a whole because when one southern black athlete starts to act fearful, white coaches start to think all black athletes are fearful. That's when you have big surprises in the meeting rooms. When a white coach has been around a lot of southern black athletes for a long period of time, and when he comes across a black athlete who has more respect for himself, a field slave, look out. There may be hell to pay.

All black athletes, including me, are descended from past

generations of slaves; however, the slaves that took off north, west, and east had no fear of their master. They refused to buy into that kind of humiliation and mind control. I'm thankful they ran with the little dignity they had because I consider myself a field slave, a runner, a man of his own identity, and under no circumstances would I ever take on the mentality of a house slave.

I remember one team meeting when a coach said some degrading words to a southern black athlete for making a mistake on the football field. The southern black just sat there like a little boy with no spine. Then I heard a coach say almost the same thing to a player who was from the West Coast. The coach almost died. That West Coast player stood up like a man and said, "You don't have to talk to me like that. Respect me like I have respected you. I'm not going to let any man talk to me like that. I like this game, but I'm not going to sell my soul to play it, and be rolled over like a dead dog in the street." That coach changed his tune that day. He let the coach know, "I'm a man before anything." I've also heard northern black athletes threaten a coach's life for talking to them any old kind of way.

Some southern black athletes have tarnished the role of the black man in football. Once there was a coach who had been fired from a college team and hired by a professional team, the same team I was playing for. During the course of the season we had a lot of injuries and the front office had to bring in some players from that coach's old college team, the one that had fired him. These are the exact words this southern black athlete used, "Boss, I see they brought in some of your boys," and the coach smiled and said, "Yeah, I see that." This attitude needs to stop. It's killing the advancement of black athletes into management at a pro level. If this southern black athlete had only realized that thousands of blacks lost their lives to their bosses, he would never have used that word "Boss." I have even heard a player use the word "master" when asking his coach a question. I wanted to kill that bastard, but I had to realize that all his hope was in his coach and not in himself. His mind was gone. He was a product of generational mind damage and held the belief, "I can only attain what my master allows me to attain." I just felt sorry for him.

❧

My experience with the outbursts and mental discouragement from coaches has been funny at times, but more often downright degrading. As a young athlete, my only coaches were Mr. Burns and my father, and they were black. Anytime they would discipline my actions, I didn't find it degrading at all. At nine and ten years old, it felt right for one to correct his own.

As I got to college and the pro level, things changed rapidly. Not only was it clear to me but all the players acted in the American way. Any time a black coach tried to discipline or talk aggressively to a black player, it always seemed funny to everyone in the meeting rooms. Every time a black coach would yell in the meeting rooms, the players—black and white—just kind of looked and said, "What's he in an uproar for?"

Black coaches treat white players differently. They act like they're scared of them or something. Usually that black coach is from the South and is an ex-player himself. And he brings his attitude of fear to the table as he once portrayed it on the football field. There is also the black coach who tells everybody how he feels about them, but then he's considered a rebel and usually doesn't stay on the team. He is said to have been too extreme on players.

I believe that black players and white players feel the same way. White players say, "I don't want no nigger coach yelling at me, because I'm white." And black players say, "I don't want no Klansmen coach yelling at me because I'll hurt his ass."

The hypocrisy in all this is when a white coach yells at a black player or uses what I call "aggressive talk." He's in his rights as a man, because the American way says a white man can abuse a black man all he wants. Malcolm X put it best when he said:

"I don't feel that I am a visitor in Ghana or in any part of Africa. I feel that I am at home. I've been away for four hundred years, but not of my own volition, not of my own will. Our people didn't go to America on the Queen Mary, we didn't go by Pan American, and we didn't go to America on the Mayflower. We went in slave ships. We went in chains. We weren't immigrants to America, we were cargo for purposes of a system that was bent upon making a profit. So this is the category or level of which I speak. I may not speak it in the language many of you would use, but I think you will understand the meaning of my terms." (Malcolm X, University of Ghana, May 13, 1964)

When a white coach is all in an uproar about a white player's mistakes, the coach always comes across passive, as if he were talking to his own son, saying, "I expect more from you, Johnny." But when he's addressing a black player, he threatens his ass and everyone gets quiet. You hear no laughter. All you can do is listen and, when the meeting is over, go into the locker room and talk within your circle, saying, "If he talks to me like that again, I'll tell him." But the coach does it again and again, until you become a spineless man. You have no words to defend yourself because you're afraid of losing your job.

My first years in the pros my coach was Al Roberts and he yelled and screamed every day and sometimes at me, but I felt it was okay because he was black and his anger only came from being frustrated about the little control he had. He took his anger out on the players and all we did was laugh when he would get into an uproar. Al Roberts is a good man with a big heart. He knew his history and his struggle is bigger than coaching. They fired Al the following year and I didn't have another black coach until I got to Minnesota. His name was Coach Solomon. He was a screamer and a yeller and he loved to threaten you. He was short and stuttered sometimes. He worked us hard and when we won, he was a different person. I never minded him yelling at me and threatening me. He was black like me and, when you're black, you're struggling to prove yourself. Consequently his struggle was my struggle.

If you're a black coach, your coaching schemes must be flawless. Your playbooks must have a solution that makes a winning unit outside what the white coaches are doing. The white coaches' playbooks are within the black players. They don't coach you; they tell you to be in a certain area and let your body and your athleticism take you from there. That's highway robbery. Black coaches are the technicians of modern-day football. In this racist system they have to be. Best of all, most black coaches are ex NFL players. They don't just bring knowledge and know-how, they bring wisdom about the doing of it all.

There have been a few times when I had to defend my manhood in front of coaches. After a game we had lost, we were reviewing the game film from the previous night and I had made a couple of mistakes, not big ones, though. As the film was rolling closer to one of the plays that I had made a mistake on, my heart began to beat faster. The coach was talking to players like they were little boys, but all I saw in the room were men. When he got to my play on the film, the coach started yelling, "Don't back your fuckin' ass up, damn it." I said, "Look here you son of a bitch. I got three kids. I don't talk to my kids like that, and I'll damn if I let a man talk to me like that." And then a player in the corner tapped me on the shoulder. I looked over, and he was pushing his hands down, as if to say, "Calm down, calm down." I looked at him, and said, "I ain't no house nigga. I cut his fuckin' head off." Just as Malcolm X recognized that a "house slave" mentality was holding back the Black Power movement in the 1960s, I thought to myself, "We today have a lot of house niggas walking around locker rooms in pro football." Then the head coach said, "That's enough." So we finished watching the film, and after the coach and I shook hands and it was over. We both knew our place. The following week we won, and the next year we won the championship.

Another time my team couldn't find that winning edge and we were struggling. So after we lost a game, the coach said,

"Look here guys, if we don't win next week, the front office says they're going to start cutting people, and they don't get rid of the coaches, they get rid of you players first." He pointed at all of us, and my heart started beating. I said, "Look here, tell them to cut me now. I don't give a shit what they do or how they do it. My father has never threatened me and I'm not going to let anybody threaten me. I don't even threaten my own kids. So you go tell them bastards that." I was upset that we were losing, but threats I could do without. The following week we lost, and all the players kept their job, even our coach. But they fired the head coach.

There was another situation when we had lost a game and during the meeting a coach was talking aggressively to a black player and told him, "Sit your ass down, Aunt Jemima." My heart started beating fast. I looked around and some players were looking at me. Their silence made me speak. I said to the player, "You gonna let him talk to you like that?" The coach looked at me and said, "Did that offend you?" I said, "We don't need that shit in here. That's racist." The coach said, "I've been called worse than that." I said, "If that comment was directed towards me, I'll get up and beat your ass right here." Afterwards, the coach and I apologized. He was a new coach who came during the season and he didn't know about the sheep he was addressing. I believe teams need to have people who question how each player wants to be addressed and treated in all situations. That way you will know who you're working with.

I once had an interesting conversation with a white player. He said that he just wanted to pick my brain and ask questions about blackness in football. He asked a question I'll never forget. He said, "A.P., I've always wondered, and maybe I'm wrong, but all the black athletes seem to be uptight and angry." I laughed and said, "You just now figuring that out? Every black man in America is angry, even in Canada. There's racism. It's worldwide. You can't change it, you just accept it, and move on.

Picture this. You find yourself in the busiest intersection in the world. Statistics show that this particular intersection has the highest pedestrian death toll, with hundreds of pedestrians killed each year because people speed through the yellow caution light and run red lights as well. Because you are very aware of these statistics, when you get to the intersection to cross the street, you push the button to wait to see if it's safe to cross, and listen for traffic noise if you're blind. When the light says it's safe to cross you still look to the left and to the right because you don't trust the traffic signal or the drivers and you're scared of getting killed. Finally you get to the other side and breathe a sigh of relief, turn around and do it again.

That's what it's like every day being a black man in this world. The only way it can change is to use our power. In the 1960s our power was in the people and we had pioneers leading the way. They were not rich; they were two ordinary men who spoke out loud for change: Martin Luther King Jr. and Malcolm X. They were never associated with violence. They never started a riot. You never saw them beating white people. You never heard of them lynching white people or bombing churches with little children inside or assassinating white leaders who spoke against segregation. And what about the unspoken violence against blacks that got swept under the rug? For all of this violence black people suffered, all we got was a chance to eat with you and use the public bathroom with you. All we got was a bill that we're still paying for.

Black Power is now within the sports arena. It's going to take a worldwide ban for us black athletes to make change. To pose a real threat to white America, we black people need to become the CEOs of the world. There is power in decision-making; no power in decisions being made for you. Look, seventy-five to eight percent of all NFL players are black but there are hardly any black coaches to come close to that percentage. There are no black owners either. Nothing has really been changed. The same thing that's been eating away at us is still doing his job but I tell you this there is a sleeping giant ready to awake and make a change and it's going to happen through athletes. That's where the money is and the black athlete is a powerful commodity. Once he recognizes his power, and two and three begin to talk, it will start to multiply. Once it starts to multiply, it will roar and when it roars it will take action and that action will lead to change.

When you start to really open your eyes, you see that the scenes of our world have changed. Time can do that. But if you look hard enough, you'll see that the situation for blacks in America is still the same. I see it today. The slave ships have turned into commercial airliners and the cotton fields have been transformed into football fields. The chains have been turned into contracts and those good old picnics, we now watch them on TV, live from our house. In the modern-day world of political correctness, Draft Day in the NFL is a modern-day picnic.

Folklore tells us that the picnic originated in slavery when the slaves would arrive fresh off the boat tired, chained, and bound. The plantation owner, the master would tell his black Aunt Jemima to fix a basket of food for him and his family, and they would sit and amuse themselves and watch these slaves, these warriors, these mighty men, walk across the podium like an animal, a commodity, a product on a shelf, ready to be sold and traded, at any cost. When the master was ready to pick his slave, he would raise his hand, with authority, and say, "I pick that nigger right there." And there it is —"picnic".." That's why most blacks, if they're educated, always say, "I'm having a barbeque." Those who are ignorant say, "Let's have a picnic." The *Oxford English Dictionary* suggests that the word "picnic" is of French origin but blacks find racial overtones in the word.

Draft day in the NFL is like a modern-day picnic. In today's world of high fashion, big cameras, and media hype, draft day has turned into a day of celebrating the new big buck on the plantation, where you get a close up look at the nigga who they say will be a star some day. The only stars I've ever seen were in the sky and they shine forever. Athletes only shine for a game or two.

To show ownership, slaves used to be branded; that doesn't happen anymore. Instead, players just wear T-shirts saying property of this team or that team, letting the whole world know who they belong to, who owns them. I myself don't wear T-shirts saying property of".. I'm a product of my parents. I own myself and set my own standards on the field and off.

I learned to write the way I feel and not just talk about it in small groups, but to write something the whole world needs to read about. The beautiful thing about today's world is that we as human beings have the ability to choose what we want to do and become. The slaves never had that option; they were brought to a foreign land of no choice of their own. Their destiny was predetermined by their master. Football didn't choose me. I decided to play the game and we have to realize when you make a choice in life you take the bitter with the sweet.

It would be false to say that being a black athlete is degrading. It does have its advantages. Women flock like vultures and, for some players, those multimillion-dollar contracts do have their advantages. If you take a closer look, and really focus on the black athlete, you will see that many think they are above racism because they are able to move from the middle class to the upper class, with big houses and big cars, moving into white neighborhoods. With pride in their voices, they say, "I'm the only black in my neighborhood." I really never understood why we black athletes feel we need to let everybody know how many of us live around us. I believe it's just a way of letting the other black athletes know we feel accepted by mainstream society. But in the eyes of our peers, we're just house niggas, trying to get accepted by the boss. Understand, no matter where you live, you'll be a nigga in the ghetto, even in the White House. You and I will never see racism on all levels disappear. White folks don't like us and it's going to take generations ten times over to change that. Until then, fasten your seatbelts and enjoy what peace you can, for peace is just a mindset and freedom in this life is only a dream for the black athlete. Freedom will only be discovered in death, not in this sunlight.

As the football season comes to an end in Canada, the place I call my new home, a place of beauty, where the air is clear and the view of God's landscape will take your breath away, I find myself on a journey of self discovery. The things I once laid to rest have awoken in my soul. I find myself needing to write these words. I have spoken these things throughout my career, but many players, past and present, are too afraid to say what they really want to say. It's easy to talk in small groups and find yourself at the center of attention, but when one person puts himself on the line for what he believes is true and what he feels, then what he needs to say must be told. If he remains silent, in the end, he will only destroy himself. The message that people need to hear will never be told. All in all, we fail as a whole.

&

Where is this taking me? Slow your mind and hear your heart beat. Take a breath and feel the life that is within you. That is the greatest gift of all.

In the summer of 1998 I was visiting my oldest son, Jordan, in Cheney, Washington. We decided to take a drive down to the local park, which holds a man-made lake. For a while we sat there, playing the game "I Spy." I told him I spy three hats. He looked and sitting in a boat in the middle of a lake were three old men fishing. We sat there for a few minutes and watched them. When the first fisherman caught a fish, the second fisherman would put his pole down, grab the net, and catch the fish as it got closer to the boat as the first fisherman reeled it in. The third fisherman would then put his pole down, reach into the box of worms, and re-hook the first fisherman's pole as the first fisherman put his fish in the bag. That fish was going to fill his tummy, feed his family, and please his soul. They continued to fish for hours, and before you knew it, they had so many fish that they could eat for weeks.

Those fishermen were like the people, companies, and even churches that use the black athlete to help build their wealth. These organizations use black athletes to benefit their own selfish desires. We black athletes need to recognize these thieves who are making money off us and giving us nothing, a free T-shirt, half off a meal, really they're giving us the tip off an iceberg.

We're just like worms for these fishermen, bait to catch their fish. Like worms, we bring in fish, which bring people to the table to eat. Those people sitting around the table benefit from the fish. If it weren't for the worm, they wouldn't be there.

Where does all this come from? If you look closely at people, then you can see them for who they really are. Ask yourself, black man, this question is for all the athletes out there, "If you were just an average black man on the street, and nobody knew that you were a football player, do you think all these beautiful women would give you all that attention and let you get away with all the things you do and don't do for her. Would she really have patience like she claims to have had? Or the big company that wants to promote their product. You're the hottest athlete right now. Let's get this worm to help bring the fish, to buy our product, drink our drinks, eat our food. This worm is good. He's making my money grow. He's bringing it in and, in the meantime, you get a tip, like an unattractive waitress.

This attitude has even crossed over to the religious world. You even have ministers and pastors trying to use athletes to help build their churches. They want the athletes to fill their churches the way they fill stadiums across America. We black athletes need to take a stand right now and let some of us black athletes start picking up some worms and doing some fishing to benefit ourselves. Many people and institutions are making millions of dollars because they put a black face on their products, in their magazines, and on TV screens for the world to view.

This world is run by supply and demand. All the great athletes we watch on the big screen do incredible hits, catches, and all the things that make your eyes bigger and make you say "wow," they're great. But there are not enough jobs out there for everybody. There is a huge supply of black athletes and demand is low. For every Jerry Rice there are 100 more around the corner. That's why when a lot of black athletes are put in the spotlight, they know it's for just a period of time, until we get slower, weaker, and our performance disappears. Football can't be played forever. It's just for a season or two. If you're lucky and have favor, you'll go beyond what's normal. And this is where the attitude is born, "Let me get what I can." With that attitude many black athletes are still selling their soul running in fear and walking in the dark, not knowing who they really are. They continue to let everybody dictate their life for them, how to eat, how to train, where to be, where to go, and even how to pray.

❧

There are many faces to the black athlete and where this is most revealed is in the locker room. Through my observation and experience in all the locker rooms I've been in, without exception, the locker room is a place of extreme pressure. Locker rooms are all the same; the only difference is the location. Across the country, locker room behavior during training camp follows four distinct patterns.

The first pattern of behavior is shown by athletes who try to find God in a desperate attempt to make the team; they carry the Bible around like it's their playbook and they become self-righteous. God becomes their lucky rabbit's foot and they walk around saying, "If God wants me here, I'll be here." My opinion has been, "God put you here, now it's up to you if you can stay here. God's not going to make you run or make you tackle. That's your job." I write this because I found myself in a place like that holding onto God, waiting for a miracle. But deep down I wasn't sure of my fate in the hands of coaches.

The second pattern of behavior is shown by all the players who have graduated from college and have their degrees. During training camp in the locker rooms, they continually say, "I got my degree to fall back on if I don't make the team." They are also unsure of themselves. They think that having a degree makes them more valuable to society? They hold their degrees as if they are more uppity than the next black athlete. Their degree makes them feel special. But a degree has no value on the football field. Value on the football field comes from performance and beating the man in front of you. One player once said to me, "Do you have your degree?"

"No, I have a semester left," I told him.

"I got mine," he said, "and that's one thing that white man can't take away from me."

I looked at him and said, "That's great. You have your degree to fall back on. You say that if they let you go on cut day that you'll fall back on your degree. Well, that's what's going to happen, you're literally going to fall back." I asked him, "You walk around screaming you have a degree, where is your faith: in your athleticism or in your degree?" He couldn't answer, because he was straddling the fence between his athleticism and his schooling. But society is going to look at him as a black man whether or not he has a degree. The system has been set. The clock has been ticking a long time and nothing has really changed but the weather.

The third pattern of behavior in the locker room during training camp is the weakest and is shown by the players who have massive million dollar contracts. They feel above the law. They walk around like kings with no crown. Players respect them because of their money, houses, and cars. They pump their egos any chance they get and young players think, "When I get that big contract, I'm going to be the man." Who is the man? I never met him. If somebody knows him, let me know. The only true man I ever known, his name is John Frank Prior and he's my dad. That's a man's man. I'm not saying big contracts, big houses, and fancy cars are a bad thing. If you have those things, then good for you, considering the worth of slaves in the past. But when they have you, that's a problem. Many black athletes are not keeping it real. If the ones with all the big millions really had clout I would not be writing this chapter; instead these players stack their chips and talk in small corners in the locker rooms. Everybody's talking loud but nothing's being heard. Too many of us are scared to say certain things and address certain issues because we're afraid of losing what we have in front of us. Open you eyes and realize what's in front of you now will be gong tomorrow. The only thing that will last is when a man takes a stand for a cause.

The fourth pattern of behavior in the locker room is the most powerful. These black athletes bring one thing to the table. Their faith is within themselves. You can see when they walk in the locker room. They bring a certain presence around them. There stature is always upright. If you didn't know him personally, you would think he was serious all the time. I've called it confidence, walking with dignity, and carrying character. You never see him telling jokes and carrying on about things that have no value, like some players in the locker room. When he talks he says things that will help you later in life. He always asks, "How's your personal life going?" A lot of us want to be this man, but the mainstream and big lights have a hold around our necks and too many of us can't break those chains. Only time and adversity can bring you to a place like this. Finally I find myself at level four. That's why I'm writing this story. I have never put my faith in coaches or players. Throughout my football career my faith has been on forty yards. Speed has carried me this far. Many players fit this category. They believe in their inner strength. My inner strength has been speed. For some, their weightlifting strength, athleticism, knowledge, and ability to relate to people have helped them make pro football teams across the country and abroad.

Another pattern of behavior in the locker room is shown by the player who acts like the centerpiece. He's the black athlete who sits in the center of locker room, not literally but figuratively. This black athlete continues to tarnish the image of the black man. He comes into the locker room, bragging of all the women he's slept with, making sure everybody hears him. He's ignorant and has no concept or self-respect. He's the first to tell a joke and try to make everybody laugh, thinking his foolishness off the field will win him some friends. All it does is give people something to laugh about. I call them "Locker room comedians." Side shows are what they really are.

The locker room takes a drastic change once training camp is over. The religious guy who was getting close to God during training camp—now that he has made the team you see a difference immediately. His Bible is put up on the mantelpiece until he finds himself injured or discouraged; then he finds God again. All he does is make deals with God all year long. When things are going well, God is nowhere to be found. But I guarantee you'll find that player everywhere but church when the storm is still. As soon as the storm begins to rise, the Bible is back and God is present for him once again.

The college graduate forgets his degree and says, "I knew I was going to make it. That degree really can't do nothing anyways but show that I'm a nigga who can follow directions. That's about it." He laughs as he mocks himself, but deep down he wasn't planning to fall back on his degree. He just felt the need to let every other black athlete out there know, "I have options, not like some of you stupid niggas out here slaving for this white man." Actually, a person's words can only go so far. His actions speak volumes. "If your degree means that much to you, then why even put yourself through this brutal sport? Why come to training camp?" I want to ask. We all come to training camp to get paid big money, hands down. The problem sometimes is those players with degrees think they have a notch above those who don't.

Nothing really changes for the weakest link. He remains the same mentally. Money has put him in the back seat of mental growth. He feels there's nothing to prove. He only has to buy the latest fashion, the newest car, a bigger house, and continue to stroke his ego. When the team travels on away games, he'll buy an expensive suit to the approval of his peers, asking the question, "Do I look good? Are the shoes flossin' or what?" Constant attention is his motive. He is always looking for the next person to accept him. I believe people will accept you first when you accept yourself and be true to who you really are.

As the season starts, the fourth kind of black athlete becomes more powerful in his own time, not only is he admired, he's respected by his peers and coaches. His consistency goes beyond the football field, off the field he continues to challenge his mind. He's in tune with human history and knows where his strength is. He not only becomes a role model to younger players, he becomes more of a man.

After training camp, the centerpiece usually loses some friends, the ones he influenced during training camp. There can be only one centerpiece and he wears many hats. He's a comedian, a storyteller, but never a person you respect, mainly because he doesn't respect himself.

The most significant aspect of being a black athlete is knowing the history of the black man first, not just listening to others tell you about history. If you look at the word "history,", it's "a person's story, his story." I don't have time to read one person's story. To understand anything, let alone your past, you have to research and read about the great pioneers who broke down barriers and took on nations, not only to benefit themselves but generations to come. As a black athlete, we look at some of the benefits we now have, but they all have come at a costly price: Blood shed, murder, lynching, all in the name of equality. Nobody wants to discuss where we came from and the past we still struggle with, but people look at black athletes like they looked at the slaves when we first came to America—as a commodity, a product, a money-making machine—on the field and off. The problem I have is off the field, when everybody is only after money and their own agenda because, think about it, if you were just an average black man walking the streets of America, people wouldn't give you any attention let alone a second look. For example, when your father or brother go into a public place and are treated less than human, you become enraged, but when you go into the same public place, they smile in your face and tell others around you, "Look who's here! Come take a picture. Can I have an autograph?" Fifteen minutes ago, they made my loved ones feel undeserving.

Athletes can't be in every public place to raise eyebrows and get cheap smiles. However, my people are everywhere. They deserve self-respect first. When they are in the presence of an athlete, people feel more accepting and befriend you, let their white daughters marry you, invite you to dinner. In their eyes, you're just a sideshow. The black athlete has made some strides and must applaud himself, because nobody else will. Learn your history, my brothers, and know the chains have been broken and freedom can be obtained only through death. Walk a little taller, knowing the system has been set. Know in your mind that you control your own destiny, and God is watching you.

❧

Being a black athlete is a marvelous thing. It happens only for a short period of time in your life, when for a moment the people across the country will love you for it. During that time, you find yourself indulging in things you never thought possible: women, money, and—the most dangerous—self-pride. When the lights turn off and the crowd no longer cheers your name, we often wish we would have done things differently. We wish when the lights went off we had a flashlight to find the door.

As black athletes, we find ourselves in a room for a while, where the walls are colorful and we feel good. All of a sudden the light goes out. We find ourselves running scared, looking for the door to open, looking for a little light to help us find our way. Being a black athlete, you're not in control of your career; it's in the hands of the people making decisions, not yours. That's why a lot of athletes, the majority of southern black athletes, are driven more by fear than anything. In my opinion, in order to gain control, we first must win the battle in the meeting rooms. Your heart starts racing when a coach says something that degrades your manhood, but the fear of losing your job is greater than your self respect, so you sit there in silence and when the meeting is over with, you sit in a small group, telling tales that will never be heard. Free yourselves, speak out when your manhood is tested. Respect people and at the same time demand respect. When the battle is won in the meeting rooms, we will become leaders and we will find ourselves battling management. That's when we declare to our team, "You're the general and you need some soldiers to fight this cause we call racism."

I've spoken to many athletes, ministers, and everyday people about being black. I have even talked to coaches about it. Of all the people I have encountered on the subject of blacks and whites in sport, none can compare with the conversation I had with a white man in Canada the fall of 2000.

The city was on fire, the team was in first place, and we were hosting the championship game in our stadium, in the city of Calgary. You would think that all the hype of football during the season would be a time of celebrating wins and correcting defeats, but I found myself thinking about making a change in the system. I looked around the locker room and I didn't like what I saw. I looked at the coaching staff and I didn't see one of my own. I saw all the black players laughing and calling each other "nigga." I saw injured players looking terrified because their fate wasn't in their own hands. I saw confusion among players. They were thinking, "What am I doing?" and "Who am I?" I saw white players huddled in their corners and blacks in theirs. I began to see how different we are, how we look different, talk different, and walk different. The only thing in common is that we come together on the field and play a game; then we go our separate ways because we are not the same, our history is different, and that's the key to unlocking the mystery.

I was running the stadium steps as many players do about once a week during the regular football season in order to maintain strength and endurance. It was cloudy day but far away you could see the sun. I was all bundled up in a gray sweat suit with a beanie on my head. Someone else was running the stadium as well, running up and down, up and down. I kept glancing at him and he kept looking at me. I believe he was waiting to see if I would tire before him. We both had started at opposite ends of the south side of the stadium. As we got to the middle, before crossing paths, we stopped at the top of the stadium and kind of walked around for a moment to catch our breath. He was waiting for me to sit down, and I was waiting for him. We smiled for a second. I said, "How are you?"

"Tired," he answered and he sat down. I sat next to him

and said, "Yeah, I'm tired, too." I folded my hands behind my head. He crossed his arms and leaned back in the stadium seat. Then he leaned forward and said, "A.P., you're always thinking like me."

I said, "I bet you my thoughts are not like yours. Your thoughts could not reach the depth nor the height of my thoughts, which I have been thinking for years and which have been so real and true."

Then he asked, "Well, what have you been thinking? Tell me about them," he laughed. "Enlighten me, A.P." So I began to share with him my thoughts of this life I'm living and reliving.

Before you can enlighten another person, you better first know your history and the history of your people. That way you will know who you are by reading and researching, not just listening to other people and who they say you are, or should be. That goes for white people and black people. We all have the racism of our ancestors in us. I don't care who you are, or where you came from, or what nationality you claim to be. There is racism in all of us and it's real prevalent in sports. All you have to do is watch black and white players interact, and hear their views on certain things in the locker room and outside of it as well. When you see a white coach yell at a black player, other black players don't like that, except the occasional Uncle Tom walking around the locker room. And on the flip side, white players don't like it when a black coach yells at him. He feels the coach should submit to him. It's not in his right. That's what history tells us, if it weren't true, why were thousands of blacks lynched because they gave a white man a dirty look or spoke his mind? Between 1882 and 1938, the recorded lynching of black men in the United States totaled 3,397, according to Bradford Chambers' *Chronicles of Black Protest* (New American Library, 1968, p. 128, caption 20). And there has never been a single conviction. Ain't that a bitch? Even truth brought him to his death, hanging from a tree. It's sad but that's history. It happened and it's true.

There aren't too many black coaches, so it doesn't happen too often, and when it does that coach is usually shipped off and labeled overly aggressive, a nigga that doesn't know his place. Oh, yeah, racism is going on in modern-day football. The same attitudes that were held in the 18th, 19th, and 20th centuries today still control the football field in the same way they controlled the cotton fields.

Oh, yeah, there's a big division between players black and white, even when it comes to women and children. The general public knows what I'm talking about. I speak for myself, but I know I'm speaking for millions who are too scared to lose a part of what they have. I'm going to let it all roll. White men hate it when they see a black man with a white woman. That shit is still not accepted. Have you ever been in a public place and seen a white woman with a black man? It doesn't even look right. All you see is people saying to themselves, "Look at this shit and then they look at their kids and say, 'Look at those mixed kids, all mixed up.' They don't know if they're black or white. They just say multi racial, but anytime you have black blood in your body, you're considered a nigga." Yeah, that's the truth. Can I keep it real?

The same is true when we see a black woman with a white man. If the black woman is beautiful, the first thing that comes out of our mouth is, "Look at that sell-out bitch." But if she's ugly, we just say, "Don't nobody want you anyway."

People think the Civil Rights Movement cured that but it didn't. Well, listen here. The Civil Rights Movement was a great thing for black people. The Constitution was written by white people for white people, but the Civil Rights bill was written by black people for black people. Now everybody and their grandma from other lands are riding our backs like a freight train. Foreigners and other groups of origin need to get their own movement established for their own people. The Civil Rights Movement was for blacks. Nowadays it's a thing of the past.

I once overheard some teammates talking about segregation and what a wonderful thing it was. I asked, "Can I get into this discussion?" "Sure, this is locker room talk and it's real," they replied. They went on to say that segregation has two aspects. In one opinion, black people were weaker as a whole in the 1960s. We were coming together and we should have just stayed together. But the other opinion suggests that I'm supposed to jump for joy because now I can sit at a restaurant and use the same bathroom. If integration is so great, why is the ghetto getting bigger, why are jails going up like new housing tracts, and why don't the school systems teach us about our own history, our great pioneers? The only black person they praise in schools is Martin Luther King. We have so many pioneers, but you have to go to the library to find out about it or go to a black college to learn your roots.

All the black men at white colleges are either tokens or athletes who will bring millions of dollars to the university. They're promised big NFL contracts, taking his mind and using his body for economic growth. Black athletes who go to white colleges all say, "A black college can't do nothing for me." Well, listen here, a white college can't either, you Uncle Tom. A black college will let you know who you are and there's power in that. A white college will let you know who you are not, and you will have to keep refueling yourself in that isolation. When you're around your own, you're at your best, whether you're black or white.

Can you imagine if segregation never happened? In my opinion, our ghettos would be smaller. Our educational system would be stronger. There would be a sense of pride of history and the understanding of it, because so many of us are walking blindfolded, believing anything anybody says about us.

If sports were segregated today I believe the stakes would be high. Can you imagine white versus black? All over the world ethnic groups competing against other ethnic groups, for money, prestige, and respect.

Your respect has always been achieved on the battlefields, when was the last time you saw one hundred thousand people attending a biology test? Never. People would come from all over the world and the violence would be praise. People would be proud of their warriors and during the battle people would live out their hatred through their warriors.

It's going on today, anytime you have two boxers in the ring. If one is black and the other is white, whenever that white man strikes that black man, the crowd jumps up out of their seats and you can feel the roar of the crowd. You know what they're saying? "Kill that nigga, hurt him. Hurt him bad." And we black folks are just the same. Whenever a brotha knocks out a white man, we think of going into work the next day and looking at our boss and saying, "Did you watch the fight?" We pride ourselves in that, because history tells, too.

My father tells me of time, way back in history, sitting around an old radio, with black folks going crazy, listening to Joe Louis fight. When he won, it was a celebration for the people, and when he lost, it was felt deep. Every victory was like a step forward and every loss a step backwards in the fight for equality.

If sports were segregated it would last for a few years and billions of dollars would be made. But white athletes would realize that they couldn't compete. Eventually they wouldn't show up and billions of dollars would be lost. Sports would be a thing of the past until something changed. This change I'm talking about is being discussed in every locker room across North America, on every level, from high schools to colleges to the pros. The black man in America wants to see changes in his ghettos, his schools, and his workplace. He wants power to dictate his fate and the fate of his people.

We came here on a boat as cargo to make a country rich. Our blood is still in the soil of America. Our ancestors' spirits are still with us. There have been many athletes thinking the same way I have, but they're too scared to express their real self. Hiding like thieves in the night, robbing their people of social change, their children, their grandchildren. Alex Haley's last few paragraphs of *Autobiography of Malcolm X* reflect this idea. I quote his words:

> "But there is much controversy still about this most controversial American, and I am content to wait for history to make the final decision. But in personal

judgment, there is no appeal from instinct. I knew the man personally, and however much I disagreed with him, I never doubted that Malcolm X, even when he was wrong, was always that rarest thing in the world among us negroes; a true man.

"And if, to protect his relations with many good white folks who make it possible for me to earn a fairly good living in the entertainment industry, I was too chicken, too cautious, to admit that fact when he was alive. I thought at least that now, when all the white folks are safe from him at last, I could be honest with myself enough to lift my hat for one final salute to that brave, black, ironic gallantry, which was his style and hallmark, that shocking zing of fire-and-be-damned-to-you, so absolutely absent in every other negro man I know, which brought him, too soon, to his death."

Alex Haley at the height of his writing career and worldwide recognition with the novel and TV mini series, *Roots*, was still holding his true beliefs within. Haley, a Pulitzer Prize–winning author had his real opinions chained within because of fear. They would take something away from him, his pen, his creativity, but most of all I believe they had his true thoughts. Unlike Haley, Malcolm X heard the echoes of his people and told the whole truth and nothing but the truth and all black people loved him. They were just too afraid to admit it, because their way of life would have been altered and, usually, that meant it was taken away. We black folks love what we have. It's too bad that the things we love don't love us back.

The experience of Alex Haley and many other prominent black people went through during the 1960s is still powerful today. We are not keeping it real in a sense that whenever there is conflict between white and black, black people always say what white people want to hear. We fear we might lose something of value. The only value a black person has is his mind. When that goes, everything else goes, too. And today I see things going straight down the toilets because of fear.

One black player I know played on the same team as me and when we were both rejected by the same team, we sat in silence looking at each other and shaking our heads, saying "What's really going on with all this football stuff?" I saw a picture of a white woman hanging on his locker. I asked, "Is that your wife?"

"No, we've been going together for about four years," he said.

"Oh, I hear you," I said, "but I really don't know what's going on. Can I share my opinion with you, my brotha? I understand your situation. I bet when you first me her it was in college, huh?" He nodded and I went on, telling him how it goes:

Y'all started hangin' out kickit, and then y'all started having sex, and the bond grew closer, with that closeness brought emotion and with emotion I bet she started expressing her feelings for you. You were okay with that because you felt time would make sense of this all. But spending time with her you began to feel obligated to her. I bet she shared her feelings with her father, that she fell in love with a black man and her father never spanked his little girl, but when he heard of her feelings for a black man, he hit her, and let her know where he really stands and you then went against her father's will, still having sex with his little pure Lily, she buying you clothes and taking care of you while you promising her the world when you go pro.

You begin to get recognition on the football field, the media has you all pumped up. The paper prints you're the next million dollar black face. All of a sudden pure Lily's daddy wants to go to a college game. The following year you meet him and he smiles in your face and you smile back like an Uncle Tom because you don't want to disrespect pure Lily. She's taking care of your sorry ass, and her daddy is calling you a nigga behind your back and you know it, and don't even address the issue, you then grow stringer with Lily and the bond is tight, but physical bonds can only last so long.

Your senior year in college, you're over for dinner at the big house, talking about the pros. He's only interested, "Can I have some of those millions they're saying you're about to make? You better not hit my daughter, you black bastard. That's my job," he's thinking, as you eat some KFC chicken he picked up for you with a side of watermelon. You still remain silent of your feelings. You walk around confused and puzzled about your life and the situation you're in. Your pure Lily tells you the truth, because deep down she only feels sorry for you. She don't respect you.

History will teach you that, if you give it a chance. A white man once said to keep the truth from black people, put it in books. Those niggers don't read anyway. Tell them anything and they will believe it. The NFL draft didn't work out for you, the big million-dollar contract was just in print for a day, the media is interviewing somebody else and now you're a has-been. Pure Lily's dad has kicked her out of the house. Lily works at a grocery store. She has your baby living in the ghetto, with state assistance. Lily's dad don't claim the baby as his grandchild. Lily cries all day long, "How did I get myself into this situation?" She tells you she hates you, then she calls you a nigga and you finally see the realness of her. What is within our parents is strong within us. You can't deny that.

You see, my brotha, a lot of black ball players have that "Popeye syndrome" when it comes to white women. I can't say only white women. Let's just say women in general. Like Popeye there are many insecure pro ball players. But as soon as they get their money right, they have the need to save a woman like Olive Oyl. That spinach always was green like money and Brutus was a constant moral opponent. Yeah, and now Popeye has a tan, he's traded his pipe for a football helmet. Well, Olive Oyl, she still has her place on Popeye's locker. Even Sweet Pea is alive and kickin'. Brutus, he's always around too.

Think about it. As soon as Popeye beat down Brutus and got Olive back, the last thing he says to her, before the credits,

"Well, blow me down." Those words were reserved for Olive's ears. From there it became a sex thing, "Okay, Olive, you owe me now." And when the curtains fell, it became X-rated.

Popeye was insecure, like a lot of football players without their money (or spinach). They feel their opponents can't be conquered except with money. They believe they can destroy their opponents and win back their women all in the name of money.

❧

Now on the other hand, if you would have gotten that big million-dollar contract, you wouldn't be in this state of confusion. You would be very lost. The people who would surround you are only around the glitter and gold. There would be no conflict with you and her father, just a silent war because you're afraid to speak your true thoughts and he just continues to smile in your face, shake your hand, eat your food and Lily then asks, "Can you buy him a car with those big dollars you have?" You find yourself in church with Lily's family and you wonder why you're here. Your body is here but your mind is elsewhere. They introduce you as a football player. They don't just introduce you as a man. They have to put a phrase with it so others will accept you for your position, not your color. Everywhere you go you're introduced not as a human being but as a spectacle, a sideshow. This nigger is ours and even though we hate him, people seem to accept us with him because he's a professional football player. If you didn't have that title on your name, there would be a lot of closed doors. And until then you will never know people's true colors, true feelings, true beliefs, and most important, where they really stand. I'd rather know the true feelings of a person before meeting them and see the most dangerous people in the world are those who get along with everybody. They don't have enemies you know of and they're always gazing.

There are some things that just hold true, like the sun will always rise and death will come knocking on every door. How do we know this history tells us this: it's just recycling, like everything else. The modern-day white woman doesn't respect a black man. During slavery the white woman was considered the white man's price and she still is. On those big plantations where the bullwhip was used to instill fear in the black man, the white woman was present and we all know women are sympathetic; it's in their nature. As the beatings grew and lives were stolen, fear grew but sadness and compassion grew in the heart of white women for the brutality her white brother put on the black man and that spirit is prevalent today. White women feel sorry for black men. They feel the need to console him. That's why a black man will cry in front of a white woman before a black woman. It was birth hundreds of years ago. There is always roots to any scenario. How do you think problems get solved? You first go to the root of it. There are pictures of white women on black locker rooms all over the world and the cycle continues. Some stay in a state of confusion; some just choose to believe "Lilly's family loves me," but her ancestors would lynch you if they had the chance, just for looking at Lily. Her ancestors would take your last breath and remember our history is within us all strong. The problem is people act like black people don't have a history and some white people think, "Oh, just get over it. How can we when the same things are going as they were yesterday? What does all this have to do with football? It's history and all aspects of it we carry with in mind, body, and soul.

If you ask any Jewish person about Hitler, they would know who he is and what he tried to do—eliminate their existence. It's a sad part of world history and Hitler is in every school history book across the world. I hate that bastard. I would have cut his throat if I could have got close enough to him. If I'm going to kill somebody I'd do so quietly, blade to the neck and just walk away.

☙

I have asked teachers and professors, black and white, football coaches, players young and old, and very few have ever heard of Willie Lynch. I have asked black teammates about him throughout my career. Some have asked, "Was he an ex-player, a rapper, an athlete?" I just sit there in disbelief. I even laugh sometimes, because of the answers I receive. Willie Lynch was the man who took the identity away from every black person walking in America this present day. As Hitler lied to the Jews, Willie Lynch was the biggest liar who every lived. Some call him a hero. The Klu Klux Klan loves him. He's like a god to them. Where do you think the term "lynching" came from? Willie Lynch. He was referred to in a well-remembered speech given at the Million Man March in 1995. Since then there has been much dispute within the African American community about the authenticity of the text and the historical existence of the man named Willie Lynch. Some people believe he's an urban legend; others say his speech was written some time in the mid-20th century. Either way, the Willie Lynch speech hit a chord in the heart of black Americans. One posting to the Afro-American History website said, "It does not matter the source of this letter. The important thing is the matter that it talks about—the fact that this is still happening to our black people. This is very relevant to us and until we erase these inner lines that 'Mr. Lynch' has drawn and we have kept defined we will never unite" (http://www.afro.com/history/million/lynch/lynch.html#reacts October 24, 2002).

Lynch was a slave owner. Some say his speech is folklore and should be erased from the psyche of black Americans. Others have said that it's myth and has no creditable effect on the black struggle in America. And there are those who say it's rumor. But for every rumor whispered there has been some truth. The Willie Lynch speech explains why black folks haven't united in centuries. Our black history is constantly put under a microscope, as if we have no history, as if we just fell from the sky.

The game has won us.

Willie Lynch's Speech on
His Methods for Controlling Slaves

Gentlemen:

I greet you here on the bank of the James River in the year

of Our Lord one thousand seven hundred and twelve. First, I shall thank you The Gentlemen of the Colony of Virginia for bringing me here. I am here to help you solve some of your problems with slaves. Your invitation reached me on my modest plantation in the West Indies where I have experimented with some of the newest and still oldest methods for control of slaves. Ancient Rome would envy us if my program is implemented. As our boat sailed south on the James River, named for our illustrious King, whose version of the Bible we cherish, I saw enough to know that your problem is not unique. While Rome used cords of wood as crosses for standing human bodies along its old highways in great numbers, you are here using the tree and the rope on occasion.

I caught the whiff of a dead slave hanging from a tree a couple miles back. You are not only losing valuable stock by hanging, you are having uprisings, slaves are running away, your crops are sometimes left in the field too long for maximum profit, you suffer occasional fires, your animals are killed, gentlemen, you know what your problems are; I do not need to elaborate. I am not here to enumerate your problems, I am here to introduce you to a method of solving them.

In my bag here, I have a fool proof method for controlling Black Slaves. I guarantee everyone of you that if installed correctly, it will control the slaves for at least 300 years. My method is simple and members of your family and any Overseer can use it.

I have outlined a number of difference(s) among the slaves; and I take these differences and make them bigger. I use fear, distrust, and envy for control purposes. These methods have worked on my modest plantation in the West Indies and [they] will work throughout the South. Take this simple little list of differences, think about them. On top of my list is "Age" but it is there only because it begins with an "A." The second is "Color" or "Shade," there is intelligence, size, sex, size of plantation, status of plantation, attitude of owner, whether the slaves live in the valley , on a hill, East, West, North, or South, have a fine or coarse hair, or is tall or short. Now that you have a list of differences, I shall give you an outline of action but before that, I shall assure you that distrust is stronger than trust and envy is stronger than adulation, respect and admiration.

The Black Slave, after receiving this indoctrination, shall carry on and will become self-refueling and self-generation for hundreds of years, maybe thousands.

Don't forget you must pitch the old black versus the young black and the young black male against the old black male. You must use the dark skin slave versus the light skin slave and the light skin slaves versus the dark skin slaves. You must also have your white servants and overseers distrust all blacks, but it is necessary that your slaves trust and depend on us. They must love, respect and trust only us. Gentlemen, these Kits are keys to control, use them. Have your wives and children use them, never miss an opportunity. My plan is guaranteed and the good thing about this plan is that if used intensely for one year the slaves themselves will remain perpetually distrustful.

Keep the body, take the mind. In other words, break the will to resist. Now the breaking process is the same for both the horse and the slave, only slightly varying in degrees. But as we said before, there is an art in long range economic planning. You must keep your eye and thoughts on the female and the offspring of the horse and the slave.

Take the meanest and most restless slave, strip him of his clothes in front of the remaining male slaves, the female, and the slave infant, tar and feather him, tie him each leg to a different horse faced in opposite directions, set him a fire and beat both horses to pull him apart in front of the remaining slaves. The next step is to take a bullwhip and beat the remaining slave males to the point of death, in front of the female and the infant. Don't kill him, but put the fear of God in him, for he can be useful for future breeding.

Therefore, we shall go deeper into this area of the subject matter concerning what we have produced here in this breaking process of the female slave. We have reversed the relationship. In her natural uncivilized state she would have a strong dependency on the uncivilized slave male, and she would have a limited protective tendency towards her independent male offspring and would raise male offspring to be dependent like her. Nature has provided for this type of balance. We reversed nature by burning and pulling a civilized slave apart and bullwhipping the other to the point of death, all in her presence. By her being left alone, unprotected, with the male image destroyed, the ordeal caused her to move from her psychological dependent state to a frozen independent state. In this frozen psychological state of independence, she will raise her male and female offspring in reversed roles. For fear of the young male's life she will psychologically train him to be mentally weak and dependent, but physically strong. Because she has become psychologically independent, she will train her female offspring to be psychologically independent. What have you got? You've got the slave woman out front and the slave man behind and scared. This is a perfect situation of sound sleep and economic well being.

Thank you, gentlemen.

(Source: http://www.toptags.com/aama/ voices/speeches/willlynch.htm October 24, 2002)

Yeah, the smell of Willie Lynch is still alive. He still lives in the minds of millions in this day and age. The black athlete is still under slave-trading system whether he tries to deny it or not. But millions would agree with me, especially current players. They realize it but they are too afraid to speak what their minds want to really say, because their body is all they really have to give. If they give their mind as well, then their body will surely follow. But if the mind is trapped in a system that has been trapping the mind for more than 300 years and counting, things haven't changed. They have remained the same since the beginning of time. Read the Bible. It says that things happened thousands of years ago and they are still a reality in this new day of ours.

So why can't these words be true? Is it my kinky hair, my big lips, or my black skin that makes you think, "I need to get over it?" How can I get over oppression that has been around for 300 years and counting. The identity crisis is so real and has been for many years.

❧

Football players are made and athletes alike are bred to play on the field. It starts at a young age when your father is absent from your life. You don't know how to be a man, for you have never been around one to identify with so you then become a person whose identity has not yet been formed and mother tells you your father ain't shit. Ask her this: "If my father ain't shit, then mother you ain't shit either." So then the little boy gets involved in sports and his mother tells him to listen to your coach and believe him. Sports will provide a better life for you and you will not have to live like this. What momma should have said was, "Son, read a book, study. Become book smart, not street smart. Learn your history. Do something mentally before you do anything physically." The boy then finds sports a god in his eyes. He looks at pro players and learns how to identify himself. He chooses the negatives icons and walks around with a ball in his hands and the bling, bling in his mind.

Didn't the black colleges tell us a mind is a terrible thing to waste?. Well, black minds have been wasting away like we waste water. This black athlete's coach tells him he's great and he believes that. His attitude is formed and his mother lets him try and be a man, even though he's a young boy trying to be a man, trying to find an identity for himself. Refueling himself, only leads to self destruction. His father is absent and he's never tried to contact him and he learns weakness through the lack of manly influence. He's a dependent man who only knows how to look after himself. He's weak and people know that and take advantage of it, for he's motivated by fear and superstition and pro players like these are bred for good economics in modern-day football. They'll do anything and everything to please their master coaches, who are picking up and have been developing this method of breeding for many years. These black athletes are like horses, chained and bound still.

Today many NFL teams have you take psychological tests

to understand how you behave and to identify how you perceive yourself. The first questions usually are, "Are your parents still married? Who raised you? Who was your major influence? What was your father's entire name? Where did you grow up: in the ghetto, a middle class neighborhood, a rich neighborhood? Do you have brothers and sisters who share the same parents? Did your parents go to college? Did you graduate from college?

They ask questions like this for economic reasons: Does this black athlete pose a threat to our organization? Or will he just be a hard-working, obedient slave who knows his place? Will we have to lynch him? Will we have to cut him, even though we know he's better than the other players we have? The only problem is that his personality doesn't match up, so we'll have to cut him or just say we don't have the money in our salary cap.

A modern-day lynching is still going on. Why, when a player who is only human gets in trouble, does his coach makes him apologize to the team and the entire world? The only apology anybody needs to make is to God and his immediate family members. I don't see anybody apologizing to African Americans for slavery. I don't hear Willie Lynch apologizing. People are still applying the Willie Lynch theory because his methods are still working on us.

Careful breeding is still going in the NFL. They try and place players by height, weight, and even where they grew up. That's just economics. If it weren't true, why have a draft? Listen to the language during the draft. The announcers always say he would have gone higher in the draft if he was a little taller, heavier, faster. Oh, yeah, he got in trouble with the law. He's considered a disobedient player, a runner not good for long-term economic growth. We don't like to trade slaves, we would rather keep them until we have taken their body to the limit. So no other plantation will get a chance to benefit from his production. Well, maybe he will run to Canada and seek refuge and they laugh in your face when you try and come back to the atmosphere that still has your mind locked into a system you call and you fantasize about a comeback, but a comeback is just a fate you can't control.

The committee in the NFL controls your fate whether or not you're a great player. You're just not good economics. Too short, talks too much. His father is a strong influence in his life, so that makes for inconsistent behavior. Not controllable, can't show him disrespect in meetings, will try and change things will tell the coach what's really on his mind, may be part of a rebel group. There are people who still think like this and they are smiling in the black athlete's face. I know, I've experienced it hands on. The committee is a strong giant and the Klu Klux Klan, well, they call themselves the good ol' boys and this system will never die.

James Hasty, former Kansas City Chief cornerback, wrote about the good ol' boys system in the *Kansas City Star* in August 2001, after he had been cut from the team because of his high salary: "Loyalty can be a great thing in pro sports. It can unify a team and create good chemistry. But the kind of loyalty being practiced in Kansas City will contribute to many losses in the near future if something isn't done soon." Hasty went on to explain that the appointment of coaching staff to the Kansas City Chiefs was a prime example of the "good ol' boy" system still going strong. Chiefs' president and general manager, Carl Peterson, a former Vermeil assistant at UCLA and personnel director in Philadelphia, repaid the man who got him into football (Vermeil) by handing the Rams high draft picks for Vermeil's services and handing Vermeil a three-year, ten million-dollar contract. Vermeil's first move as head coach of the Chiefs was to reward his friend and former Rams assistant Al Saunders with the offensive coordinator's job in Kansas City. Vermeil and Saunders quickly agreed that they'd like to pursue a quarterback who would be familiar with and loyal to their high-flying offensive system. A first-round pick was shipped to St. Louis for the quarterback Vermeil pegged Trent Green for stardom with the Rams, Hasty claimed. He concluded by saying, "Do you notice a pattern here? Friends are hooking up friends."

Similarly, as Malcolm X said at Oxford University on December 3, 1964: "The reason that these men from that area have that type of power is because America has a seniority system. And those who have that seniority have been there longer than anyone else because the Black people in the areas where they live can't vote. And it is only because the Black man is deprived of his vote that puts these men in positions of power, that gives them such influence in the government beyond their actual intellectual or political ability, or even beyond the number of people form the areas that they represent." (Malcolm X, "Any Means Necessary to Bring about Freedom: The oppressed masses of the world cry out for action against the common oppressor." In *Malcolm X Talks to Young People: Speeches in the U.S., Britain, and Africa*, Steve Clark, ed. New York: Pathfinder, 1965, 1970, 1991, p. 28)

To eradicate the good ol' boy system, black players would need a new system for coaches. Coaches in my mind should be like presidential candidates and the players should be able to vote for who they want making the decisions. The players have no power. They're expendable, so they live in the abuse and suffer in the meantime until a losing season will bring about a change and the cycle just repeats itself over and over again. That's why we don't burn bridges. We would rather take the bullwhip and keep our tails in between our asses.

If you really want to put an end to this, boycott their system and demand changes. Form chapters around the athletic world. Pick a Sunday to demonstrate your seriousness and when the whistle is blown to leave the locker room to pick some cotton, stay inside until there's a change. We want to vote for our leader, our coach, our minister, our man in charge.

Have you ever seen black coaches doing this good ol' boy system? Isn't it ironic, for his people and his continent are producing big bucks for the football industry, for black people make up and create this industry.

W. E. B. Du Bois, the most important African American leader of the first half of the 20th century and the cofounder of the National Association for the Advancement of Colored People (NAACP) commented on this trade in men:

> "There was thus begun in modern days a new slavery and slave trade. It was different from that of the past, because more and more it came in time to be founded on racial caste, and this caste was made the foundation of a new industrial system. For four hundred years, from 1450 to 1850, European civilization carried on a systematic trade in human beings of such tremendous proportions that the physical, economic, and moral effects are still plainly to be remarked throughout the world. To this must be added the large slave trade of Mussulman lands, which began with the seventh century and raged almost unchecked until the end of the nineteenth century.
>
> These were not days of decadence, but a period that gave the world Shakespeare, Martin Luther, and Raphael, Haroun-al-Raschid and Abraham Lincoln. It was the day of the greatest expansion of two of the world's most pretentious religions and of the beginnings of the modern organization of industry. In the midst of this advance and uplift this slave trade and slavery spread more human misery, inculcated more disrespect for and neglect of humanity, a greater callousness to suffering, and more petty, cruel, human hatred than can well be calculated. We may excuse and palliate it, and write history so as to let men forget it; it remains the most inexcusable and despicable blot on more human history."
>
> (W. E. B. Du Bois, *The Negro*. New York: Humanity Books, 2002, pp. 152–3)

It's strange to me how people don't want to believe that slavery existed. I believe that the purest form of this modern-day is on the playing fields across this globe. The black man isn't and never will be in a position to make big decisions until he realizes that wealth is not measured by gold and silver.

As Malcolm X said at the University of Ghana on May 13, 1964:

> "I had to write a letter back home yesterday and tell some of my friends that if American Negroes want integration, they should come to Africa, because more white people over here—white Americans, that is—look like they are for integration than there is in the entire American country. [*Laughter*] But actually what it is, they want to integrate with the wealth that they know is here—the untapped natural resources which exceed the wealth of any continent on this earth today.
>
> "When I was coming from Lagos to Accra Sunday, I was riding on an airplane with a white man who represented some of the interests, you know, that are interested in Africa. And he admitted—at least it was his impression—that our people in Africa didn't know how to measure wealth, that they worship wealth in terms of gold and silver, not in terms of the natural resources that are in the earth, and that as long as the Americans or other imperialists or 20th-century colonists could continue to make the Africans measure wealth in terms of gold and silver, they never would have an opportunity to really measure the value of the wealth that is in the soil, and would continue to think that it is *they* who need the Western powers instead of thinking that it is the Western powers who need the people and the continent that is known as Africa. The thing is, I hope I don't mess up anybody's politics or anybody's plots or plans or schemes, but then I think that it can be well proved and backed up."

([Malcolm X, "I'm Not an American, I'm a Victim of Americanism." In *Malcolm X Talks to Young People:*

Speeches in the U.S., Britain, and Africa, Steve Clark, ed.
New York: Pathfinder, 1965, 1970, 1991, pp. 15–6)

As a black man first I see the racism in people's eyes when I walk down the street or take a stroll in the mall. I feel their eyes like vultures getting ready to eat a dead animal. But at thirty-two years old, I'm used to it. All the stories about being black in public places I've experienced, in big cities as well as small ones. I'm not writing to complain. I write to bring awareness and solutions. It's easy to complain, but history is real and our present-day history hasn't changed too much for the black man in America or any place on mother earth.

Anytime a black athlete signs a major contract, it's known all over the world and we black folks have pride in that and some envy black athletes. In the game of life, you have winners and losers. I feel the black athlete has been losing for a long time. Why when you look around the country you see many great black athletes on the field playing but on the sidelines there are only a few black head coaches? Look at the college level, where all those souls are being misled away from the pot of gold at the end of the tunnel. Look at the pro level, all those mighty African warriors who have taken football to a million, I mean, billion dollar industry, not with their minds, but with their bodies. They have been a vessel to victory on the field. It's their bodies that have changed the way we play football.

Africa is the richest continent in the world in natural resources. They even have parts of Africa that haven't been tapped yet and that would be a whole new discovery within itself. People were brought from the richest continent to be enslaved and used for profit. In the marketplace, slaves were trendsetters, just as black people are today. We are Africa. We are rich within our souls, for our continent is the richest. That makes us rich as well. America has put Africans on every playing field across the country. Our blood is in the soil.

As black athletes we have been muttering for years and years. I hear the echoes of my brothers. It's time for a change, a real one this time. It's time to make a statement, to change the course of history again. This time we must create a change that will benefit future athletes, such as our kids and grandkids. To level the playing field, if black athletes realize that their most precious natural resource is their body, then not having control of it is slavery in a whole new way.

Just look around. No black man owns a pro football team in the NFL or in all of big-time sport. But it's the black athlete who sets the standard and breaks records. Black athletes feel that one of our own should be in a position to seal our fate. Our fate in America has been in the white man's hands for more than five hundred years.

If the world wants to breed us for sports, ask the owners of these big sports teams to give some of their millions of surplus into our school system and education programs. We don't need another basketball court or sports arena. We need millions poured into our schools and ghettos. That way the prison system will get smaller through education, not through new playing fields. For a change, put more black coaches in head coaching positions and more assistant coaching positions as well. People tend to respond better with their own kind. Who wants to listen to a coach who has never even played at a pro level? That's the conflict going on in pro football. That's the meat.

Why is it that in locker room conversation across this country, players are talking about an uncle, or a cousin, or a friend they know who could outplay all of us? Well, we need to level the playing field so it's fair. I'm not crying because steroids have taken glory away from the honest athlete. The good ol' boy system is the steroid that needs to be stopped. I have told tons of players and ex players about this book and they all agree that something needs to be done before a revolution rises from locker rooms across this country, pitting players against coaches and coaches against players. People hold the power and power has been given to the black athlete. He knows this, he's been calculating. A sleeping giant lies within every black athlete. He is ready for change. He is ready, not for a small change but a big one, a change in the course of history not only for himself, but for his kids and those who will come after him.

The fireworks go off. The crowd is electrified. Billions of people around the world are watching, for people of every language can understand the meaning of the Super Bowl. It's time for family and friends to get together, even though they don't like each other. But it's the Super Bowl and billions of dollars are about to be made. There's a black man singing the national anthem, and he sings it so well it brings tears to your eyes. And the people of America are proud to be American.

The players come to the center of the field for the coin toss. The team that is favored to win succeeds at the coin toss and the crowd is electrified once again. The players shake hands and walk back to the sidelines. They bow their heads and pause for a moment, then they begin to look around. They players' hearts are beating out of control as they look at their brothers. Their eyes speak of power and determination, and through the silence they know what has to be done.

The coach calls the unit to go on the field, and the referee blows the whistle to get the game under way. The referee begins to blow the whistle uncontrollably, and the coaches are stunned, because all the black players refuse to play. The coaches go crazy, "Get your black asses out there before I get the bullwhip." But the players walk, realizing their coaches had the bullwhip all along.

The world is stunned. Billions upon billions of dollars have been lost. The economy has been affected by one single act of bravery. The Super Bowl has been boycotted by black players and even some white players who walked alongside of them. The world knew the black man, the athlete, the slave, the hero, was once again ready for change and change came. Players began to vote for their coaches and a couple of new teams had black owners. The cycle went on for another thirty years until another change was needed.

I once heard a black man say that a boycott will be impossible. Players have too much to lose. The sleeping giants are in prison. I believe that we all owe something to our ancestors who were beaten, raped, lynched, the list goes on. They have suffered so that we may have a better tomorrow. I'm still looking for that tomorrow. Change comes only when you have a purpose and the purpose for the black athlete is team ownership.

It would be nice to see a group of retired players pull their money together with other investors and own a black franchise. I once heard a white man say, "I love black people. I have no problem with them. I just believe everyone should own one. Their skin has been their sin."

I'm a thirty-two-year-old man. My father started getting gray hair in his early fifties. I believe that, by the time I start spotting gray hair, the ghetto will be so big and the prison system will be larger. They will merge the two. It will be called "Mecca's reservation." You will need a pass to get out. Only whites and Uncle Tom will have unlimited access. That way we black folks will smile real big for you, make you laugh, dance for you, and entertain you. Some may argue that point. Some may say the NFL is not a slave trade. Others will say, "He's just angry." Has a slave ever owned a plantation? No, just forty acres and a mule. Today that's forty yards and a helmet.

Understand that this book is inspired by something greater than me. The modern-day slave of professional football today believes he has won the game. In reality, the game has won him. As equality of opportunity has steadily increased on the football field, equality in administration and coaching has actually declined. The opportunities to participate have been extended only to the white middle class.

It is known historically that a slave never owned a plantation, the plantation owned him. His labor has made his master rich, as today's black athletes make team owners filthy rich. Journals indicate the need to reactivate the Civil Rights Movement of the 1960s. This might best be accomplished by awakening the sleeping giant and banding together today's black athletes.

Chapter 10

The NFL versus the CFL

When you look closely at the NFL's hiring practices, you know why it's called Niggas Freedom Living (NFL). The only impact to ensure more opportunities for black coaches will come from the players' actions. They need to shout and take a stand for the generations that stood before them. Or is the silver and gold in front of them more valuable than carving a place in history for the next pioneers?

Johnnie Cochran Jr. is the Lone Ranger. He needs some modern-day troops to fight on the cotton fields. Of the thirty-two NFL teams, thirty head coaches are white and thirty-two owners are white. That's strong white supremacy. There are 547 assistant coaches who are active in the NFL. Only 154 are black, which is twenty-eight percent. "In more than 80 years of doing business, NFL teams have hired only six black head coaches—five since 1989 when Art Shell became the first of the modern era," said *USA Today* sports columnist Jon Saraceno in his October 1, 2002, "Keeping Score" column.

You have too many Uncle Toms in the locker rooms allowing this hypocrisy to go on. These are the same Sambos who kept us in slavery so long, perpetuating the "We got it good, Boss" syndrome. It's still as powerful as it was centuries ago.

The college statistics are an even greater disappointment. Of the nation's 117 major college teams, only four are being run by black head coaches. This is so disappointing considering football wouldn't be football without black athletes generating millions for universities and corporations nation wide.

Whenever the sleeping giant awakes, change will come in a hurry. It's funny, when we black folks want justice, we usually have to wait years and years. Patience is starting to run thin, but one man can only do so much and when a group comes together and demands change, and when billions of dollars are on the line, change is inevitable.

The pioneers of the Civil Rights Movement of the 1960s are old and tired. They gave us some open doors and now those doors are beginning to close. We need some new young guns, new soldiers to take on a new giant. Let our elders rest, for their work is done. Martin Luther King, Jr., and Malcolm X are looking down saying, "Come on, somebody."

The NFL has become the National Freedom Living. It's the capital of football. The athlete dreams their whole life about competing in this arena. When I played in the NFL it was all it was cracked up to be. At first I believed I was a privileged man who had a part of God within him. I felt more of a man but actually I was sleepwalking, living a fisherman's lie about the reality of the system. I was contradicting myself, playing for the lifestyle but also taking a cowardly approach to what I saw and how I really felt about the treatment and the ongoing life. Build you up, let you down, and so on, making you believe in them not in yourself.

❧

I guess I know why most black men hate the dark. Slow your thoughts for a moment. Forget about what you know about football and think about this story. I can feel the strength of a man lying in bed. As a door is forced open, he awakens as he sees a lantern. His eyes focus on the light. Above the lantern he stares down the barrel of a gun and hears the words, "Come on, boy, we'se got some fightin' to do, you'se gonna make us some money."

Barefoot and all, the slave rises up from sleep. His companions, his family, his people cry in the night as he goes into the dark at gunpoint. Not knowing his fate, he is placed in a carriage with a gun to his back while chained and bound. You hear the whip on the horse's back, "Yah, yah," is shouted to the horses as the slave sits there chained and bound. He feels every bump on the dirt road and his body sways from side to side. The night is black and the lantern that sits on the carriage is the only light. The slave raises his hands to swat a mosquito. The master presses the gun tighter to his back, "Hey, boy, no sudden moves now, you hear? I'll shoot you now."

The slave is spooked. His eyes never blink. The night has frightened him. Others have left during the night at gunpoint, but have never come back. So the slave takes a deep breath and a tear comes down from his right eye. A frown comes over his face.

As the carriage moves through the thick trees, the moon is full and lights the night. The slave says, "Massa, where's you take me?" The master says, "We gonna go nigger fighting tonight."

The slave then looks into the distant night and sees three men huddled by a fire. One is a slave, who looks to be a mighty man, a big buck. With him are two white men, one holding a gun, the other holding chains. The slave in the carriage gets restless, like a pit bull, not out of anger but out of fear. He says, "No, massa, I'se don't want ta fight."

The master presses that gun to his back, "Listen here, nigga, you fight and kill him, you'se be a free nigga."

The slave standing by the fire hears the carriage and looks into the night to see if he can size up his competition. But the night is too dark. As the carriage gets closer, the slave by the first is told the same thing. "You fight and kill this nigga, you'se be a free man."

As the carriage comes to a halt, the warrior steps down, still chained. The two slaves stand by the first, ready to annihilate one another. Power against power, shoulder against shoulder, still chained, the plantation owners talk strategy and money with the other two white men, who are holding guns and scratching their ass. They make bets themselves. As two slaves stand in the middle between life and death, the ropes are cut and the two slaves charge each other like wild beasts of the night. They let out shouts and roars from Africa as they try to kill each other with each blow in the night sky. The fire roars as the slaves continue to unleash hell upon one another. The devil seems to be in the midst of it. The fire starts to flame stronger. As the slaves bleed, they see the blood and more energy is within them. The sign of blood to them means freedom. The loss of blood may make one weak, but blood loss makes the slaves fight even harder. The need for freedom was greater than death.

The men holding the guns were jumping up and down, saying "Look, these niggers are animals." And the master was moving from side to side, watching every hit, every strike, wishing he were fighting himself.

The carriage slave began to tire. He began to lose. With every step, every swing he started to miss and the fire slave that was waiting began to slowly take his life. With every act of violence the two white men that were also on the carriage began to shout, "Come on, boy," as he shot his gun in the air. Immediately the slaves stopped fighting because of the sound of the gun. Then the gun holder says, "Go on fight, you coons." So the slaves once again began to unleash hell upon one another until the carriage slave was so badly beaten and couldn't fight anymore.

As the waiting fire slave began beating the carriage slave, the white man with the gun kicked the first slave to the side, "Get back, boy." The fire slave stepped back and the gun holder stood over the carriage slave, who was badly beaten, and said, "Open your eyes, nigga." The carriage slave slowly opened his eyes. With the barrel of the gun in his mouth, the trigger was pulled and a part of Africa was dead.

Money was exchanged between the owners. "I'll come burn this dead nigger tomorrow," his owner said. The fire slave asked, "Is I free, boss?"

"Hell, no," his owner replied. "You gonna make me more money." The fire slave was escorted back to his bed a gunpoint, with bruises and once again chained and bound. As the fire slave lies down he feels the spirit of Africa. He feels a discomfort in his mind.

Solitude becomes his comfort until the looks of a woman start to motivate him and console him. The fire slave receives humiliation from his white master, but receives love and comfort from his white woman. The white women on plantations are a slave's rebuilding tool. After being torn down and beaten by the head master, white women are a refuge emotionally and physically, like cheerleaders on the football field.

Across America, white women are a motivational tool, a prize to win. But they are never won, only imagined, and if you imagine something long enough, you'll become insane. Think about it, whenever a football game is about to start, in the NFL or the CFL, players run out onto the field between two rows of cheerleaders, who call your name and jump up and down, as if you're the Sky God himself. (That's what we called God in Africa.) The cheerleaders are always in your vision, constantly moving around the stadium. As you watch from afar, you imagine all kinds of things. It constantly drives you and inspires you to play harder so she can cheer your name, console you, accept you, with all your blackness. The cheerleader is just another tool to keep you fixed, like a production labor force. Keep the slave motivated until he's exhausted and fill him up with long legs, short skirts, long hair, and a beautiful smile. He will be refueled for more production.

Football players all across this world are taking that carriage ride. They're being told of a freedom that doesn't exist. It only drives them insane. We no longer carriage rides to meet the fire slave, we take high-end buses with TVs. Now the stakes are much more intense. The fire slave doesn't just sit by the fire waiting for a death match. He has a team now. There are no longer small fires and lanterns to light the violence. It's now lit by million-dollar stadium lights. The master is still protected and surrounded by guns. There are not only four in attendance; now it has reached an audience of a billion worldwide through television and satellite. Not only can you watch one carriage ride, you can tune into multiple death matches at your fingertips.

The history of football only goes back about 100 years

or so but my ancestors have been playing football for more than 500 years. History is only one man's story. That's why I believe you have to determine your own history by doing your own research. Instead of listening to people's opinions in what you should believe. I constantly felt the spirit of my ancestors while writing this book. I hear their cries. I feel their pain. They huddle around me as I try to sleep, protecting my soul in the midnight hour. I believe their spirit is still alive in every black American walking this earth. I hear the old hymns. Their voices of desperation pierce my heart with amazing courage and words of wisdom. I tell them, "I'm just a little man, trying to stand tall." They tell me to stand, for I am not alone. I can now see my sister and brothers little, big, young, and old, barefoot and with rags for clothes. I ask them, "How do you plan to fight a giant with only sticks and stones? The giant has weapons, guns, missiles that can destroy a city with just one touch of a button. I look into the redness of their eyes. They're tired and weary souls. A little gust of wind could have blown them all over but together they were strong.

I was taken back into time and there I saw my brothers playing football one on one, with no rules, no coaches, no referees, just a little fire, a lantern, and on the edge was a carriage strapped with two horses. There were no contracts or signing bonuses, just another lie, promising freedom in the name of violence. But the original carriage slave who lost his life, actually regained it in the end. The slave who lost his life won his freedom through death; the slave who won actually lost his freedom. That is how football is played. Sometimes you think that because you made the team, you won a prize or something like that but you really give up your freedom, your life is exposed, and every move you make can either make you or break you, on and off the playing field. You're constantly trying to prove your worth, and you will tear down the man next to you in order to stay a step ahead. That's only bad karma and that will always come back to bite you in the ass.

Slaves were the first football players and they will be the last. They haven't stopped playing the game. They even go across the border to play in the CFL. American players call it the Cash-Flow Low league, some call it the Cheap Football League. I say to them, "What ever happened to 'If you love what you do, it shouldn't matter where you do it'?" But money and prestige make a fool of us all and in the CFL many fools never really get to enjoy playing in their CFL games because they are constantly trying to get back to the NFL. I tell them they're insane, "Why attempt something the same way? You're gonna have the same results." The NFL has a committee that will look for a white CFL player before a black one. Colleges each year have young talent cropping up like wild fire. Black players are like economy cars: they're plentiful; meanwhile little or no talent white players are regarded as Lamborghinis, a rare commodity that can be posted around the country. The myth of the Great White Hope is still strong on the playing field.

Countless players who are axed from the NFL go across the border into the CFL. There they constantly tell themselves they can't wait to get back into the NFL. They feel they got a raw deal. I say to them, "The people, the coaches, the committee that took your job away from you are still there in authority so what makes you believe so strongly that they're gonna just change their mind? Your fate is in their hands."

Young players who get cut from the NFL and arrive in the CFL are so in constant conflict with reality and fantasy. The dream of becoming a NFL player is so embedded in their minds they are blinded by the reality of politics and bullshit. All they do is say, "I can't wait to show them. I tell them you already showed them, so get over it. You didn't fit the bill economically so take this time and enjoy what's right in front of you. This experience only comes once so enjoy every minute of it. Stop dreaming for a moment of the things you want and what you don't have. Focus on this day, this moment that God has given you. If you feel the need to dream, dream of something attainable, which all of us can enjoy. Too many black folks and athletes dream of a self uplifting experience. The same politics that are present in the NFL are just as strong in the CFL. The scale is smaller but the weight is the same.

Chapter 11

The NFL Combine: A Monkey Show

The NFL Combine has become one of the biggest events for senior college football players. The Combine takes place once a year in the state of Indiana in February. It's when all potential draft picks are invited to come together for a range of tests: running, jumping, strength, agility, acceleration, catching, and stamina.

When you first get the news that you're invited to attend the Combine, you realize that the dream you've held since you were a young child is almost a reality. Soon after the college season ends, you find yourself training, missing classes, breaking promises. You become almost paralyzed, because everything you do has a timeframe. You chalk on the calendar the day you leave and the day you return. Until then your mind, body, and soul have been purchased.

The day you arrive at the Combine, you either become a leader or a follower. Arriving at the airport, you find that you're competing against about seventy other guys for the next three days. So many players have been invited to attend that some athletes look at the competition and feel overwhelmed. They lose confidence and their childhood dream becomes a distant memory. Some say, "If it's God's will, I'll be here."

Players like that make me nervous. They don't know where they stand; they're in between God and the NFL. I tell them, "God didn't give you an invitation to play a violent game with violent men. The NFL didn't choose you. You chose to play the game and you either have to deal with whatever comes with it or just walk away." God doesn't care about football. People care about this child's game that grown men play and get paid for.

My experience at the Combine in Indiana in 1992 was a great one. Getting the opportunity was a satisfying feeling. On my arrival, I was a little stunned considering I got a later invitation. I wasn't a big name coming out of college, nor did I have statistics that would make you look twice. I didn't become a starter until my senior year and, on top of that, I only had about four good games. But during my senior year I showed some skills that had potential. I could hit, but what stood out was that I could run like a deer and, if speed was going to be my ticket, then so be it. Let's ride it out.

At the Combine, ex players and players who are currently playing talk about their NFL experience and what to look for out in the community while playing. Players talk on various subjects that rookie players will be faced with after signing an NFL contract. The NFL player who speaks during the NFL draft is usually a big-time player the whole world knows about. It's a very encouraging thing to listen to NFL players who some of us watched as children. During the Combine you see him from a distance and you pause and the guys around you have their attention fixed on him. They whisper words in your head such as "I want to be like him someday." That's great, but if you and anybody else ever put their faith in man, he will fail you every time. The whole purpose of the Combine is to get drafted or have a successful football career. Some players don't even get invited to the Combine, but to turn out to have great NFL careers, it's just the way life is when you have no power, no say. You have no heart, no mind, and you can't find your soul.

❧

The state of Indiana where the Combine is held has an interesting history. In 1818 rebel soldiers slaughtered native Americans, men, women, and children. They didn't want to live with them or try to negotiate an equal claim to land. Those rebels took the land with force and the native Americans had no choice but to sign their treaty. They were given gifts and large reservations, where they have been stuck ever since. It was called "The New Purchase" back then, but another new purchase is now going on. It happens once a year during black history month — February — and the new purchase of the 21st century is young black football players. You purchase their eyes with money, gifts, and fame. You purchase their minds by making them dream of what they don't have and what they want. Once that purchase is complete, you purchase a whole new machine that will always be at your disposal to keep your pocketbooks fat and the economy going and the NFL industry will have players knocking on the door for an opportunity to play. They will have their agents calling us, begging us to take a look at their new black face. Players will call and leave the message, "I'm ready when you need me." Players will even just show up and say, "Can I have an opportunity? Watch what I can do." All the NFL industry needs to do is take your name and number and ask you to wait in line. We took the native American's land for our use in this beautiful state of Indiana, so let's take the black man's body as a new purchase to build our industry. We'll take his mind in Indiana, where we took the native American's soul. The state of Indiana has a history all its own. In 1831, a new law was introduced that all blacks moving to Indiana had to post a five-hundred dollar bond in advance for their good behavior. If you didn't have a bond, you were sold to the highest bidder. For six months, you were their slave. That really hasn't changed too much.

⌘

The most memorable day in America is Independence Day. Back in 1848, on the Fourth of July, a black man named John Tucker, described as a soft-spoken man who had purchased his freedom in Kentucky a few years before, was walking in downtown Indianapolis when a group of white men beat him to death for walking too proudly. (See "A survey of Indiana's African-American history" by Lynn Ford (Originally published in The Star, February, 1990), now available on the Indianapolis Star website at:

http://www.indystar.com/library/factfileshistory/black_history/ December 14, 2002.)

The Klu Klux Klan, which started as early as 1866, was centered in Indiana in the 1920s, and the Indiana Klan was the strongest chapter in America. During that time, the KKK took 150 hooded horsemen and tried to purchase Valparaiso University. They were trying to establish the first Klan college. Thank God they weren't successful. But their terror and destruction was not slowed a bit and for decades they brought death and the devil to every non-white American. They are still going strong with their Christian values today.

On September 16, 1968, a beautiful, young black woman was out doing her job, selling encyclopedias. Carol Jenkins was brutally beaten and stabbed to death. Thirty-four years later, Shirley Richmond who had been an eyewitness to the murder, came forward. At the age of seven, she had watched her father kill Carol Jenkins out of the back window of her father's car. Detectives were convinced by Shirley's statement because she remembered a clue that had never been made public: that during her murder Jenkins wore a yellow scarf. For thirty-four years, that yellow scarf was tearing away at Shirley Richmond, like the cancer that took her father's life. It was said that her father, Kenneth C. Richmond, the murderer was an affiliate of the Klu Klux Klan, but he went untried and died on August 31, 2002. That's justice in the eyes of God, because all of us will suffer for the wrong we put on humanity. The Combine is a strong form of white supremacy and Indiana has the strongest chapter of the Klu Klux Klan.

❧

The NFL Combine is a recipe for endless riches. The recipe goes like this: You take a large number of black men in order to establish a joint purpose and then you can contain them in a fused state of mind. Bring them to a powerful state where white supremacy is still prevalent, still obvious, still strong, and they will feel its presence everywhere. Bring in a top NFL Uncle Tom so he can help dictate the brainwashing, telling all of them, "You can make it if you put your mind to it." Let him be a step-in fetcher for a while and let the players buy into what he is programmed to say.

When you're knocked out at the Combine, Charlie tells you, "Don't worry about it. We'll be at your college timing again on such and such a date." That's when scouts go for a second look and, in turn, take a look at the juniors, next year's new purchase. They give you time to keep on dreaming about what you don't have and what you want.

Picture yourself in a dark room. You stretch your hands trying to touch something and you can't. You hear a loud voice that says, "You can run in the dark. You can scream, for you are alone." You start running in the dark in all directions and there is nothing to slow you down.

"The only thing that will slow you down is your own will," the voice tells you. "Stop running and look up for just a minute. I want to show you something."

As you look up into the darkness, a light appears and before you know it, above your head you watch scenes of the way you want your life to be. You see a big house, with five cars in the driveway. You see yourself on a pro football team with all your friends. You're healthy, your wife and kids love the man you've become. You feel successful with the NFL on your right shoulder. You feel accepted by society because you're a pro athlete and everybody loves you. Your whole family is taken care of: brothers, sisters, mom, dad, cousins. You even have your own little business on the side and it wouldn't be possible without the NFL. With your last thought the lights go out again and you find yourself running in the dark, desperately trying to see a light that will help you find a pathway to freedom.

That's what happens to so many black athletes after they go to the Combine. They get brainwashed into thinking about how their life is going to be and their own thoughts paint beautiful pictures. They hear the voices they choose to hear. We all feel good when we dream. It only becomes a problem when we get out of balance and focus on a single purpose. You shit on everyone else and forget about those who really love you and care about you.

The NFL has a strong system, strong values. You will never see who is really in charge but he has a name. He sells empty boxes, empty dreams, and empty promises. That makes him The Undertaker.

The NFL Combine is a slavery day picnic, pickin' niggas at will. It's a monkey show. When you go to the zoo, everybody loves to look at the monkeys. All they do is run around, jump, and swing. They're always making noise talking shit and smilin'. That's what Charlie wants us to do.

At the yearly Combine purchase, if you don't smile enough, Charlie says, "You got a bad attitude." If you don't feel like running or doing drills, Charlie says, "You're just hurtin' your chances to be an NFL player." Those are Charlie's tactics to control your fate. He lets you know where your black ass stands. "You're here in Indiana, boy, and you need to start showin' us that you really want to be here." Then you start being a step-in fetcher, dancing for that white man and smiling the whole time. That's The Undertaker's approach.

The NFL Combine is strong and kickin'. You can still see the monkeys in their cage, running and jumping. A Combine is a place to form a substance that is different from what it really is. What that means is when players attend the Combine, they are made to believe that as long as they wish for this opportunity, they will get it. So even if they don't make a team, they will keep on training and running in the cage like the monkeys in the zoo. Sooner or later, the gatekeeper will release them to the outdoors. Some monkeys make that transition, but the majority of monkeys stay in the cage and the gatekeeper has a great economic system. When the outdoor monkey's business is done and all the people in the stands get tired of seeing the old, wiry monkey and refuse to pay to watch the monkey run and jump, the gatekeeper puts the monkey to sleep. He goes into the cage and realizes he has so many monkeys at his disposal that he'll never go out of business. He has all the caged monkeys believing they will soon be free. If a new monkey turns out to be an economic loss, they put him to sleep as well, and the cycle goes on.

❧

They should hold the NFL Combine in Africa, in Zimbabwe. That way, young black athletes would get a history lesson. Let them compete on their ancestor's land and see the motivation like never before. See the spirit of Africa rise up in players.

Instead, the Combine is held in Indiana where it's cold in February. When you look around, every step you take during your visit to Indiana, you see red, white, and blue. The NFL and all its independent clubs join forces to set guidelines for young players, so when their opportunity presents itself, they will be very well prepared. The city, the teams, they treat you great in the state of Indiana during the NFL Combine. There are treats and lavish gifts in your hotel room.

❧

Why is it that we are so quick to listen to people who have "MD" or "PhD" behind their names? MDs haven't even found a cure for the common cold, just temporary relief for the symptoms of your cold. PhDs usually comment on things they never even experienced — a study they call it. Some even have the nerve to try and break down the black experience in sports but have never even played the game. And most PhDs are not even black, but they seem to know how it is to be black. Their external opinions are just that, an opinion: secondhand information. How can someone comment on something he or she has never seen or experienced? Just because a person reads a book, doesn't make them an expert on the subject. An opinion based on experience has much more credibility and meaning. For example, take a read on my theory of what I call "color shifting" in the NFL.

Anthony Prior's Theory of "Color Shifting"

To appeal to the mass market football fan, pro football practices a color coding system as follows:

o White Caucasian Player

2 Tan (Light skinned Afro American, Hawaiian, etc.)

3 Dark (Standard Afro American)

5 Black (Dark skinned Afro American)

Color shifting is a new strategy to control the game once again by a system that can and will revolutionize football. This theory has come from the "stacking" that many people do, sometimes unconsciously. Diane L. Gill writes in Psychological Dynamics of Sport and Exercise, 2nd ed. (Champaign, IL: Human Kinetics, 2000), p. 266: "Many athletes are not white and middle class, yet power remains solidly white and middle class. Sport's glass ceiling keeps all but white middle-class athletes clustered at the bottom. The popular media and some scholars have referred to such practices as 'stacking' (e.g., African-Americans in positions such as running back or outfields but not quarterback or pitcher) and to the nearly exclusive white male dominance of coaching and management."

If that doesn't raise an eyebrow, then you're just a son of a bitch. This method of color shifting analysis relates to thinking that the darker the skin tone the more powerful the slave. A very dark, black slave was considered rich, aggressive in NFL terms. The blacker you are, the better player they think you are. You have some players who have been diluted through interracial marriages and they're looked upon as weaker athletes all around. And if you're tan, light-skilled, well, hell, they don't even have a place for you on the bench unless they make you a safety, because when you're a tan player, and have been diluted with some good old white blood, then you're considered smarter than that dark, black buck. Or they will make you a wide receiver. That way some fans will mistake you for a Charlie as long as you keep your helmet on. Players can't take off their helmets on the field, only on the sidelines. The fans aren't looking when you're on the sidelines; they're watching the action live on the playing field.

After a day of trying to sell yourself at the Combine, you get on the phone to call back home. Some players have conversations full of negative outbursts. They say, "I was too short. I had no speed, no strength, and my color rating was a two. They seem to love those dark skin niggas. They gave them a five on the skin-tone scale." I've heard black players wishing they were darker. The color code scale says blackness is superior on the field. It's powerful when undiluted. A half black, half white player, is seen as weak and not aggressive enough. He's not pure. The purer the man's blood, the stronger he is. If his blood is diluted, it's weakened. His aggression isn't consistent. His emotions are pulled in two directions. He thinks he's white off the field and tries to be a nigga on the field. The NFL's not looking for that. Economically that's not good. The next thing you know, if he thinks he's white off the field, he's gonna try and take my job. He's gonna want to be president or general manager. Next thing, when we look up, he's gonna want to be an owner. If that happens, then the NFL will be a different league. There would be more black coaches on the field and in the front offices. Until then, I guess I will keep on listening to Marvin Gaye's "What's Going On?" and hearing Sam Cooke in the distance singing "A Change Is Gonna Come."

❦

When you look at the color shifting, you think racism. Maybe you think, "Why even mention color? Why even acknowledge color, if the objective is to win? A color line, or the shades of gray of a player's skin, shouldn't even be a thought, considering the history of America and its injustice to African Americans and others of color. Why is the color line such a factor? Well, it's not a mystery. If you look at its dynamics as I have, it's a masterpiece. I have figured out the puzzle. The color line is only part of the changing NFL system. Why do you think more black quarterbacks have been playing? Why do you think there are more white free safeties in the league? Why do you think there are more white wide receivers? Why do you think there are more white linebackers? White fullbacks are soon to lock up that position and your white tight ends will soon take that position in full swing. This is the new silent revolution that has been going on for some time.

When rating the color line, take this example for offense. If you're a quarterback, you can either be a zero or a five. If you're a zero at quarterback, you must always put the ball in the hands of a five to make up for the zero's weaknesses. If you're a five at quarterback, then you can revolutionize the game of football. But the managers are not ready to see a five at quarterback. It will change a game's dynamics and that will only prove that the five was held back as a quarterback only because of the darkness of his skin. If you watch games today and see a five at quarterback, running like a slot back and throwing to a five like him, that's a winner. That's something. When a five throws to a zero at wide receiver, it may take the zero at wide receiver longer to get open than it would a five at wide receiver. But as long as you have a five at quarterback, he can scramble and stall time until that zero at wide receiver gets open. That's how you make up the weakness of a zero. But zeros will always have the kicking jobs. They even get paid more than some fives on the team and they don't do shit. Kickers should only get a bonus if they kick well. If they don't, dock their pay. Fine their sorry asses.

In my lifetime and even into the next generation, there will never be a zero at the tailback position to lead the NFL in rushing. The same goes for boxing — there will never be a white heavyweight champion of the world. Genetics just won't allow that. But the color shift can compensate many factors. That's how team sports can be manipulated so that zeros can play in the battle, even though they are below average.

Don't get me wrong now. There are many great white football players in the NFL. Color shifting just makes room for more white players who may not be up to par, making room for potential players to develop their skills.

The way you do that is through match ups. You notice lately in the pro football arenas it's all about match ups and the guy you will be responsible for each game? It's a new player, but with the color line, you can match up color. That way blacks will be playing against blacks and white players will be playing against white players.

This is how you do it and you people thought all coaches were intelligent. You don't need to have a college degree to figure out this one. All you need to do is watch, open your eyes wide enough and question, "Why aren't all the good players playing?" It's because you have to make room for Charlie, the zero on the color line. This is not make-believe. This is happening today in modern-day football. For example, look at all the zeros at lineback. Their responsibility is to cover the zeros at fullback. Sometimes the zeros at free safety cover the zero at tight end. They usually switch responsibilities to have one or the other free safety covering the fullback. The linebacker covering the tight end and the zeros playing those positions compete with each other. Charlie says, "If you black faces keep on complaining you want more fives at quarterback, okay, we'll just take four positions to your one. It all balances out." Charlie will always balance the table to benefit his own, so why can't we blacks come together and demand more of our own in administration jobs: as general managers, presidents, and a hell

With the new color line in full force, watch the upcoming draft. Watch the rosters begin to have fewer blacks. And with fewer jobs on the field for blacks at certain positions, competition will be so intense for other positions because there will be other positions reserved for whites only. This color line will only bring segregation to the game and the game will take on a new challenge. It won't be about the team. It will be about players at certain positions. Their one-on-one battles will be better than the game itself. Why has this come about? Color shifting is a new renaissance of the game of football. Color shifting is the new league world order. Whites go up against white players, and they play their big slow game within the confines of a game that is dominated by speed and power. If you watch carefully you will see this happening today. Look at the color shift and look at rosters around the NFL. Tell me if I'm crazy or just bold enough to recognize a scam when I see one.

The color shift is systematic device to enable more zeros on the field. Even though their placement will determine the outcome, there are some pieces on a chessboard that have higher rank and can outperform other pieces. On the other hand, you have weaker pieces that have a role to play as well.

And it's all maneuvered and strategically planned to enable every line of color to have its input. As long as zeros control other zeros, you have quality. As long as fives compete with other fives, you balance the game of football and everybody looks great.

Chapter 12

On the Plantation

Nat Turner is said to have been a rebel without a cause but I argue that he was a slave who tried to abolish slavery with a sword, through bloodshed and death. He started off with a whirlwind of violence and his sole motivation was to put to death those who were supporting slavery. Nat Turner led one of the largest slave revolts in the United States in the 19th century. In the early morning hours of August 22, 1831, in Southampton County, Virginia, Turner led between sixty and eighty active rebels in the death of approximately 200 people (*The Confessions of Nat Turner and Related Documents*, Kenneth S. Greenberg, ed. (Boston: St. Martin's Press, 1996). Turner was what some call today "nigga off the chain" but niggas today are still on the chain. Nat Turner was willing to die and ultimately did die for his cause.

The slave in the modern-day has invisible chains. The slave of today talks and talks but never really acts upon his motives. He has been equipped only to mutter words of action but never to put them into action, always waiting for a new song, a new movie, a talk show to promote his cause. But Nat Turner took his cause in his own hands and the repercussions were not only his own death, but the death of those who supported him. Beyond shallow words, Nat Turner's actions were those of a man who got fed up with the hypocrisy and took lives in trying the change it. That happened in 1831 and we are still talking and reading about his action that took place more than 140 years ago. Imagine if Nat Turner were alive today. Would he try and change things once again or would the welfare system make him complacent? Would he go on a 21st-century rampage as he did in 1831? I can't say, but the prison system would love to chain him up and lock him in a cell. If we could clone Nat Turner so that he came alive in the 21st century, he would put fear in the eyes of white America.

The black man in America still faces the kind of humiliation Nat Turner faced during his time walking in chains on American soil. Some say he was too smart for his own good. I believe he was highly intelligent, considering he could read and write. For blacks in the early 1800s, that was forbidden. Intelligence was something to fear. If a slave could read and write, he would question slavery and tell others, "Put away your Bibles. 'Obey your master' is not the only verse to recite in the Bible. What about the verse 'Do unto others as you would have them do unto you?'" It's funny that plantation owners use the Bible to introduce slaves to their destiny, "Obey your master." That's not scripture; that's brainwashing. It places fear in people in order to derive service in order to keep an economic system strong and prosperous so that it benefits someone else. The problem with the enslavement to millions is that you can't fool everybody; there will be a man that will get fed up with all the humiliation. Education will explain that slavery is an inhumane service done to humanity. Plantation owners called themselves Christians and believed God had ordained them to enslave millions of innocent men, women, and children. This is just another ploy to justify an unjust industry that has been bleeding money out of humanity. This method of labor still exists in America. It may not be labeled slavery, but there are new names in the equation. I'll give you one: football. This occupation has slavery written all over it. The reason nobody has spoken out is because the master syndrome is still in the minds of athletes on the football fields across this land of ours.

The layout of a typical practice facility was influenced by the big house, which in days of old was the massa's house. The plantation homes still stand strong in the 21st century. Big and spacious, the plantation home has a backside view that shows the field hands at work in the fields, practicing for an upcoming game. Owners and managers sit in the shade on second- and third-level balconies, watching you sweat and running while they relax in the shade drinking lemonade, determining your future on their plantation. As you glance at the managers drinking their lemonade, you feel the looks and sense the need to work a little harder, but really what you're doing is slaving for the man. You glace around at the layout, understanding why the coach said, "All players use the back entrance, not the front. We don't want traffic coming through the front doors of the plantation. We the administration will be the privileged ones to go through the front door. As in days of old, slaves use the back entrance. And if you're caught using the front entrance, you will be fined. Now that you know the plantation's rules, don't make me repeat myself."

If it's too hot outside, the managers sit in their air-conditioned room while they watch you sweat and run. Their parking lot is right in front of the plantation and the slave's parking lot is either on the side or in the back. Your car will be towed if you try and park in a place not permitted for slaves. You would think players would have privileges to park anywhere, considering they're the ones who fill up stadiums all across the country. The fans come to see the players, not the administrators. You would think players would be running the practice facility. But have you ever heard of a slave running a plantation? The only slave who tried to run a plantation is a dead slave. If a player tried to run a facility he would be considered off the chain and not a team player. He would be labeled uncoachable because of his bad attitude.

Players are still being lynched, not physically, but on paper, and what is on paper follows you like a bad habit. Every little act of disobedience is chalked up, like a criminal rap sheet. With high-speed internet, your acts of disobedience are sent to every plantation. Before you even get a chance to gather your belongings, you're tagged, labeled and shipped off like a thief in the night. For some odd reason we never hear of you again. A team never picks you up even though you showed great talent on the field. You were consistent, aggressive, everything a team could ask for in a player. That's what you were but for some odd reason your career was cut off, like a surgeon cuts off a leg or two for diabetes and you're never the same person after the surgeon cuts your limbs.

You still feel the need to compete. Your peers call you and ask, "Why aren't you playing? We need you out here on the battlefield." But the surgeon has done his work and you will never be the same because you got a raw deal. Players know it, coaches know it, fans know it, and the surgeon continues to stay in business, cutting off limbs to keep you from the game you were bred to play.

If you pay close attention and look at the head master, the chief in charge of facilities and pro plantations, why is it that pilgrims are so often recycled? There are coaches out there coaching who have been in charge of different plantations all around pro football and who continue to have losing season after losing season. Although they may be fired they are not thrown in trash cans like slaves and players but are actually thrown into the recycling bins and are given second, third, fourth and so on chances to produce a winner. But to continue to have defeat on the battlefield, this is white supremacy in its purest form. Despite a white coach's incompetence to produce a winning plantation atmosphere, he will always be in charge as your coach, your boss, your massa.

Players, and more so black players, who are unsuccessful on the plantations are often thrown in garbage cans across America. Even when they are productive on the battlefield, they are carried away, seemingly thrown away, never to be heard of and seen. In some odd cases, you'll find him pop up here or there to help pick some cotton at the end of the season because some other slave's either injured or just rebelled. So the administration grabs this player for a few weeks, uses his body, throws it away and grabs a new body in the upcoming monkey show, the NFL draft. That new player may have a tremendous few games as a fill-in, but his likeness usually will never be remembered. Only the moment he showed greatness will ever be implanted in his mind and he will live with the moment as a constant reminder of a possibility of a comeback. But the moment in his head is just that—a moment captured, but never forgotten.

Whatever happened to the old saying, "If you're not a winner in your present environment, what makes you think you're going to do something great in another one?" That philosophy goes right out the door when it comes to black and white on the plantations across America. It's this hypocrisy that is starting to cause a sleeping giant to rise. This hypocrisy is pro football, where the slave ships are now commercial airlines, and the cotton fields have been transformed into football fields. Look at the dynamics, the plantation layout. Look at who's in charge. Look at pro football and see how it relates to the history of slavery, the industry that has brought billions on the cotton fields is bringing billions on football fields. Pro football facilities got their layout and plans of influence through slavery. Nothing has changed under the sun. The same things that happened in past centuries are still prevalent and they are operating in a very productive manner.

The plantations of old are still admired on how they would treat the slaves during the end of the year when the holidays would roll around. There would be ceremonies and festivals when master and slave would gather together at year's end to show a sign of appreciation. The master would prepare a gathering, sort of like the way NFL teams do after a football season when you get dressed up and cut your hair so your smile looks good. You even go out and buy a suit like master's so that you feel a sense of acceptance and pride in your appearance. That's how Somerset Place, a North Carolina plantation, was run. Slaves were to gather wearing their finest clothes, those suitable to wear in the presence of their master. Satisfying the slaves with a party and sense of equality would lessen the chance of a rebellion against the slavery system. After the holidays the slaves would return to wearing their old rags, go back to the cotton fields and into hell's kitchen, but they will constantly remind themselves of the ceremony. It would be for a conversation piece until the following year.

❧

A lot of players in pro football remind me of a slave I read about. "Old Peter Law" was considered a hard-working, obedient slave who refused to disobey his massa and at year's end, during the Christmas holidays, "Old Peter" would climb the front steps of the big house and shake his master's hands as if he were shaking the hands of Jesus himself. It was a privilege he was allowed after the festivities and he prided himself for his heightened acceptance to shake the hand of the man who had his destiny in the palm of his hand. "During the year, the only slaves who could cross into the white world were house slaves and other with special privileges. Yet on Christmas day, slaves not only entered white space, but they also performed a ceremony that was uniquely their own while in that space. They were so confident in their self-assertion that they requested money from whites at the end of the ceremony. The custom of shaking hands on the front porch before or after the Jonkonnu performance is further evidence of black assertiveness in what was considered white space." (Elizabeth A. Fenn, "Slave Society and Jonkonnu", *North Carolina Historical Review* LXV, no. 2: 138)

I believe if somebody had my destiny in the palm of his hand I would love to shake that hand and take my destiny from him. I believe that's what "Old Peter" tried to do. Think about it. Black folks love reading horoscopes and dialing up psychic hot lines, trying to figure out what the future holds and then turn around on Sunday morning, claiming the Holy Ghost, hollering and shouting, saying, "I see Jesus." Anytime you allow the devil's demons to camp out with you and turn to God on Sunday, letting everybody know you're saved, the church audience becomes your fans and they believe you're holy. But the devil's horoscope shows your faith is as weak as the paper you're reading it from. Black folks were very superstitious back then and would believe anything. That spirit is still hovering around the blackness of America.

There are high-profile and not so high-profile players who attend their annual season-ending party or Christmas party. They get a chance to mingle with those in charge of their fate on the fields. They meet the owner, shake his hand and are proud of themselves, as if they just shook the hand of Jesus. The only time players and the administration get a chance to intermingle is during the holiday party. Until that time the philosophy of Somerset Place, a plantation in North Carolina and other plantations across this country hold strong. Somerset Place used a white picket fence to set boundaries between slaves and masters of the plantations (Elizabeth A. Fenn, "Slave Society and Jonkonnu," *North Carolina Historical Review* LXV, no. 2: 138). Pro facilities use brick walls and separate entrances, separate parking places. That way you keep order. You instill white supremacy and black obedience. But during Christmas we will all have a little party for a moment, shake hands and when it's all over get ready to pick some more cotton.

As in days of old, separation was a big part of the ceremonies and festivities. It's still strong today during Christmas parties: blacks sit at their tables and whites sit at theirs. We all complain about the food. Blacks want black-eyed peas and greens and white folks want hamburgers and fries. The music is either too white or too black. That's not conflict, that's just unique differences. It's the hypocrisy I can do without. When you look at the administration, they're all white, considered brainy and smarter than we laboring brute black physical specimens, who bring millions to their dinner table.

Think about it. Players of color dominate pro football. After we retire, why is it that we can't find employment within an industry we have helped create, to bring billions to owners and thrill fans worldwide? From my research, interviews on the subject in private conversation, with a huge phone bill to prove it, I know that many ex players say that every time they fill out an application to continue their careers in a field that they have dominated, year in and year out, they say they get rejected. The white administrators say they don't have enough experience to either coach or be a scout. "But how can I not have enough experience?" they ask. "You just hired a person who has never even played football, who has never seen or heard about talent. You send white pilgrims all over the country to find black talent and they've never even sat at the dinner table with a black person. How can you send a person to find a great athlete and he's not even an athlete himself? Remember that it took a slave to catch a runaway slave. Coaches are coaching color and scouts are only looking for a new black face. That's all you can do. How can you find something you don't possess yourself? You would not know what to look for, you wouldn't."

People are in positions of authority because of shades of gray. Talent has nothing to do with it. That's why players who get huge signing bonuses usually turn out to be horrible players. They are garbage players and teams feel obligated to keep them around because they have already invested millions in this product. That's not the player's fault. He can't contribute on the battlefield. It's the scout's fault, thinking that because he's blacker than the next athlete or his head's bigger, his hands seem real big to catch the ball, he has big feet, or a big nose to bring in more oxygen. That's not it. It's the four corners of hell, the field in play, that determines the valuable player. So how can the scout find a player when he's never been a player himself? Do you see the hypocrisy in this? If you can't, then read a little slower.

It's not that I don't like authority. I just hate seeing a coach or scout dictating my career despite their lack of wisdom and the fact they have never played or even put on a helmet.

The facilities are laid out just like the plantations of old, and when the players get excited, they are like the slaves anticipating a trip to the big house. Now the big houses are multi-million dollar stadiums and billions of dollars are being made from players on the gridiron, sacrificing their bodies to attain acceptance and a sense of freedom, just as the slaves did on the cotton fields.

A hypocritical system can only go on so long until there is

a person or a group of people ready to sacrifice their lives for a cause. In the history of America, there has been one man who is said to have been the most fearsome slave. His name wasn't Malcolm X, he was not affiliated with the National Association for the Advancement of Colored People (NAACP), nor did he have ties to the Black Panther Party. He was Nat Turner, who you read about earlier in this chapter. Let me tell you more about him now. In 1831 Nat Turner was responsible for slaughtering fifty-five white men, women, children, and babies, for their support of enslaving his people. He is what some folks would call a nigga off the chain. Black folks use the term loosely when referring to another brotha, either being loud or just acting ignorant or not obeying or refusing to conform to the coach's plans or the plantation's rules. He's off the chain, he's just a slave in his own right. The only true nigga off the chain was Nat Turner. I suggest you read his confessions (*The Confessions of Nat Turner and Related Documents*, Kenneth S. Greenberg, ed. (Boston: St. Martin's Press, 1996)). Nat Turner tried to end slavery with his own hands. Strike by night and spare no one was his philosophy. He was educated by his parents but his genius set him above the rest. He could articulate without struggle, which made him more of a threat. You couldn't brainwash him. He witnessed the eclipse in February 1831, called black February. Now we call it black history month, for African Americans. Nat Turner's mother said he was a prophet and intended for some great purpose. He was convinced that with his intelligence he would never be any service as a slave. But religion was his truth to live out the duties to slaughter those willing to enslave his people. He spent time praying and fasting. During a meeting he heard a passage, "Seek ye the kingdom of heaven and all things shall be added unto you." After praying for two years, Nat Turner confessed that the spirit of God spoke to him, that he was chosen for a great purpose under the sun and the spirit of God was with him. A couple more years rolled by and Nat Turner was convinced of his duties due to the events he saw. The horror, the death bestowed upon his people and the enslavement of himself reaffirmed his date of death. As he spoke of things of the spirit, Turner's fellow servants were convinced of his revelations. They believed his intuition came from God himself. He let the servants know that something was about to happen in the eyes of God, but at the time of his early gatherings he was placed under an overseer. He actually ran away and lived in the woods for thirty days, an act of disobedience. On his return to the plantation his fellow negroes were amazed and somewhat shocked. They believed he had escaped to some other land of freedom. The spirit of God came to him in the midst of the night, telling him to direct his attention to the spirit and not to this world. So he returned to his master's hand, "For he who knoweth his Master's will, and doeth it not, shall be beaten with many stripes, and thus have I chastened you."

The other slaves started to lose faith in Nat Turner, and began to talk against his will, saying, "If I had the intelligence of Nat Turner I would never obey a master of this world." Nat began to pray for holiness, for the Day of Judgment was near, and his hand was ready to bring death. He told these revelations to a white man (Etheldred T. Brantley), who was attacked immediately, and Nat prayed for him for nine days, and he was suddenly healed. The spirit spoke to Nat. As the savior of the world was baptized, so he took it upon himself to baptize other slaves. They walked down to the water together, and in the sight of people that hated then they were baptized by the spirit and shouted greatly. "Give thanks to God." Nat Turner believed white plantation owners were the serpents of the world, here on earth to do the devil's work. He believed the time had come, for the first should be last and the last should be first. Nat believed in his spirit. Knowing his fate was peace within himself, he believed God was instructing his steps. He kept his intentions quiet from his enemies and from the fellow slaves. Nat kept to himself, and his plan of action to destroy slavery was silent within his own thoughts for years, until the time came to relay his message from God to four brave slaves: Henry, Hark, Nelson, and Sam. They believed in Nat Turner and were willing to die in their quest for freedom in order to put an end of slavery. On Saturday, August 20, 1831, the group of men prepared a dinner far off in the woods, late in the evening. As the sun was about to fall, the four men arrived. Ambitious as they were, they sat and waited on their commander and chief, Nat Turner, who was the last to arrive. As he saluted his men on his arrival, he spoke about liberty and how it was dear to him. If he couldn't attain it, he was willing to lose his life.

There has been much speculation and different theories as to what these slaves were planning. They all met on a Sunday, deep in the woods on August 21, 1831, to discuss their methods of death. I have wondered what actually was said during that meeting. I spent time praying and fasting, asking the spirit to come visit me and take me there to meet Nat Turner, who was refused to be ordained by white priests but the slaves ordained him and made him their prophet anyway. Although the white priest refused to baptize him, the slaves walked beside their prophet, took him down to the water and baptized him and made him their savior, for slaves were surrounded by hell and death and not considered human. They saw Nat Turner heal people with the touch of his hands. They saw God in him but on Sunday, August 21, 1831, his will became greater than God's will.

Semi-conscious, I lay in the blackness without sound or sight. Frightened, but with my mind still alive, I didn't know whether I was dead or alive. I felt the sprit of a timeless vessel. I wondered, "Do I really understand my own thoughts or does a man really fully understand himself?" For some reason, I comprehended and articulated the spirit's vision. I was ready to be there and behold I was surrounded by trees. As I looked to the sky, I saw the clouds above the Virginia woods. The leaves were green and the air was thick with humidity. I couldn't feel it, but I blew the hot air from my lungs. The air went cold and left a mist of smoke as I saw it vanish in seconds. It reassured me. I was in the presence of the meeting that took place in 1831, for I had prayed and fasted for this moment. As I stood wondering in what direction the spirit would lead me, I could hear voices in the direction of my left shoulder. I was not frightened but curious about the voices I could hear. I began to walk slowly and the voices got louder and louder as I got closer. I stopped and doubted myself but the spirit insisted I observe this moment in history. As I approached the center of the woods, I saw a space in the woods. It was a circular clearing in the woods and when you looked up you could see the sun and the moon. In other areas of the woods, when I looked up, I could see only the thunderous clouds ready to strike. I had found the middle of the woods, a most unusual place. Although I tried to speak to the seven men in my presence, they didn't see or acknowledge that I even existed. They just carried on as I sat and leaned against a tree, I put my knees level with my shoulders and let my forearms rest on my knees.

I didn't understand what I was seeing at first. I saw four men sitting on a log, listening to one man speak about salvation. I saw one man chopping up a pig and cooking it. Another man was pouring brandy for everyone. None of these men really looked to be in charge, but the three men who were standing seemed to know something and the four men sitting on the log seemed to be students trying to learn about it, seeking meaning before a task, looking for answers before dying. I sat there for a while and a sound came over my right shoulder. It was an unusual sound, as if it were an animal. It was an indescribably powerful sound. As I turned to look over my right shoulder towards the men, I saw the four men sitting on the log stand and look towards the mysterious sound that came from the east. I saw the three men that were already standing suddenly come to attention and forget their tasks at hand. They stood still, looking towards the trees in the east.

Suddenly the man who was standing addressed the four men on the log. His voice was not powerful, but it made the sound from the east roar again. With that second roar, all the men stood in a straight line, facing the east. As I saw the men standing, I stood up myself, looking towards the east of the trees, wondering who was coming. What force made these slaves stand at attention? As I heard the crackling of branches, when a man walks through the woods, the crackling got louder and appeared a man, strong in stature, with the face of a general, the heart of a rebel, and the spirit of God. And behold I saw Nat

Turner in the flesh. The seven men saluted him. As he saluted back, I began edging towards the center of the woods so that I could see every angle.

Before they ate, Nat Turner said a prayer. Then the men began to eat and drink brandy and discuss their plan of action. The plan that was spoken was simple, "We leave a trail of destruction and death. This trail will lead to the city of Jerusalem." Nat believed that Jerusalem was the Promised Land, just as the Israelites believed they had to get to the Land of Canaan. Nat Turner spoke to these men who were fed up with enslavement and torture and hypocrisy and who believed that God was speaking through him. He opened the Bible that evening. I couldn't make out the words, his deep, intense, intimidating voice was overwhelming. The men all sat around. As they looked up at Nat talking and pacing around, he was certain of his duty. But I needed to see what he was reading from the Bible, so I decided to walk up behind Nat Turner and look over his shoulder to see the passage he was reading to make these men feel the need to unleash hell upon those who have been enslaving them. As I began to walk towards Nat I saw that the night was coming fast. The darkness was overtaking the sun and it became darker with every step I took. I was determined to see the passage Nat Turner was reading. As I reached his back, there was barely enough light to read the passage. Light shone only on the pages of his Bible and darkness filled the woods. I looked up one more time and saw that the light was fading fast. The moon covered the sun. I looked over the shoulder of Nat Turner and behold I saw the passage of Genesis 9:5 — "Whoever sheds man's blood, by man his blood shall be shed."

I turned around and walked back to my sitting place and behold I saw the men camped by the fire. Some were praising God walking back and forth, ready to glorify God in their life's mission. I saw Nat sitting, rocking back and forth. Others offered him brandy but he refused it. Instead, he stood up and commanded his men to get ready to kill with the sword and end slavery. "Spare no one in our trail, for this is the great purpose my mother always talked about."

As the men began to leave the woods, I stood up and followed them to see what was next, and behold, Nat Turner stood in front of me and said, "Wake up, my soldier, you're not ready to witness death like this. My will has become greater than God's will and, right now, I'm about to ride with the devil. For the injustice that has been bestowed upon my people, the negro, the black face, the African, but most important, the slave." I awoke immediately and my pen flowed with grace.

There has been so much speculation of these men's conversations before their rampage. I believe I have a god-given right to give my opinion of these slaves for I am a modern-day slave in the 21st century. The same things that brought these men to a rage are still roaring in the hearts of black America. I believe that while in the woods, planning out their executions, Nat Turner and his men were deciding between God and guns, but their will became stronger than God's will. Once that happens, the beast will awaken in the body and the mind will close out all reason. Then the only passion burning in you is death and destruction. The body becomes a tool of the devil and you're controlled by your emotions, which only makes for bad decisions.

Nat Turner spent many hours praying and fasting before his rampage, I believe. God's words from Genesis 9:6 uplifted them and reassured them that their will was God sent. "Since my master has shed my people's blood, I shall shed my master's blood, his wife's, his children's and his baby's blood. They shall suffer that which they have dealt." From that moment, these men decided to leave the woods and end slavery with the sword. They felt they were instructed by God. Ultimately they were motivated by anger, which only leads to death. As they entered the first plantation, Nat Turner threw the first blow. Some say he beheaded a plantation owner. Fifty-five lives were lost. They started off with five men, but built to a force of about sixty. They were all captured, but the last to be captured was Nat Turner. He was captured on October 30, tried on November 5, and hung on November 11, 1831. They skinned him and made lampshades, which sit in the Smithsonian. They took his remains as souvenirs and chopped his corpse and even spread it along plantations around the areas he took white blood. Innocent slaves were beaten and tortured just because they knew him. Some were even hung in front of other slaves to instill fear in them, to avoid another rebellious attack on slavery, and more than 200 slaves were killed in retaliation for Nat Turner's murders.

Then on the plantations a new system was created. New laws were written prohibiting the education of slaves. The governor even insisted the slaves be taught religion. Pastors and ministers poured into all the plantations worldwide, because of the rebellious Nat Turner. The master believed religion would keep the nigga obedient, give him a God that says "Obey your master." Give him Jesus to show his white supremacy.

❧

There was another stronger aspect developing. I believe this aspect was most powerful. The master had a snitch in the group, to whom he had promised better clothing and a better life. This is the house nigga, your Uncle Tom, the one who is always smiling in front of massa.

Oh, yeah, Nat Turner is long gone, but he lives in the memory of millions today. There are Nat Turners on the plantations of today, but are never quite capable of staying on the football field. They're good players, but they can't be controlled. They ask too many questions, when the answers are buried in the ground. You even have players on modern-day plantations who can't get a job because they knew or had heard of Nat Turner. Nearly 200 slaves were slaughtered after Nat Turner's death just because of speculation that they would rise against their owners. Players in the NFL are not playing because of speculation. It has nothing to do with talent. Some players get the shaft by association. That's bullshit. Then you have that Uncle Tom around the locker room, lying, telling tales to secure his own job. (You know who you are, bastard.) You have players in the locker rooms, mainly black players, start to get all nervous when other black players speak their minds about the rights of black players. They say, "We got it good. No need to causing an uproar." That's the same nigga who confessed seeing Nat Turner kill people to save his own ass but was hung himself. That's what I'm talking about. You may be a nigga in an all-exclusive white college but you were born a nigga, so stop trying to be white and accepted. It's not gonna happen in this life. The same hypocrisy that Nat Turner faced is being played out all through the world. But the NFL is something special.

Why is it that there has never been a movie made about Nat Turner, the most ruthless nigga to walk on American soil? I believe white American isn't ready to envision a man like him. The history books make you believe he never even existed. He's one of the worst mass murderers in history, so why do we never read about him? Because America doesn't want blacks getting any ideas. They just let us get some laughs on the big screen, never really making a statement.

The plantations haven't changed too much. They still bring religion in to make players obedient, cut their hair, wear nice clothes, conform to new standards, not allowing you to think for yourself. Brainwashing, I call it.

Some say Nat Turner was a savage beast who had it coming to him. There were rumors he was a prophet, a saint, even a martyr. I'll leave that conclusion to God. We can talk and try to articulate a man's motives, but until you slide his shoes on and take a walk in his path, hold your opinion and let God have the final say about this man's life, and any other man at that. There are two things we have to do in this word: take up space and die. The space you take up will ultimately bring shape and form to your life. It may even bring meaning if you decide to move. And dying, well, I'll let you and God determine your fate there.

Will there be an uprising of violence in the NFL? Is there gonna be a player who will get fed up with the hypocrisy in the NFL and take matters into his own hands? There is always a spirit of Nat Tuner within the black athlete. Religion has done that. Just as religion was Nat Turner's motive, ordained by God to put an end to slavery by the sword. I don't agree with Nat Turner's way of putting to death men, women, and children, but I do understand.

Chapter 13

Searching for Democracy

Some players of color feel useless and insecure in their careers because of a lack of power to control it. Whether or not you're a great player, your worth to the committee in charge has no validation because they can replace you at any moment, no matter what caliber player you are. The only way to nullify all this hypocrisy with the system is to form a powerful democracy on the football field, in the slave quarters, on the plantations, and, yes, in the cotton fields that have been transformed into football fields. The committee now watches you pick cotton in your uniform and they pay to watch you sweat. That's great, but democracy means the people have power to aid their own endeavors. The people call the shots and understand their true worth. The people take complete and full advantage of it. A true democracy on the football field will bring increased awareness of the rights of individual players. The sleeping giant has risen and wants to claim what is his.

The sleeping giant has an opponent: the ruler versus the ones under rule. The rulers, owners, bosses, masters: they are all the same. Our modern-day NFL owners are like the dictators on the plantations of old. Even though you hardly ever see them, you think they're too busy or have other business to attend to, they still call the shots. Big money never takes a backseat.

Players of color are bringing in big money for owners and, through all their pain, these players are just puppets on a string, cargo that is bought and sold, traded, or even cut loose. Players of color have never had the power on the field to make democratic decisions. Decisions have always been made for them by white owners, head coaches, position coaches, and trainers. They even bring in a white team chaplain, and he gives the black player a white Jesus. Come on now. Can we keep it real?

A weak democracy is currently in place in the NFL, where black players are still slaves and still under the control of their white masters. Black players, like the slaves of yesterday, hold all their hope in their body and what it can do and produce for their master, the white coach, the brains behind the operation. The media has it down pat: every time you see a player of color score a touchdown or make a terrific play, seconds after you watch that black player accomplish that incredible feat, the camera goes straight to the head coach while you watch him talk into the microphone as if he were the brains behind that play. The body belongs to the master and the master's brain I can't do without.

That's the democratic system under way on the playing fields of the NFL — "Niggas Freedom Living" — for that's what the NFL means to me. Freedom has a price that can be costly. Like the slaves of yesterday, many players don't want to be free because they don't know how to take care of themselves, let alone think for themselves. They think they need a boss to tell them their fate. That spirit still lives in the hearts of many black football players today. They're merely robots beings twisted and turned in directions they have no clue about.

On the other hand, there could be a strong democracy on the playing field. Black folks could stick together. If we know a problem exists, we could use our wisdom to do something about it. Once we recognize the problem, we should have sense enough to change it. But we say this over and over again and continue to stand in the same place. NFL players who are standing in the same place, hoping for results, are insane with inaction.

A strong democracy can be developed in many ways. It can be achieved through violent means or it can be achieved through nonviolent means. Players don't have to threaten revolution in order gain control. A revolution would be bad economics. A revolution requires the taking of the committee's land, which would require blood and the loss of life. It would ruin football's economy for years to come.

A nonviolent approach would prevent the loss of billions of dollars, which makes cowards of us all. To form a strong democracy, players would have to boycott games. They would do so completely unannounced, without threats or accusations. Threats are met with the dictator's plans for such events. The owners would prepare for an economic hit, a loss of millions.

Instead, imagine that one Sunday players of one NFL team decide not to play. Just before the game is about to start, they decide not to go out on the field. The crowd would demand its money back. The television broadcasters with contracts would have lawsuits so big they'd try and bankrupt the industry. Fights would break out all over the stadium. With 80,000 screaming fans looking for a show, maybe ten fans would lose their lives. Ten families would sue the stadium, the owner, the city, and millions would be lost down the drain. Other teams would play and millions would be made for that plantation but soon other players would boycott their games. It would become an uproar across America. Black players would refuse to play just before kick-off. All week they would dance and make you laugh, smile for the camera, but this one time, they would be silent in order to change the system. And people would start to talk about what players of color want. "Look at the system," they would say. "Look at how it's manipulated."

With players forming their own democracy, this is how it would be. The big cities would work to fill their empty stadiums. There would be black owners and, on game day, with 80,000 screaming fans, when a player of color did his incredible feats on the field of play, the camera would turn towards the owners' box and we would see one of our own standing and clapping with his family and business associates.

Players of color would have a new coaching system. Coaches would be like presidential candidates and players would vote on their coaches and determine their worth on experience, not skin tone. That way there would be more coaches of color in the NFL. And the good old boy system would not exist. I always believed football was a team sport, but now I've seen and learned politics and bullshit play a major role.

If the object of the game is to win, then we must have the best players on the field at all times. That's not the case today. You have horrible players out there. They're the players all the other players wonder about thinking, "How in the hell is he still playing?" I call them Uncle Toms. They're always smiling and talking to the boss man, telling him everything: who's shitting, who's partying, who's sleeping with white girls. You can spot these Uncle Toms a mile away. Usually while you're having an intense conversation with your teammates, he'll bring his Uncle Tom ass over and say, "What y'all talkin' about?"

"None of your damn business," you reply. "Go somewhere else, we're talkin' business."

Uncle Tom then just sits there watching your lips move, hoping to decipher what you're talking about so he can go tell the headmaster chief. That's stronger in the NFL, but it even goes in the CFL. Remember history has a way of explaining the future.

The new rule would be that before a player is let go into the streets, players would vote on a list of his qualities, including his weaknesses. Vote him in, vote him out: that's democracy. Maybe a coach doesn't like a player because he chooses to hug trees for spiritual strength. Well, that's not a good enough reason to let a player go. Our object is winning on the field and what you choose to do off the field on your own time is your business. Players would never let great players go if the object is to win. There would be hundreds of new faces on the football field if players had the fate of their teammates in their hands, not in the hands of committees. I would still be playing in the NFL if my fate were in the hands of my teammates. This holds true for hundreds of players sitting at home right now. I could call up some warriors this weekend and put together an elite group of men: current players, retired players, players sitting by the phone. I could assemble them and I promise you that I could beat ninety percent of NFL teams, hands down. I wouldn't even need coaches to help me because anger would be my motivating tool. Anytime a man is in a place he shouldn't be, he will unleash hell when he arrives at the place he should have been all along.

◈

Remember when you were a little kid and you would take a baseball bat, lean over and spin until you got so dizzy you couldn't walk? Imagine everything around you spinning while you stand and watch. Imagine I climbed a tree and sat in it and watched everything spin around me. When it stopped I heard drums and singing. I saw animals in the distance. The sky was as blue as a priceless stone. The landscape was Africa. From the view of the tree, I could see a group of African boys playing with a stone in their hands. They were tossing it to and fro. Whoever had the stone, they would chase that particular boy. Whoever caught him was given the stone and this continued until they saw a group of white men in the distance. They slowed their play when the men approached them. They looked to be journeymen travelers from far away. They asked the group of boys if they wanted to trade their candy for the stone they had been playing with. The boys glared in confusion but traded the stone for the candy.

The stone the children were playing with was a diamond. They were throwing around a fortune and they didn't even know it, ate the candy and got a stomach ache. The group of white men talked a bit and took the group of boys on a boat to America. They put them on a football field, replaced the stone with pigskin, and told them, "If you want your stone back, it can only be won back once a year. The men would call it the Super Bowl. If you win this game, I'll let you wear a part of that stone on your finger." I find it strange talking to some black football players who say, "Africa can't do anything for me. I'm not one of my ancestors. I've never even been there." Yet these players put their lives on the line to win a championship ring. They put their lives on the line to win the very thing they're running from. The diamonds, the silver, the gold, and all the precious jewels are found in the soil of Africa. When showing friends and family the ring of a champion, you're not just showing off a ring, my brotha, you're showing off Africa.

Look at us. Can you see the sunrise? Can you look into the eyes of our ancestors in Africa, where we ran free and lived off the land? We lived in Africa, the richest continent in the world. The black athlete is the dust of Africa. We are rich within our bodies. History has beaten that into us and sports teaches us that at an early age and now here in the 21st century we are still controlled by our bodies. If we feel good, life seems to be cooperating with us. That's the heart of an athlete. For a black athlete, that's all he has. That's why when black athletes get hurt or injured, there is more fear of losing his job than getting healthy. It's a reality. That needs to change. There has to be a strong democracy formed on the playing field. Until then the committee will have you on a string, running for your life and the same things will continue to happen over and over again until the sleeping giant starts to awake, there will never be change, just continued disappointment. The weight of this situation relies on the black players.

I often think about those African boys with the diamond and wonder, Do they still have a stomach ache from all the candy the white men traded? It's strange to me during the NFL pre-season games. They take the slaves to play abroad to show off their prize-winning machines. They don't use boats, but commercial airliners take them to distant places. They have gone to Australia, they have played in Europe, Mexico, and even Japan, but not once has the NFL take the slave back to Africa to play on their land, their continent, where it all began. With democracy I would hold an NFL game in Ghana in Africa, where we once ran free.

Players of color are going to have to rise up and take a stand like the Haitians did during their revolution between 1791 and 1804. Howard Winant describes that revolution as "an independence struggle of unparalleled importance, not only for that country but for the hemisphere and the emerging world system. Only in Haiti was a black-led revolution successful. Only there did independence and abolition coincide. Only there did black insurgency intersect fully with the dawning revolutionary ideal of popular rule" (The World Is a Ghetto: Race and Democracy Since World War II (New York: Basic Books, 2001), p. 68). The Haitian revolution not only created the first free black nation in the world, it brought revolution to colonial nations throughout Latin America and the Caribbean. "News of the revolution inspired opposition to slavery everywhere in the hemisphere, and greatly fueled the abolitionist movement" (Winant 2001, p. 68).

To form a democracy you need not violence or bloodshed. Boycotts, refusing to play, are the only strong push for change. A Super Bowl boycott will be the most powerful push for democracy, with players forming their own democracy on the field. Once you affect the economics of corporate America, you will be heard. Money makes us all talk.

Strong democracy is when players decide.

If you look back at it, there are just two forms of democracy: a weak form and a strong one. On the football field today is a very weak democracy, with little or no power given to the players, no control of their future or their peers. When you look at owners, they are dictators and the middlemen are associations that make rules to try and keep the labor force happy, but the labor is the most important entity and usually goes unnoticed.

❧

During the Civil Rights Movement of the 1960s, my favorite singer was Sam Cooke, who wrote and sang the song "A Change Is Gonna Come." He wrote that on behalf of Martin Luther King Jr. and the millions of people who were fighting change in a system that for centuries has given black folks a back seat and a bad check. There are so many frustrated black pro football players, they have been getting robbed of their worth and have been selling their souls to sport. They only get so far until they run up against not a glass ceiling but an iron wall. You see the hypocrisy clear as day and teammates see it as well but are too afraid to lose what they have, too afraid to voice real issues, too afraid to burn a bridge that may lead into a job within the industry after walking away or retiring from the game. But silence only makes a giant grow bigger.

Too many pro ball players are driven by fear because their destiny isn't in their own hands. They hold no power over decision making, and the cycle goes on. You're cut for no apparent reason. You're better than your competition. The coaches know, the players know, the player who has your job knows. Then why is this happening? Why are the coaches who never even played football coaching? How can we listen to a coach who has never gone to battle? Why do white coaches have a hard time when black players point out on the field that the plays they're calling are insufficient? Why is it at times when a players speaks his mind, he's blackballed and never steps on a field again? Why is it that so many players are called into the coach's office and let go, with the coaches usually saying, "We're upgrading the team"? You think, How can you upgrade a team and let a player like me go?

It's called a dictatorship and how you overthrow a dictatorship is two ways: boycott the system and demand changes or billions of dollars will be lost. This is a revolution that requires a radical approach. A man who is serious about his intentions and his people back him one hundred percent. They agree that change has to come. The other approach is to sit back and let fear continue to be your biggest motivator. Your children will be the same way: spineless, just like you, smiling all the time in the face of people who hate them. Remember it's easy to mingle with people you need. There are millions mingling with us black folks.

I really love the song by Marvin Gaye "What's Going On?" That's the question I'm asking. Football today is a modern-day slave trade. Look at the colleges — all those black football players on the field, on the plantations, all that money, millions of dollars, are being poured into those colleges, through the labor of slaves on the field, and being motivated by fear, by white coaches. Why is it that we see great college athletes, blackballed for speaking their mind? They label them uncoachable and when pro teams call down from the big house asking about a player, a slave, a negro, not in their minds a man, he then is labeled and tagged and his career will either be rough or nonexistent. And some players in college are disrespected so bad and humiliated. They take the abuse for fear of not getting a chance in the NFL and then they find out about politics and bullshit. The two go hand in hand.

These players get to the NFL and realize their talent is being controlled by a committee. Their destiny is not in the hands of their peers, which it should be, but in the hands of people who never even played the game. There are scouts who go across the country looking for talented football players. They even go around the world and ninety-five percent of them never even played football on a pro level. So who in the hell do they think they are?

During the 18th century, slaves would run from plantations, trying to escape the brutality. Some even took their own lives as a means of escape. That's desperation at its bleakest hour. Herbert Aptheker in American Negro Slave Revolts (New York: International Publishers, 1943, 1993) tells how self-mutilation was sometimes used to shorten a slave's misery and hurt their oppressors. "Notices of acts of self-destruction also [occurred]. ...Because of the possibility of imitation, planters tended to keep news of suicides from the other Negroes. On at least one occasion, in 1807 in Charleston, mass suicides occurred;" (p. 142).

Some plantation owners would gather up a mob to find the runaway slave. Often times the mob would come up short, so they started sending a slave to catch the runaway slave. In order to find a great football player, you have to send out a player who was great on the field. You have to send somebody who knows his own people.

Height, weight, speed, skin tone are not a measuring tool to weigh talent. And running, jumping like a monkey for an hour at the NFL Combine isn't a measuring tool either. And if college players don't participate in the NFL's yearly Combine monkey show, where all the scouts come watch you run and jump, then they label the seniors who refuse to do that undisciplined, bad attitude, not a team player.

All this system is based on fear and fear will keep you quiet, and silence never changed anything. You gotta say something loud. Look closely at colleges, look at all the black players slaving. Then look into the press boxes, on high, above the fields of cotton. The press box is the big house, where the white folks watch in air-conditioned rooms while they watch your black ass run towards a dead end dream.

You ever notice all those big posters and signs saying, DREAM BIG? People who dream, dream two things: What they want and what they don't have. All the black warriors on the college level are on the field fighting like dogs for something they want and what they don't have. That's not motivation: that's good economics.

During the 1960s Civil Rights Movement, white folks believed the black man was moving too fast, demanding too much change. White folks said that it's just physically impossible to make changes that sudden. When black people said, "Freedom now!" they didn't mean in the next hundred years. They meant this present day. We have been losing our dignity and self-respect for four hundred years. It's time to once again shake something up. Whenever a plantation owner wasn't reaching his desired cotton weight, he'd bullwhip a black man in front of all the slaves and demand his cotton weight, because he wanted his money. And through fear some slaves would continue to work in the night hour, tired, weary, hungry, with no power or influence. The slave would show physical strength and the next morning driven by fear he would rise early and waken the rest of the slaves to avoid another violent episode. Slaves would work harder and faster, just to stay alive another day, to reach that desired weight of cotton for their master. During a football game, when the master of the stadium is losing in his own plantation field, he calls down to his commander and chief and, if that's not enough, during half time he comes into the locker room and there is instant fear and silence. And he says, "Come on, boys, pick it up. Run a little faster. Hit harder. Be soldiers out there. Let's turn this game around." He goes back into his air-conditioned press box, watching, drinking lemonade, and counting his millions while you wonder if you will even have a job the next day.

Then you find yourself the first one to rise in the morning and the earliest at practice, you find yourself in the weight room, hoping a coach will see you there all bright and early. That way he will say good things in the meeting. "Looks like so and so wants to be here, he's downstairs in the weight room working out, all by himself. Now that's dedication." Hell, no. That's fear that has been passed down like a bad habit.

Let's call a spade a spade. I'm hearing the echoes of thousands of players. Do people actually think I've thought of this myself? I and many other players have been living it. I have even put myself in situations to see the reactions of this system and feel the repercussions. During the 1995 football season, the New York Jets were in last place but there were a few outstanding players on the team who were having great seasons as individual players. I was considered a great special teams player and during the 1995 season I was having a break-out season. I was consistent on the field and players and opposing teams knew it. I even heard fans yell while warming up saying, "Pro Bowl Season Prior," and I was proud of that.

But one Monday morning after a loss the head coach at the time was Rich Kotite. (I started calling him Kotex after that meeting.) During the meeting he was complaining about how he couldn't go to the same gas station or take his wife to their favorite restaurant because we were losing and we were embarrassing him and his family. Their way of life has been altered because of some of you players are not playing hard enough and I have named you players and if you want to see the list come into my office and I'll show it to you.

I knew what he was doing. It's a tactic that has been used for years. It's called lynching in the eyes of the Klan. "Peek-a-boo, I got a nigger with his eyes in the headlights." After that meeting, players were doing the usual complaining, muttering, like a pack of slaves with no direction. I said, "Hey, y'all. Do you guys want me to go into his office and see the list?" A few players said, "Your career would be over." I said, "My career was over when I started playing football. My destiny has been in the hands of others for centuries. History tells me that. Take a read, brother." I knew this would be a modern-day lynching, but I let my teammates know that fear wouldn't be my motivator. Threats I will not tolerate. My father has never threatened me and I would be damned if I would let another man threaten me. I couldn't even face my kids if I let that happen.

As I started walking towards the head coach's office, at first a bunch of players were following. The closer I got to his office, of the more players vanished, like cowards going into a war. By the time I got to the head coach's office door I was all alone.

That moment I didn't even hesitate. I walked right in and I looked around. I was amazed at the size of the office. It was a corner office that looked out over the playing field. You could see the slaves on all the fields from that office. Even I felt powerful in there until I asked to see the list and was deactivitated until the last two games of the season. My pro bowl year for special teams was ruined. Players saw firsthand the power of the iron wall. It put more fear in their hearts and made me go to the library and read about things that people feel is nonsense, but I tell them, "You're living in nonsense and you're driven by nonsense and the sad thing is nobody's doing anything about it."

I could have turned around and lied to my brothers about the list but I knew what I was getting into. I was walking into a lynching. I was tying a rope around my neck, but also I was about to show my teammates who they are really dealing with — that their coach is a racist man and a dictator driven by controlling their bodies like a machine and controlling their minds for economic growth and keeping their eyes in the fog so they couldn't see too far ahead. That's when you begin to see that it's not good economics.

So let's do like Willie Lynch would do — gather all his peers and teammates, gather two horses — one facing east and the other facing west. Tie one leg to the horse facing east and tie the other leg to the horse facing west. Whip both horses on the ass violently and watch his body rip apart like an animal. Do this in front of all the black players so the next time one of them will think twice about speaking out or taking a closer look. He will have fear in his heart. That way the empire shall go on. Let's make an example out of him as we did with Squire in 1837.

"But, A.P.," my teammates say, "I got a wife and two kids, a house I can't afford, a few car payments I don't need, but I'm trying to keep my wife happy. She came from money and she likes nice things. Her mom never worked so I don't want her working either and even though she's white I really love her and I just don't want to jeopardize what I have right now," he says, an ex teammate of mine. Can you believe that? He walked away and the only thing I could say was, "I know you're concerned about right now but what about tomorrow?" and I ended it with "You punk bitch."

❧

That same day the chaplain of the team was holding a Bible study across the street at a restaurant. A few players were on their way over and asked if I was coming. I said, "What's the topic of the day?" "Living in obedience," they replied. I said, "No, I don't feel like letting people try to brainwash me today. Besides they shouldn't even call it a Bible study, more like hypocrites in action. Later."

I decided to go on, and later I sat down with my roommate and we talked about things. I did most of the talking that night and we laughed as well. We even just sat staring out the window, looking for the next thought to spark more conversation. I came up with one. The reason people dream is two reasons: it's something they don't have or it's something they want. Literally thousands of athletes think along these lines. They spend their entire life reaching for something that's not there. People, and more so athletes, try to accomplish so much and try to prove things to people who don't even care about them. They do this because parts of their life have been unfulfilled. Their need to achieve is overwhelming. Their need for fame or fortune may flow from parts of life in which they don't feel fulfilled. But if they're lacking love in their life, the only substance to fill that emptiness is love. Neither a contract nor a big hit nor the roar of the crowd can replace that.

Dreaming is like being hungry. Your mind lets you know this. So why do athletes dream of worldwide attention, championships, money, women, cars, all that stuff that really doesn't even matter or have any significance? It's called wanting to be accepted, wanting to be the best, wanting all eyes on me. How do you feel when you're hungry? Some of us get headaches or our stomach starts growling because our body is letting us know that we have no food, no energy, no enthusiasm, no motivation, and no desire. This is the cycle of all athletes, black and white. We usually spend time daydreaming, or we're hungry and our bodies and mind are in constant conflict with each other. Our minds dream of fame and fortune, but our bodies continue to disappoint us through injury. Oftentimes our bodies are in conflict with our minds. Our mind says we can, but our bodies let us know we can't.

Team sports can and has been manipulated for decades. For some sports a committee grants athletes privileges even when their talent isn't so great. That's why you will see below-average white players make the team before an average or even above average player of color. And teams will surround that white player around great players of color to compensate his weakness to allow him to play on the battlefield. Now I understand what my father talked about growing up. You have to work twice as hard as that white man to make it in this world. I think it's bullshit, but it's reality. Life's not fair so what can you do? Sit in a corner and cry, or move on and try to make the best of this day and hope for a better tomorrow. But don't hide from the truth — acknowledge it and let it be told boldly.

People of color have been in a position of second-class citizenship for centuries. This is nothing new, but in today's world of sport, a thundercloud is ready to strike a blow. Many dissatisfied players of color are sitting at home across the world, wondering why they're not on the field playing their sport.

They're scrambling their brains, fighting with their family, all because their way of life is being changed because the system is unfair. These players feel the need to say something but they then find themselves dreaming of what they want, dreaming of what they don't have and they remain silent because they're hungry again for another chance to play again, to once again be fulfilled with accomplishment, to make a comeback. But if you look at it, the cycle just goes on.

I'm writing this book as a current player and I have seen this and experienced it for a decade. I have seen players triumph, but I have seen players' hearts, minds, and souls defeated. That's more crushing than any loss, more serious than any injury. Well, he was just a weak player, you think. No, that's not it. If I had to do it all over again, I wouldn't play team sports. I'd rather pursue boxing or track and field. Those two individual sports would suit me fine. You still could manipulate boxing but I'd illuminate that. By knocking all my opponents out, I would clearly win. I would train on my own schedule. I would not have to watch what I say or be politically correct because the crowd would be more interested in a good showing than sitting next to me at a fundraiser. Just ask the great black singers of the 1950s and 1960s. They would perform and their voices were as soulful and elegant as you can get. Those big white crowds weren't interested in their civil rights, they just wanted to be entertained, nothing more, nothing less. The same attitude is present today. We athletes are just entertainers who get dirty.

Track and field is the same. The closer the gap between winning and losing, the more easily it can be manipulated so that the winner's cup falls out of your hands. In boxing where I'd knock the competition out to eliminate the manipulation, in track I would outrun the competition so bad there would be no dispute. I wouldn't have to think about a committee deciding on my behalf. My destiny would truly be in my own hands. I wouldn't have to worry about teammates, salary caps, experience, age, or, most importantly, politics and bullshit. Triumph in an individual sport means you truly are a champion, a world champion, not a piece in a puzzle. The only true champion is the heavyweight champion of the world. All of us playing team sports and winning team championships are just athletes coming together who couldn't win or compete at an individual sport. We depend on each other, which isn't a negative thing. If you're an athlete and feel appalled by that comment, maybe you ought to check yourself.

The politics and corruption of team sports have taken sport in a whole new direction. Players of color are feeling the strength of this giant. The problem with team sports at the pro level is that the players on the football field have no clout, no say-so, no input, no control of their fate. These are the emotions of players and the thoughts we really have when we first get a taste of glory in the NFL. Imagine that since you were seven years old, you have played outside in the streets. As a teenager, your peers would pick you first when choosing teams because they knew you were good and you could help them win. In high school you became a legend, a hometown hero and once again your peers told you, "You got what it takes. There's something special about you." You don't believe it until you're offered a football scholarship. Your college career soars like a roaring lion. The state you play in is proud; then the thing you have always wanted comes calling: the NFL. You celebrate your struggle to get to this point, this level.

This game has become a celebration in your heart. You reflect on all the friends who helped inspire you to reach this pinnacle in your short life. You walk into the stadium holding your helmet. You glance at the people screaming and cheering in the stands and your heart starts to beat faster and faster.

And out of nowhere, you feel a force come upon you like a tornado. You begin to shout with emotion and during the course of the game you're overwhelmed with joy, you feel light on your feet. You don't even get tired. You say, "I can play this game forever. I was meant to be a football player. I'm certain this game is my calling in life." You continue to make great plays during the game, and when you jog off the field, the crowd roars, giving the notion of a job well done. You stand on the bench, take off your helmet, place it in your right hand, and raise it towards the crowd. Once again they give you a roar. You sit down next to a veteran player and he tells you, "Wait until the regular season. It's even crazier in this stadium, louder, even more people."

You say to the veteran, "I hope I make the team."

He says, "You're the best linebacker we have. Everybody knows that. We all know you're gonna be here."

The next morning, after the lights have gone off and the crowd has gone home, the coach calls you into his office and says, "Sorry, we're gonna have to release you due to the numbers game." Or it could be due to the salary cap, an unexpected roster move, an injury, all kinds of lame excuses. You're given a one-way ticket back home, with no handshake, no entourage, and no mercy. It's just, "Get your ass outta here." And while you're at the airport, waiting for your plane, you see the coach that just let you go picking up another player, smiling in his face, shaking his hand, and promising him the world. During your flight home, you think about what people are gonna say about you. Are they gonna call you a failure? Some might, some may even say, "I'm glad they cut him." Those are the jealous ones who never really went out on a limb.

You think back to when all this started, when you were just a young boy, playing a game in the streets. Now you find yourself in tears. That saying is so true, "What will make you happy will also bring you to tears." That's hard to swallow, when you and other players knew that you outplayed and were just a flat-out better player than your competition. It's a confusing thing, a mind-damaging thought when you then start to question your own capability.

You finally get home, call your agent, hoping some other team will call, and you even hope that a player will get injured so you'll get a call to replace him. Finally your agent calls and says, "There's a flight for you leaving in two hours." You hang up the phone and scramble a few things together in a bag and get to the airport in a sweat. You realize you forgot your workout shoes and, to you, that's like going to war with another person's gun.

You worry yourself and the next morning you meet a few players working out and with the fear of their job on the line, due to their loss a couple of days ago, the players currently on the team ask, "What position? How fast are you? Where did you play before this? How many years have you been playing?" And you soon recognize in their eyes the fear that drives them. They ask questions so they can measure themselves against the new kid about to work out and possibly change the roster.

Adding the new guy will mean letting another player go out the door to fend for himself. It will mean unhooking him in deep waters and letting him find the shore alone. That's the level of loyalty you find, playing team sports at a pro level in the NFL. Once you realize they don't care where you come from, as long as you can produce, that's great. If you're okay and have potential and you're of color, they say, "See you later. Don't let the door hit you in the ass on your way out." The positions of potential players and okay players are reserved for whites only.

You don't realize that until the team that just flew you in a couple of weeks ago decides to let you go back home. And, once again, your negative emotions get the best of you. You break the lease you signed a couple of weeks ago at the apartment complex. You call the rental furniture company to come pick up their furniture. You call the moving company so they can track down the truck driver who is shipping your car across country, to tell him to turn around. You have a new destination, a different route to take. You finally get home and you wait another week for your car to arrive. The phone rings and it's your agent. He says, "They need you to catch a plane in two hours. One particular team had some injuries. Are you ready?" You get all excited again. You run and scramble to pack to make that flight and, once again, the cycle begins. It goes on and on. This is reality, but you don't hear about this side of the game.

❧

Have you ever been trying to take a nap on a beautiful spring afternoon? You turn off the TV, the radio, close the window and let the blinds down. You sit back on the couch and then you take your shoes off, lie down and face the ceiling. Just before you're about the fall asleep, the noise of a fly distracts you. You look up towards the window and you see that fly trying to get out but the glass is getting in between the fly and flying free outside. You get up and decide to let the fly live. You really feel like killing it, but you're in a good mood, so you open the window, but the fly just stays in the same place, flying into the glass, trying to fly free outside. The fly can't see the window. You use your hand to try to guide the fly to freedom. Just a few inches and the fly will be on its way to freedom. You give the fly a few more chances until you lose patience and decide to kill it. You try one more time, then with one swipe you kill the fly and its intentions for freedom. You lie back down and just before you're about to fall asleep you hear another fly. You look up and realize that flies have got to be insane. That's all. When you're insane, you're just like the fly, staying in the same place, doing the same things, hoping for different results.

Football can do this to a man. Sports can make you do this. People can make you do this. When you chase a dream, you're chasing what you want and what you don't have and when your dream comes to a halt, too many of us are insane for football, the NFL, we just become slaves all over again, in the mind, body, and soul.

Chapter 14

The Committee of Five Fishermen

I have always found clear nights, when you can see the stars clearly, peaceful. As I relax on the bed and watch TV I look out my window and see the stars and the fullness of the moon and its stillness causes me to pause for a moment. It's breezy, and cool air is coming through the window. At first it's refreshing but then uncomfortable. It's too cold to really relax and fall asleep so I get up and close the window and just before I close it, a breeze comes through like none other breeze I've ever felt, much colder, much thicker. I stop for a second to wrap my arms around my body before I close the window and say, "Damn, it's getting colder."

As I close the window and get back into the bed a feeling comes over me, a force I've never felt. I just sit on the edge of the bed and start to doubt myself. Why should I write this book? Who's going to read about me? Nobody wants to hear this. I find myself confused when, just hours ago, I was writing about the seeds of me. Now I feel the need to burn the book all because of a force I just don't understand.

I try to ignore the feeling but it's hovering over me like a thundercloud, trying to take away my creativity. So I go into the kitchen and warm up some milk so I can go to sleep like a newborn baby. I drink the milk, go back to bed, and turn off the TV. As I lie there I suddenly feel my eyes grow weak and then I smile a little for I know I'm about to fall asleep.

Drifting into unconsciousness, I can still sense a force around me. Now I'm sleeping and the force is within me. The thundercloud is ready to strike. These moments are when visions are discovered and most important reveal. It to the world if you can there may be a message.

While I was sleeping the Committee of Five Fishermen came from the clouds to visit me. They came down slowly, laughing in my face and I found myself standing by a river so wide and deep. I knew I must have been dreaming. The men suddenly appeared in a boat and one of them started to talk to me as the others looked on with fear. "Look here, nigger, I know that your thoughts are not your own. I see that many of you niggers feel the way you do, but the system of things are already set. Nobody wants to hear what you have to say. For what you want to say has already been said and has been going on since you stepped foot on this soil we call great America. Too little, too late. Just go sit and read something of old and stay in your small groups, for that is all you have. The great black pioneers were dealt with in the 1960s. The ones living now believe it's paradise." For some reason I just sat there for a while looking at them with nothing to say until I felt another force come up me and this force must have been a force from the 1960s.

I began to speak. "I know the system of things have been set, no question, but I'm here to bring awareness to the players across this globe and for future players to come make them realize their destiny is in their own hands, not coaches on a football team, for they are just human like you and me.

The same forces that have discouraged blacks visited me on a cold night. There are forces out there that will work for you and again you what we have to do is recognize them.

The next night the fishermen came to visit again in my dreams and they asked, "What is it you want? You can't change anything."

I said, "I know the system has been carved in stone. I'm not here to blow up your stone or carve a new system." The fishermen said, "Turn around." I turned around and when I saw the multitudes of boats, I stepped back. I wished I could wake from this dream but the force of courage was with me. I stood there and I saw thirty-two boats and on every boat there were five men and they said, "Speak, boy."

"I'm writing to bring awareness," I said. "I'm just a voice that echoes the hearts of many black athletes who don't want their careers sidetracked because of their feelings." I also told the five fishermen, "You knew you would be in for a fight if the forces of the Civil Rights Movement of the 1960s were to pass through some of the hearts of black athletes." Then to the left I saw a Sunday in the NFL when there were no more fans in the stands. All the TV networks were just playing movies and the fishermen were puzzled, and the next Sunday was the same thing, movies in place of football. America's real pastime, when we watch players in motion doing their craft with elegance and grace, with power and strength, added with courage and you have football. The fishermen ask me, "What's going on with these niggers? Have they lost their minds? Why aren't they playing?" I answered them saying, "They want a black owner of a pro football team. We worms that you call us, are football, we are the record setting, the ticket sales that make you fat to your stomach. Let us enjoy the feast as you all do." I then said, "We are saying we want a black owner of a fishing boat.

As I turned towards the men sitting in their boats looking at me as if they were going to lynch me, I said, "I'm trying to wake up but the force that is around makes me feel the importance of this vision." In the distance, I see some movement. I look beyond the fishermen who are staring me down like a junkyard dog. I point in the mist behind them. They turn and the movement in the distance appears and I saw five black men carrying their own wood, their own nails, a hammer, a fishing pole, and they even had some worms of their own.

The fishermen then looked at me. This time their eyes were fiery red, but they couldn't get out of the boats to kill me. I told them, "I can run real fast and you all look out of shape." The fishermen asked me, "What's going on here?" I said, "You have been fishing for many years and there is room for more boats. You even have boats that are not being occupied. Why are all of you so greedy? It must be a power trip from way back when, a force you just can't let go, huh?" The fishermen asked, "Where did this force come from?" I said, "It was said to have died in the

1960s when the pioneers that tried to bring equality and justice to all were slain in the name of freedom." This force came on like a mighty wind, bringing courage and the will to change history one more time to be pioneers, to set new standards, like the ones that were set in the 1960s. Until then, nothing has been done to change history for the black man. These men, these athletes, these warriors, were ready to do something to make change where there was none. They recognized their power and took advantage of it. The force was great and these men once again changed history and people wrote about it. They came new pioneers of a new black movement and what inspired these men most was their children's children were going to glory in it. And the spirit of the late Walter Payton is still with us.

Some say Walter Payton was the greatest football player to have ever put on a uniform. Not only does he deserve this honor, but he should have been the first black owner of an NFL franchise. The NFL's all-time leading rusher, Walter Payton played for and then served on the Chicago Bears' board of directors, and became part owner of an Arena Football team after unsuccessful efforts to buy an NFL franchise.

After he was asked to retire, not of his own free will, he wrote his autobiography, *Never Die Easy: The Autobiography of Walter Payton*, with Don Yaeger (New York: Villard Books / Random House, 2000). Payton writes that he wanted to play two more seasons but his tremendous career was cut short by the committee making the decision for him. For four years, he struggled to become an owner, actually just part owner of a franchise. But big egos of men changed the course of his life. When his attempt to become a part owner crumbled, Walter went into a depression for more than three years. Walter wanted to be a franchise president and he desperately spoke about how he would interact with the upcoming new players. He spoke about how he would motivate them and inspire them. He talked about the things that need to be done and he would have changed some things in the NFL had he succeeded. In Walter's words, "I was very devastated that other people were in control of my destiny again. I was not in control" (pp. 147–8).

Walter's spirit smiled down upon them and the third week I saw a group of black men sitting in a boat fishing and football picked up where it left off: sell outs, records being broken, bones broken, too, and the fishermen added to their committee and they carved it in stone.

When you look at the Committee of Five Fishermen really closely, you see them fishing on a beautiful day, Sunday to be exact. The committee sits in the boat and it's made up of one owner, a president, a general manager, and coaches, the boat represents the big million-dollar stadiums luxury seating, press boxes, the whole nine yards. The fish represent the fans and the only way to get to the fans and put them in the stadium, you first need good bait. And the bait represents the black athlete you would think that worms have no value but when you look real close and understand the meaning behind the worm, you find that the worm is a powerful thing to be. Without the worm, no fishing, no fans; without fans, no money; without money, no football; without football, boredom; and with boredom you become broke and being broke is no fun. It's okay to be a worm as long as you know your worth.

The morning after my dream of the Committee of Five Fishermen, I walked into work and for some odd reason I was cut by the team. I had been playing for the Oakland Raiders. I was a little stunned but not discouraged, for players said and I knew I was playing pretty damn good. A few days later, I decided to pack a little bag, go to the lake, and chill.

The Committee of Five Fishermen were discovered like this. I found my soul uneasy with football and I wanted to do something about it. Just because a few men say I can't play for them doesn't mean it's the end of living because watching my competition I was definitely better than they were, so why am I out here sitting in a park overlooking a lake?

Listening to the radio and hearing the announcer say negative things about the team that just cut me, I find satisfaction in that team that cut me is losing. I feel they would be winning if I were out there. So as they continue to self-destruct, I find joy in that. I find peace knowing they're losing for they deserve that because they cut me and I was clearly better than the person I was competing against. Am I happy for the player who has my job? Hell, no, I want to be on the field, but then it dawns on me, "Did I really have control of the situation? Was I part of the decision-making processes? No."

As I'm lying on my back with the radio towards my right ear, I raise up quickly for there is a wasp in my midst. So I throw up my hands, trying to kill it with a single blow. I'm feeling aggressive for I should be on the battlefield right now, not in some park, lying on the grass trying to fight a wasp. As I raise up I turn the radio up and relax my arms on my knees and in front of me I see five men fishing and the man at the head of the boat looks to be the oldest man. I guess he owns the boat, like owning a plantation or a football team. To his right is the fourth man. He looks to be more of a long-term friend, the kind you know for a life-time, sort of like a company president. The third man looks like he's in conflict because he's in the middle. I guess his role would be the general manager, reporting to the owner, who's ahead of him and always in conflict with the president. Then there is the second fisherman on the boat, you would think he has power because he stands out. You see him all the time, but he's just the head coach, taking orders and he's the last of them. I saw a little man and he was just a coach but he seemed to inspire you and get your hopes up and in the end he would just disappoint you because really he has no clout or say so, who stays or goes, whatever product from the shelf was put in front of him, he was going to coach it, no matter what, no matter how fast you can run forty yards or how great of a talent you are, your fate sits in the hands of other people, in this case, the Committee of Five Fishermen. Although I saw them in a vision years before, I would not think about them again until the winter of 2000.

ॐ

I found myself packing in the midnight hour. My team, the Calgary Stampeders, just lost to the B.C. Lions in the western final game. My girlfriend's upset because I'll be leaving her. However, she insists that I take a few of her belongings, because in a couple of weeks she plans to come down and meet my family for the first time. It's six in the morning and the alarm clock goes off. She squeezes me tight for it's time to say goodbye for a while. She's in her red nightie and she walks me to the front door. We hug and kiss as tears are going down her face. I tell her to run upstairs and I say I'll see you later. I turn my back and never look back.

I plan on driving to Salt Lake City and get some sleep and then make it home the following day to Riverside, California. As I'm driving my truck I can start to see the sun about to rise and then I begin to reflect on the season and I tell myself, Canada has been good to me. Up until this football season I never been on a pro team where I was a full-time starter. I accomplished that in Canada and had the best season of my career. But I say to myself I'll never get the credit due until I accomplish the same feat in the NFL. I'm thinking back when I showed up at the college campus at UCLA on their pro timing day when all the scouts are present from various NFL football teams and I remember I blew everybody away in the forty yards and the drills, but for some odd reason, many of the scouts said, "You cost too much. You have too many years' experience. We can pay for two rookies with your years in the league. Your minimum salary is too much. We'd rather get two rookies for we can pay him cheap." I said to myself, "Don't they want the best players on the field. Shouldn't the best players be playing? I said to myself the system is changing, but who am I to try and change a giant? I'm just a little man. Then as I drive for hours and hours, through Montana, I leave her a long message telling her what I'm feeling and the scenery around me is breathtaking for there is not a cloud in the sky. I tell her and out of the clear blue sky I see a rainbow in the distance. For there must be some mist in the sky to bring something out that beautiful. I leave her some music from Otis Redding on the rest of her voice mail.

My thoughts are all over the place. I'm thinking of some of the players who I know in the NFL who play my position. I can't believe they're playing in the NFL and I'm not. You would think

I would be excited about my tremendous season in the CFL but I'll tell you this. Driving along for thirteen and a half hours you'll begin to think of some of the most ridiculous situations in the past and present. Finally, I find myself in Salt Lake City, my resting place. The city seems real busy considering they are getting the city ready for the winter Olympics. I come across a cheap motel, the kind my Dad would love to stay and my mother would refuse to. The night is cold and as I enter the room I find that somebody must have left the heater on. It feels like a sauna in there, so I open the window, locked the door and ran across the street to grab a hamburger and fries to go. I was hungry and by the time I walked across the street to my motel door, the fries were gone. I sat at the edge of the bed and turned on the TV and ate my hamburger. I wasn't even paying attention to the TV I was so tried. After I swallowed the hamburger I jumped into the shower and took a long hot shower. After I got out of the shower I called her to let her know I was safe. As I hung up the phone I kinda dosed off for a minute and the coldness of the night woke me. I forgot to close the window as I got up and walked towards the window a gust of wind came through and my spirit became uneasy. I said to myself I haven't felt that kind of a chill in two years and right then I thought of the Committee of Five Fishermen and just before I started to lie down I thought to myself each NFL teach has about sixty-five million dollars to pay fifty-three players. I know some teams can use a player like me because some of those players are garbage and they come at a cheap price. Damn, they need a new solution that's all I could think of before I drifted into sleep.

Blackness. The stillness of deep sleep when you don't know whether you're dead or alive. Some call it unconsciousness. I say it's getting in touch with God. Suddenly, I find myself in a familiar state of unconsciousness and then appearing in the mist from a far off place I can see a group of black men building their boat and some swimming to empty boats. I try to yell but they can't hear or even see me and then appeared in the water on a boat the five fishermen had come back to visit. One fisherman said, "Look over your right shoulder." Appeared a little brown wooden shed where they buy their worms and I saw a short old man with a big nose and balding hair. He sat behind a little counter with a cane in his right hand and behind him the wooden shed with a single door in which he sat in front of it. I looked back at the fishermen in the boat and pointed towards the group of black fishermen. He turned towards then also and then looked at me and raised an eyebrow and said, "In due time, in due time." The fisherman said, "We have a problem." I said, "What is it?" "Go talk to the old man with the cane." I turn towards my right and start walking towards the old man. When I got to the counter it dawned on me this old man must be in charge of everything because behind him, were bucks and bucks of money. The old man says we have major problems. The worms don't want to act right. Sometimes the worms that are bought at a higher price seem to be arrogant at times and the worms that are bought cheap seem to always be in conflict with the other worms. As they are carried to the boat they seem to be fighting in the bucket and when they get to the boat they both are gonna get hooked anyway. They have the same job, maybe they should be bought at the same price. Every fisherman has this problem on their boat and when the committee picks out the worms they seem to be in conflict also because they feel the worm that cost the most should be able to bring in the most fish. But sometimes the cheap worm gets the job done better than the expensive worm and then the committee is all in an uproar because they feel they're not getting their money's worth. The old man said, "I think all the worms should have a single flat rate, from the greatest to the least, because when you look at it, they're all in the same bucket, getting ready to be used as bait."

The old man then says, "What's so great about these worms is that if one of them doesn't perform or get the job done, we just unhook it and let it fend for itself." I said to the old man, "That's cruel, don't you think?" He just smiled and said, "Come around the countertop and look into this old wooden shed of mine. The old man got up with the help of his cane and opened the door then stepped to his left. I then walked around the counter and before I looked into the door I saw that the floor the old man was standing on was solid gold. As I stepped on the gold floor and looked into the door. I could see there were so many worms at his disposal, as far as my eyes could see. These worms were in constant conflict with each other everywhere they were screaming and scattering everywhere. He then said, "Peak your head in and look to the left and then to the right." When I looked to the left, I saw the sun and it blinded my eyes and then I looked to my right and I saw the moon and it was gloomy. I stepped back and the old man said, "Do you understand what you just saw?" I just stood there puzzled. He smiled again and said, "With the sun shining on one side and the moon on the other side it keeps the worms confused and they're constantly in conflict with each other. Some look to the sun and think it's day and some look to the moon and think it's night. Some want to move towards the sun and some want to gather towards the moon. It makes them confused and when you're confused, you always want to be unconfused and it's easy to believe things when they are not even true."

I then said, "Don't you think that's cruel. How long has this been going on?"

"Since the beginning of time," the old man said. "Where do you get these worms from?" I asked. "Look towards your right," he said, and I saw a group of men holding shovels in their left hand and a bag in their right hand. They had big snouts with big teeth and long whiskers. They had human bodies but the head of a gopher. I asked who they were.

The old man said, "They go out and find the worms and bring them to me." I guess you can call them scouts. They work for the fishermen but I work alone for I control the money and that's power. "So why am I here?" I ask the old man. He said, "We need a solution but all the worms do is complain. They never say anything but mutter all day long. "What's the problem?" I ask. We're trying to make all the worms happy but they don't appreciate their worth. The little worms says he doesn't make enough and the big worms always want more. He's not happy unless he makes more money than the other worms

235

on the other boats. It's getting sloppy out there, "But you seem to be out of ideas, I said. "The old man answered, "You're just sitting there looking like a dummy." I ask, "What is each boat's maximum they can spend on worms?" The old man said, "Sixty-five dollars during the fishing season and I tell you fishing season is exciting. The world starts to move. Records are seen broken with the human eyes and some triumph and other feel defeat but all in all fishing season is spectacular.

The old man said, "Do you have a solution?" I said "Give me the equation." The old man said, "Listen, I'm only going to say this once and you will never see the five fishermen again. "On any given Sunday there are thirty-two boats in the river in front of you and five fishermen in each one of them. Each boat can have fifty-eight worms on it at one time. Five of those worms can't be hooked on Sunday no matter what. That leaves fifty-three. Now from that fifty-three, another five you have to make a choice whether or not they're good enough to get some catches on Sunday. You would usually make that choice if some of your best fish catching worms are not up to par for Sunday's event. So from that fifty-three you take the five weakest worms and leave them in the bucket. Now that leaves you with forty-eight worms to work with. Now with sixty-five dollars how can you level the playing field for the fishermen and make the worms see that the game is fair and the best worm in the world is always on the boat with the fisherman on Sunday?

I sat there for a moment and ask the old man to come around from the counter. He slowly got up, came around, and stood there, I picked up a little stick towards my left and I said, "Look here, old man, this is my solution. In order to catch some fish and beat the other fishermen in competition you gonna need a group of worms that can play defense so in the dirt I drew up eleven worms and the first eleven worms, I paid each worm two dollars a piece so when they're out on the boat they can play like a family because they know they're worth is equal and behind that first eleven was a second eleven and they were considered back-up worms, just in case one worm got bit. They would replace the first worms next Sunday and I would get each back-up worm on defense fifty centers. That way the back-ups would know their role and there would be no conflict between the first eleven and the second eleven worms. They all would be satisfied.

"Now in order to catch fish in abundance, you're gonna need a well machined offense. In an offensive system, one worm is going to have a lot of responsibility that worm is like the general. I would pay that worm seven dollars and his back up four dollars and there would be no conflict only togetherness. The other ten worms on offense have their role also and I would pay the first ten worms two dollars a piece and the second ten I would pay them fifty cents. When you're second you rest a lot and you often don't get hooked unless a worm from the first group is bit and like on defense the offense knew their roles and they were happy. There were also another two worms that help out. They usually were cast out to see where the offense and defense would set out. I would pay them one dollar a piece. That leaves a total of sixty-four dollars and the ten worms that were not hooked. I would give each of them ten cents and that leaves a total of sixty-five dollars. And on that Sunday history will change once again."

The old man said, "Wait, what do you call this system and why?" I said, "I would call it the slotting system. The worms' contracts were based on where they would be slotted on any given Sunday. It wouldn't matter how much experience you had or how old the worm was and how young the worm was. Contracts were not about money. They were about how many years you can hold down that two-dollar spot or fifty-cent spot. There would be no signing bonuses, because the fishermen would tend to lean more on the worms they already gave money to, already invested in, and from week to week your slotting can change just like your money would if some worms on the second team start to perform, better than the worms on the first team, that first team worm would find himself slotting second the upcoming Sunday and it can change that was when a worm Is hurt he loses his spot and his money drops to about ten cents every week until he's back healthy and then he's still not guaranteed to be in the first slot.

Then the fisherman asks, "What about when my gophers bring in new worms?"

I said, "They will be drafted but there would be no money up front. They would have to try to work their way into the slotting system. The only contract those worms would sign will be a chance to get into the slotting system. If a new worm beats an old worm we have no choice but to hook the new worm and let the old worm go. The slotting system is just that, it's fair: no obligation, just yearly contracts to try and get.

Playing in the new system and I found team morale up. The worms felt equal with one another. The old man and the fisherman asked me, "Where did you get that system?"

I said, "It just came to me. Why you ask?"

They said, "Come here and look into this mirror." I said, "Why?"

"No reason," they said. I looked into the mirror and I saw that I was a worm and the old man and one fisherman shook my hand and said, "We never thought a worm would have the courage to do what you have done. We can't guarantee you that your system will ever come to reality, but your concern for the worms has you in a class all by yourself. Good luck. I hope to see you in a few years and maybe those black fishermen will have their boat in the water soon and be courageous and tell the story about us, the Committee of the Five Fishermen.

The next morning I got up, fueled my truck and drove for another twelve hours until I got home, where my family and my two sons were there to greet me. They asked, "How was the trip?" I smiled and said, "You'll read about it some day."

Chapter 15

Moments with God

Listen to counsel and receive instruction, that you may be wise in your latter years. — Proverbs 19:20

It's a Sunday morning in December 1978, about eight minutes before ten. Church starts at ten o'clock and my mom and I and the rest of the kids are only now getting into our green wood-panel station wagon. We all jump in and drive off, with no seat belts and no concern for safety. We just can't wait to get back home again. I'm sitting quietly in front, still ashamed for wetting the bed last night.

There's a light drizzle left over from last night's rain. It's cloudy and gray and one of the windshield wipers won't budge from the middle of the windshield. My mother says, "That damn Frank hasn't fixed this windshield wiper blade yet." We can barely hear the music on the radio because, in the back seat, my brothers and sisters are having it out. "Shut up," my mom says, as she brakes at a red light and swings round to give them a few words to straighten out their behavior. She even looks at me, the quiet one, just to let me know, "I don't want no mess from you in church either."

As always, the service is in session when we arrive and we've missed a few songs and some announcements. The same usher who greets us every Sunday morning raises an eyebrow and gives us a church bulletin. As the song ends and the choir sits down, the sanctuary doors open and everybody looks back to see who is late, thinking "Yeah, here come the Priors." We always sit near the back on the left because those seats are reserved for people who arrive late, and yeah, we're always late, but we're never absent.

Every Sunday our family's seating arrangements were pretty much routine. My mother, my older brother Joseph, and my older sister Stacey would usually sit in the seat directly behind me. To my left would be my sister Simone. I always sat next to Stanley, who would sit next to the aisle. Stanley would lean his head to the right and go straight to sleep. My mother would smack Stanley on the head from time to time and I would even give him a nudge or two. Once he even snored and that made us laugh out loud. Mother gave us something to think about.

Stacey and Joseph were boring during church. Simone, Stanley, and I would often entertain ourselves if the minister wasn't yelling or the choir wasn't singing. Simone and I would play Last Lick. We would hit each other really, really lightly, almost with just a touch. If you couldn't feel a touch, you'd lose the game.

I often saw my mother cry in church. Sometimes the choir would sing a hymn from her childhood or the pastor would preach and say words as if they were coming out of her father's mouth. The weird thing about that was that whenever I saw my mother cry, I would start crying myself. Whenever my mother would feel the tears of her youth, and the water would pour down her eyes or she would shake her head remembering something that got her emotions all stirred up, I would immediately look somewhere else, because if I looked at the tears in her eyes, something in me would get all worked up, and the water wanted to pour out of my eyes as well. I was just too ashamed to let people see me cry in church. I believe those tears were my first moment of understanding the compassion God had put into my heart.

Those were my moments with God during my youth. I didn't start to really listen in church until I got to high school, when I was scared of the uncertainty of my future. I needed something to hold onto. It's strange but so true — during high school I prayed so hard for a football scholarship and, you know, I got one.

I once got so drunk in college that I started crying because I thought I was going to die if I went to sleep. That night I just walked all night long until I was sober, and during that time I started making deals with God. I said out loud, while pacing from side to side, trying not to fall over, "God, if you let me live I'll never drink again, and I'll go to church in the morning." I kept my promise. The next morning I went to church, but as I walked in I saw a picture of a blond-haired, blue-eyed Jesus instead of the black Jesus we had at home. The next night I was drinking again, saying Jesus used to drink wine, so I guess a little beer in moderation won't hurt. Well, it did, and before I knew it I was back in the same situation, too drunk to have fun, too scared to sleep, and once again walking all night long to sober up. I was wrestling with God, trying to fit God into my plans, looking for ways for God to adapt to my way of thinking, my way of living.

I remember calling my mother one night in March 1990. I was at my lowest point in college. You think I would have been having the time of my life but my girlfriend was pregnant, I was on academic probation, and they were kicking me out of the dormitory for numerous noise violations.

The words that came out of my mother's mouth were heaven-sent. Her words were harsh but they needed to be said. "Anthony, my son, what you do in the dark will always come to the light. We all have to reap what we sow. It may not come right away, but eventually it will catch right up to you. If not you, it shall fall on your children."

Hearing those words over the phone made me realize God is in the midst of the storms in life and they too shall pass. That's what my mother left me with. You would think that conversation would have put everything intro perspective. It did for a while. I got off academic probation. They decided to let me stay in the dorm, and once again Susan and I were on talking terms and trying to make it work again. I said, "Where is God in all this?" Listening to my mother revealed the answer to me, that in the midst of my confusion, God was right there. It would be great if I could gather all the great moments with God and take each positive moment and stretch it out to the next one, but God doesn't work that way. Times of trial and tribulation are suffering that we all go through, and through our hardship, we elevate to higher ground.

I studied philosophy in college. I remember my professor once said that in this life there are two circles: the circle of influence and the circle of concern. I think he was referring to Stephen R. Covey's book The Seven Habits of Highly Effective People: Powerful Lessons in Personal Change (1990). My professor said that if you choose to live in the circle of influence, you'll find yourself inspired and enthusiastic, because the circle of influence is a positive lifestyle. On the other hand, the circle of concern is a place of stress and confusion and the only end is self-destruction. I was amazed by those words. I felt more powerful and for some reason closer to the meaning of life. During college, no matter how bad I messed up or how good I did on the football field, I had a message from God. That message was that the better my relationship with God, the better person I am, and the better player I would be on the field. I have struggled with that for years, that my failure on and off the field were just an indication that my life wasn't lined up with God. I even struggled in my years as a pro football player until I picked up this pen and prayed to God to give me only words of truth.

❧

On game day, whether in high school, college, or professional football, my routine has always been the same. I put on some good oldies music and clean up my space, wash my clothes, vacuum, and do the dishes. I even pay the bills. I guess it's a way of setting aside distractions while I'm on the road, traveling to the playing field.

One particular game day stands out and it's spoken to me for years on end. I have kept that game and the thoughts I had after to myself until now. I can still hear the chatter. I can still feel the intensity. The locker room looks like lunchtime on a New York afternoon, with players scrambling for equipment and the equipment manager running frantic. Everybody needs something. Coaches are looking for certain players to make sure they know their assignment. Some players listen to their Walkman radios, and you can hear the music from their earphones. Other players are sleeping, some tell jokes, and the player I hate the most is the one that says, "Don't get scared now." He's the one who's truly afraid.

Then there's the preacher man, the Christian player, who seems to be more of a Christian than everybody else because he's holding his Bible and reading it. A group of players who believe in Jesus always gather before each game and pray. They pray for protection over their bodies. They pray to be victorious in the end. They even pray for the other team's protection. Just before they say "Amen" they grab each others' hands a little tighter to let the one bowing his head next to them know that they believe the words of the man praying. Afterwards, there is a sense of strength and the will to be courageous in the name of God.

On one particular day, the person who led the prayer broke his leg right in front of me. Afterwards he said, "It was God's will, a way of slowing me down so that I can learn to lean on Him more."

That night I found myself wrestling with God. I lay in bed and thoughts began to come to me in simple ways. I began to retrace my athletic career and God started to reveal not just my moments of understanding, but also moments that have confused me. I could see the track runners getting ready to run. They all pray for victory but only one wins the first-place medal. Two boxers get into the ring and, before they come out fighting, they both bow and pray to God for victory, but only one wins and celebrates the misfortune of his competitor. A baseball pitcher prays to strike out the next batter and the batter prays to hit a home run. The batter strikes out and the pitcher jumps up and down, excited at the batter's failure to hit. Two football teams in different locker rooms get ready to play a game. Each team prays to God for victory and protection. But there are a ton of injuries and only one team wins. The players on the losing team lower their heads in disgust while the other team celebrates their mistakes. During the night we see highlights of players scoring touchdowns and raising their hands to the heavens, saying, "Thank you, God, for blessing me and answering my prayer to score a touchdown. Thank you, God, for embarrassing the man who also believes in you."

The prophets in the Bible were mighty warriors, soldiers appointed by God, men who God wanted to fight to spread the Gospel. Joshua, a great Old Testament warrior, led the children of Israel to take possession of the land of Canaan. He was victorious at Jericho. Likewise, David, another great warrior, set out to do God's will and spread the Gospel. These men took lives in the name of God for a cause. They weren't playing a game. They were the real warriors of God.

I've often thought of these great warriors in the Bible as men of courage. What separates today's athletes and yesterday's heroes such as Joshua and David is that these men were instructed by God to fight battles in the name of God. We athletes are instructed by our trainers and our coaches, some of whom are athletes, to execute plays they've drawn up that often don't work. Why do we think God is out on the field of play? It's because we often believe that when we score touchdowns, dunk basketballs, or even hit homeruns, we're bringing glory to God's name. Actually we only heighten ourselves in the name of personal glory.

Baseball, football, track, whatever sport it is, it's only a game to be played. You can't glorify God on the misfortune of another player, who also believes in Him. When we're on the field of play, we choose to play that sport. Why pray for protection from God when the human body isn't even meant to play the game?

The real reasons we play are many: money, fame, prestige, time in the spotlight. When a player does magnificent things on the playing field, the crowd roars his name, not the name of God. God roars your name when you help somebody, feed somebody, clothe somebody.

When we celebrate sport, we celebrate ourselves and our hard work.

༺ঞ༻

After the slave uprising Nat Turner led in 1831, religion started to play a major role in the lives of the slaves, not to save their souls but to prevent another bloody uprising. "Give them Jesus to keep them obedient," the slave owners said. "Put a Bible in their hand. Brainwash them; then we can go on with the slave trade." A Bible to prevent an uprising?

Now you have the same thing happening with players. They get all religious for the sake of a woman. The weakest motive for getting closer to God is letting the beauty of a woman deceive you and then you turn around and put a Bible in her hand to keep her sanctified when you're not around. You have just flipped the script, my brotha. Your motives are as weak as your game on the field. You know who you are, sucka.

We have put all our insecurities on women. All our anxiety and emotional strain we have placed on her left shoulder. Our actions and lies awaken a spirit so destructive and overpowering that we think we've got it going on, but the negative things we instill in other people, especially in women, will visit us and camp out on our right shoulder. All the things we have done to soothe that spirit of confusion and emotional strain will sit on us so powerfully that we will become insane to our own understanding, which leads to foolishness.

It's often funny to me, but sometimes I see the anxiety in the eyes of so many ball players when it comes to their wives, girlfriends, significant others, or just their occasional whores. I've asked the Shepherd about the motives behind all the hype, fancy cars, expensive suits, and watches so expensive the average man could not afford to pay his monthly mortgage. These men will never be at peace with women until they learn the true beauty of a woman. She can make you do things you normally wouldn't do.

That's why some men think that women are destroying the

world, making men act in such a way that they would sell their souls for a woman's beauty and a nice ass. A man will spend his whole paycheck just for a woman's time. He stabs his best friend in the back just to lie with her. Players will take a whore out of her environment, just because she's so fine and she will look so good on his shoulder while they're living in their newfound freedom in the NFL. Until they learn, she will just be a whore in a new environment.

But you must understand about women. Even though she's in a new environment, she will constantly reflect and remind herself about who she really is. You may take that creature to a new land and a new way of life, but the thoughts of old remain. The cautious will never let us forget who we really are.

That's why all these fake players, black and white, put Bibles in the hands of their women, trying to keep their minds and hearts pure. The truth of the matter is that those players have slept with every woman known to them, sowing their oats. Now they make their woman go to church so they feel secure. They hope the preacher will turn her mind away from the lust of temptation and sexuality. That player's motive is fraudulent; we know who this player is in the locker room. He's the one leaving meeting rooms frequently to call her really quick, asking her questions he doesn't need to ask, hoping she's reading God's word to stay sanctified for all his insecurities.

❧

I often wonder why we do the things we do. I believe it's all about a person's motives, whether they're an elite athlete or just associated with one, because there is reasoning behind every action. Whenever I'm wondering about something, I ask and pray to the Shepherd to come into my presence so I can speak to Him, asking questions to heighten my understanding of myself and the real motives of people around me.

As the rain falls in the blackness of night, I find myself staring out the window. I can't see the rain, but I can hear it. Sometimes I can't believe my eyes, but I understand that what my eyes have seen and ears have heard, I have come to believe.

God gives us moments to let us know He is with us through our difficulties and to tame the beast that's within us all. God is not complicated. We complicate our own lives and then, when things aren't going our way, we call upon the name of God as our lucky charm to bring us good fortune or to relieve us from a negative situation. I never blame God for my misfortune or pray for wealth and riches. If that was the case, God wouldn't give us free will to attain these things. Whether misfortune or riches, they come at a price. Time and action, our actions, lead us into misfortune and wealth, and time reveals our actions in their purest form.

Moments with God are not limited to just a feeling or a change in circumstances. The thoughts and concerns and the power to articulate your thoughts are powerful, because then you can share those thoughts. Some people, athletes among them, never share their thoughts, and I'm sure some players have thoughts more powerful than mine. God doesn't want us to hold His secret when He inspires us to say something. If you're gonna preach, preach the whole truth, not just what fits your lifestyle.

Sometimes we have moments with God and don't even know what we are really experiencing. I have the ability to recognize when God is trying to tell me something. Many people have too many distractions going on in their lives. They have too many people telling them too many things and they don't have the time to hear God's words for them or to see the vision God wants them to see.

The biggest and clearest vision I ever had from God was in August 1999, the same year I didn't play any organized football. I wasn't working, my phone didn't ring that much. I wasn't going through the stress that comes with football. I had no film to study, no coaches to impress, nothing to prove to my teammates. Most important, I was in a state of consciousness that God could take advantage of. There were no excuses to hear Him loud and clear. I heard Him speak volumes to me. I just never thought I would write about it.

It was a gray September morning. I did my usual go-on-a-little-jog-and-lift-some-weights routine, all the while wondering about life and the chaos going on in the world. I ran a few errands and called my friend Steve to say, "Let's go see a movie tonight." I told him, "You pick the movie. I'll talk to you later." I jumped on the couch and turned on the television (sometimes I call it "Hell-ivision"). With the remote in my hand I was channel surfing until I saw that nothing was on. So I went into my prayer closet and prayed to God for understanding and wisdom. After, I jumped back on the couch to take a nap.

As I was sleeping, I dreamed I saw in the distance, as far as my eye could see, miles and miles of cotton fields, all around me. In the distance appeared a white church, with five windows on the right and seven on the left. It had double wooden doors, a steeple, and a cross on top. As I looked around and walked up towards the church, I wondered, Where are all the people?

Opening the door, I saw the church was empty, with old wooden benches side by side. In the center an aisle led to the altar and the pulpit. Above the altar hung a picture of a blond-haired, blue-eyed man, with his hands all stretched out wide. I guess it was supposed to be Jesus. The walls were dirty and full of holes. As I looked up towards the ceiling, to my right I saw a ladder leaning against a window, leading up to the roof. I climbed out the window to sit on top of the church and get a better look around me. I saw that the cotton fields had turned to snow, the sun had turned blue, and the sky was black.

Looking back into the church through a hole in the roof, I saw slaves coming in through the front door. They look tired and hungry. Some just lay on the benches; others sat on the floor, leaning against the wall. Some were saying, "Lord have mercy. I don't know how much longer I can hold on in this place." Some were talking about coming together, for their time in this building was the only place they can unite. "This is ours. We own this," they said, "for this is the only thing massa has really given us. Let's keep this." The slave who spoke seemed to be in charge, for all the slaves were listening to what he was saying.

All of a sudden a slave came running through the front

doors, breathing hard and sweating like he'd run away. He said, "They's coming, y'all!" I looked up to see who was coming and saw that the cotton fields had turned to dirt. The sky was an ugly gray. I saw a group of white men striding towards the church. Some walked faster than the rest.

As night fell suddenly, candles light the church inside as groups of white men stood grouped at each window, watching the slaves inside. The slaves saw the white men's eyes watching and through fear they began singing and shouting the name of Jesus. Some were running down the church aisles, falling and shaking on the ground, saying words they couldn't even pronounce, screaming, "Hallelujah," jumping up and down, out of control as if they were possessed by a demon. The white men began to laugh and said, "Yeah, these niggas are getting the message. It's working. We're making them insane and crazy. They shout because they're trying to convince us. They scream so we can hear them. They dance so we can watch them. They fall to the ground and lie there so we can laugh at them." This went on for a while. As the sun came up and the white men walked away a slave who had been spying on the white men from a corner threw a piece of wood to tell the slaves they could come together and stop all that nonsense, which they did.

Now you know why black folks like to scream and shout in church. I think we're just trying to convince somebody out of fear that, "Yeah, we got it." In reality we've been hoodwinked.

❧

I once had another dream. I dreamed I saw the sun but my eyes were not blinded by its powerful rays. A man appeared. He had brown skin and a white robe with red rubies for buttons. He was barefoot, with nappy hair like mine. We stood there looking at each other. I was waiting for him to say something to me, for this man had come from the sun. He was no ordinary man like myself. He was special and then he began to speak. "I know your thoughts," he said. "Don't be afraid, my child." He spoke with such clarity I asked him, "Who are you?" He said, "I see that you are a man of simple things, so I shall be simple with you. I am the Shepherd." I asked, "Why is there so much evil and destruction in this world if you are all-powerful? Why don't you end it?" The Shepherd looked at me and said, "If I were to get rid of all evil and death in the world, there would be no sheep, my child. It's the sheep that are destroying this world of mine."

"Why don't you stop the sheep?" I asked. The Shepherd said, "There are things that have to happen first, my child. My prophecy has to be fulfilled, and what you see in today's world is mass destruction, evil, murder, killing of brothers and sisters, of family. It's all a prophecy that needs to be fulfilled. I tell you, my child, it's going to get even worse."

I then said to the Shepherd, "As I look at you, I see that you look like me. Why is it that you let your flock suffer so much?"

The Shepherd answered with these words, "My flock is the last prophesy that needs to be fulfilled. They are the lost tribe of Israel and they have been in captivity for many centuries as my prophecy said. They have to suffer until I come back to gather them. When I do, the biggest sign will be the weather pattern. The multitudes of people shall be confused, but my flock will know my voice and see the signs as clear as day and they will not be afraid. I'm not coming in the name of religion or institutions that claim to believe in the Shepherd, for they are as corrupt as the world. I'm not coming for those who say they are Christians. They will be dealt with on Judgment Day, the day I will come. Tell the world, my child, that the Shepherd is coming for his people. The real sign of a shepherd is that he takes care of his flock. His flock doesn't take care of him.

"My child, you prayed to me and I have come to you to answer the concerns of your heart. Now realize it didn't cost you anything. I need nothing from you for I walk on streets of gold. All I ask of you is to love my sheep as I have loved you."

As I awoke I felt peace all around me. I have never told this story until now. I believe the time is right. Now I understand and see corruption everywhere, even when going to church I see the hypocrisy within. I see things I don't like. Why is it when pastors and ministers come from a distant place to give us a word from God, first we have to give them money and they have the nerve to pass around buckets and trays and say, "This is God's money and you're in God's house." I don't think so. Man has built these buildings. You notice that during tax season, before you get your income tax check back, pastors and ministers all over the world start talking about tithing to the church. What they're really saying is, "Give me some money to help me pay for the new house I bought, the car in my driveway." Tax season is a time when the value of the stock in some of these churches rises. Pastors, just like CEOs, should have public financial records to let you know where your money is really going. Their financial statement might read something like this: their kids are going to private school; yours attend a backward public school. Their kids already have their college funded, yet you struggle to buy your child a pair of pants. They get rich, but your lights get turned off and your kids go hungry because they make us feel guilty for not giving. I see scams going around like tidal waves.

Whatever happened to somebody talking about loving one another? When the Shepherd spoke in front of the multitudes, He never asked for anything. People felt the need to give out of love. Now greed has become as evil as Satan himself. I'm not saying that all ministers and pastors are like this, but most of them are, and they come in all shapes, sizes, colors, and creeds. They're all human like you and me.

The Shepherd told me, "Spend most of your time loving people. The only lasting thing is love. Everything else will fade, my child. Love with no limits and no conditions, and I will return. On my return the earth shall be on fire and death will come upon billions: women, men, children, babies, animals, and fish, for this you shall know I'm coming."

The Shepherd wants the world to take a good look at the holy age today. The churches are institutions now. They have conformed to the world's standards of living. Like the change of weather, the Church has also decided to put Christmas lights around her steeples and Christmas trees in her churches. She has brought Easter bunnies into her midst, hiding eggs like

Satan has hidden the truth from millions upon millions. She has Thanksgiving feasts. She sits with savages sharing stories of greed and death, and yet they say they are not conforming to this world. These pagan rituals have caught more interest in the minds of millions who claim to be holy. We can only be holy if we possess holiness.

A new kind of holiness is walking around locker rooms: white pastors. They prey on black athletes, claiming God has given them a platform to spread His message. Ask a white pastor, "Where did that platform come from?" He will tell you how great you are and how God has destined you to do great things on the field of play to demonstrate his glory through your body. Ask the white pastor about your mind. Ask him, "Why is it when you want me to give my testimony around your people, you critique my words and tell me what to say? You also tell me what not to say, so I don't make your people uncomfortable. That's saying, "You're on my agenda, slave. I'll put you on that platform like my white ancestors did." These white pastors don't tell you that, when your ancestors came off the boats as slaves, they were put on a platform to be bought and sold at any price.

You then became an athlete and once again a white man puts you on a platform to show off his black Sambo, takes you to the NFL Combine, lets you walk on a platform to compare you to other slaves, just as he has done since the birth of America. Then you come to a NFL plantation where you have been sold, too. A white pastor says, "I got a new platform for you to help me fill my church the way you fill a stadium. Economically I need you. You're not the average black man on the street. He can't do shit for me, but since you're in the paper and on TV, you'll bring in some people just on curiosity alone, to see a slave up close and personal. God don't need us. We need him. A platform is for an athlete's accomplishment, not an opportunity for white pastors to pimp black athletes.

I had a discussion on the topic of white pastors and black athletes with one pastor I met. He told me that I had a problem, that I was angry. I told him, "You can't entertain me with Jesus."

He then told me that I need Jesus, that the devil was present in my life, and that I should repent. I then asked him, "Let's just have a conversation. Why is it that at chapels across the athletic world, there are always more black players than white players?"

He told me, "So many of you come from broken homes, you men need Jesus to fall back on." I just laughed and said, "And you will be the man to give us Him, huh?"

"Oh, yes, you can accomplish so much with Him in your life," the white pastor said. I asked the white pastor, "Can I open your Bible?" He put it in my hands, gently, as if it were about to fall apart. I opened it up and saw Jesus and the prophets all painted up white as snow. I handed it right back, looked him in the eye, and said, "All you're doing is promoting white supremacy and you need to stop."

He said, "How can you say such a thing, Anthony?" saying my name as if he loved me.

I told him, "Before we can understand something, we have to get to the root of it first. Look at our beautiful country. We slaves helped build the White House and what do you see when you tour inside its walls, all painted with white men you call the founding forefathers? The slaves helped build white churches as well. When you walk into those buildings, you see paintings of a man called Jesus and all his prophets. They're all white. That's why we black folks, when we see a picture of a white Jesus, we feel the need to feel all serious and righteous, responding to the moral influence of the painting, like it has power or something." And you see that spirit lives on in many black athletes as it lived in the slaves of old. "I need a white man present to worship Jesus," they say.

I have nothing against white people, or white pastors for that matter. I have two older brothers who are married to white women. I have nieces and nephews who are mixed. So if I hate you, in turn I'll have to hate my own family.

But I can't forget history. In 1831, just before Nat Turner's revolt, the Virginia Assembly enacted new regulations that provided "no slave, free negro, or mulatto, whether he shall have been ordained or licensed, or otherwise, shall hereafter undertake to preach, exhort, or conduct, or hold any assembly or meeting, for religious or other purposes, either in the day time, or at night," under a penalty of not more than thirty-nine lashes. "Whites, however, were allowed to take Negroes to their own services, and a licensed white preacher was permitted to address Negroes during the daytime... If any Negro should commit assault on a white person with intent to kill, death without benefit of clergy was to be his punishment" (in Herbert Aptheker, American Negro Slave Revolts (New York: International Publishers, 1943, 1993, p. 314).

I told the white pastor that when he comes into the locker room with his holy Bible, all I see is his cause: white supremacy. He comes in here, all excited about what? Putting a nigga on a platform, telling him how to dress, where to speak, what to say, and how to say it. He calls that a testimony from God in front of his congregation? Pimps do the same things to prostitutes, but when I question things, I'm a devil and he and other players get mad when I ask questions they can't answer. Just because a player has knowledge in his head, mainly from what people tell him to believe, what comes out of his mouth has no significance. "Get to the origin of your knowledge," I tell him. "Try reading the original Hebrew scriptures and not the Bible translation of the Hebrew. Get to the root. Fill yourself from head to toe with knowledge, and mouth phrases that you do understand. Make yourself holy."

Chapter 16

Behind the Sun

There are so many things I don't know, so many things I haven't even figured out yet. But there are some things I am certain of. My life, as yours, begins with a single breath and every breath we take brings us closer to understanding the meaning of our lives.

I watch the rain come down like the tears of a silent warrior. The football season has ended. Our coach has been fired, and I wonder about next year. As I arrive at the facility to clean out my locker, I look around at my fellow teammates. Some look excited to be going home; others are anticipating new contracts because they're free agents. Yet others are injured and can't wait to prove themselves next year. One player is saying, "I'm happy to be leaving here. This organization is all in an uproar." That player fails to recognize that all teams have the same kinds of problems, where loyalty is just a word. Some players are wondering what their fate will be as they clean their lockers real slow, they wonder, "Will this be the last time I ever do this, be on a team, go to war, be a player?"

I wonder as I take my belongings from the plantation, "Will I ever get a chance to play again?" I talk to myself. "I'm still strong and fast. I still have the desire to play. But will this book be the end of my career? Should writing about what my eyes have seen and my ears heard be silenced on the gridiron? Should I put this book away and let it collect dust on a shelf or should I be selfish and wait a few more years to pass by?"

I can't do that. It's time for awareness to get out, for the locust has stolen but the shepherd will restore what has been stolen.

A rock is significant. You can't manipulate a rock's mind or even persuade its vision. A rock has seen the rain crash down like a beast from the sky. It's seen the rays of the sun beam down, bringing heat and fire. It's seen wars and watched millions being slaughtered. It's seen everything under the sun and, I tell you, the rock says nothing has really changed. Everything is recycled, like trash.

Like the rock, I have seen things as well: players getting cut who should have been playing, coaches coaching who weren't even qualified. I have witnessed the hypocrisy in all facets of the game. My eyes have seen and my ears have heard, for this is not hearsay but my own words from my own mind.

I often wonder why people and black football players in particular say that they have a preplanned destiny. If that were the case, why did God grant us free will to make intelligent choices? I'll tell you the truth, Destiny is what you make it and with whom you make it. Only a slave would say such foolish words. His massa had his destiny in the palm of his hand. That's why slaves were superstitious: they would think that if they shook their master's hand, then they could take their destiny back. We still have superstitious people today.

To write this book, I have spent time in prayer, asking for the timeless vessel, the spirit of God, to come and witness to me the things I need to understand. Spirituality is a powerful force. You can call upon the spirit of knowledge and understanding. You can even call upon the spirit of death and destruction. One must be careful about what he prays for. God says, "Whatever you ask of him, you shall receive it." I often tell people, "Ask yourself: Are you living or just existing?"

We all have a purpose. If you know your purpose, the things you do in accord with God's purpose in your life will flow with grace and your struggles will be at a minimum. But if you don't understand the purpose of your life, you will ultimately abuse it. How can you not abuse something you don't understand? I have made it this far entirely by faith and faith alone. With real faith, a person will risk being embarrassed at times. We all have been there.

On this side of the sun, the world has been tainted by greed and hypocrisy. When I look around, sometimes I'm happy and sometimes I'm sad because it wasn't supposed to be like this: killing, war, greed, all the horrible things people do to on another. Too many people get self-gratification from the fall of other people. Ask yourself, do you even really truly love your own family? Ask yourself these questions: Why am I here? What's my purpose? Who am I? These questions are in the hearts of millions on a daily basis. To find the answers, you first must understand your motives.

My motive in writing this book is to echo what my teammates have told me, and to tell of the blackness of their distant voices. I have heard on the banks of rivers and streams, "Why have I only been the first to write a book like this?" It is not my voice but the voices of the negro, the black face, the nigga, the African, the slave. They have brought me to an understanding that little murmurs and small talk in locker rooms and shouts in the distance have never changed. When you articulate those thoughts and write them on paper, you make them come alive for the world to read and understand. It is not my will but my ancestor's will to carve a place in history and give the modern-day slaves of pro football something to share with the world, that nothing has changed on this side of the sun.

There will always be problems between black and white. History explains that to us, for history repeats itself and the recycled life continues. Face it, and move on.

Faith on forty yards has brought me here. Maybe this is the last time I'll play football, but this book stands as an act of free speech. Black athletes see the hypocrisy but are too afraid to acknowledge it. They hear the abuse but are too spineless to correct it.

When you're flying in an airplane, the clouds above seem to be a danger, but then you realize there is the peace of the sun beyond the clouds. There will never be peace until we go through the clouds of confusion, fear, and despair. Athletes have the slave mind. They have been in chains since the 16th century and the playing fields of today continue a modern-day slave trade.

Realize in life and love that there are always two sides to every story. No matter how thin you slice it, we have seen this side. It's ugly, wouldn't you agree? But behind the sun I would like to think is a world so beautiful that my eyes would confuse my mind of its beauty. The colors would be as bright as the sun, but it wouldn't blind you. So remember each breath you take. Look often towards the heavens and to the sky, for you are a breath away. One day you will take your last breath, which will take you behind the sun. Until you take that last breath try to love one another. Until I take that last breath, I'll continue to write, kiss my kids, love my family, and know that this book wouldn't be possible without faith on forty yards.

Acknowledgments

I would like to thank God for giving me health and a sound mind to write this book. I would also like to thank the people mentioned throughout this book. Some may not agree with my views, but I'll leave it up to you to share your own opinion of the subjects discussed here.

Writing this book has been a great experience. Thank you to my editor, Ann-Marie Metten of Vancouver, British Columbia. Book publishing is a new environment for me and Ann-Marie has patiently helped me believe I could complete this book, even when I've been overwhelmed by the enormity of the task.

I have written in the late night hour and even in the early morning sunrise. My background music has been an instrument to my eyes, a soothing to my soul. The lyrics of Sam Cooke and Otis Redding have inspired me to write through days of sunshine and rain. These two musicians died three years apart on the same day, less a day. Yet I can still see Otis Redding "Sitting on the Dock of the Bay" and Sam Cooke singing, "A Change Is Gonna Come."

The writing of the great pioneers Malcolm X and John Baldwin have heightened my knowledge of myself but also of racism and the struggles of the black man.

The people not mentioned here should know that you have inspired me. I acknowledge your contribution to my life, even if not in my writing.

Anthony Prior
December 11, 2002